הגדה של פסח

A NIGHT
OF TEACHING

MOSAICA PRESS

הגדה של פסח

A NIGHT
OF TEACHING

An elucidation and guide to
the text of the Haggadah for
the Seder leader and participant

RABBI ISAAC RICE

ISBN: 978-1-957579-52-8

Published by Mosaica Press, Inc.
www.mosaicapress.com
info@mosaicapress.com

Dedicated by Laura and Dov Hertz

In honor and in memory of those who survived the Holocaust

המקום ריחם עליהם והוציאם מצרה לרווחה,
מאפלה לאורה ומשעבוד לגאולה.

Their strength and commitment stand as a guiding light for all generations.

Dedicated by Gilla and Yitz Stern

לעילוי נשמת

אוריאל ע״ה בן הרב שמואל אילן

Who, during his brief life, inspired so many Jews around the world to expand
their performance of תורה, עבודה, and גמילות חסדים
ת.נ.צ.ב.ה.

Dedicated by Lani and Shimmy Tennebaum

In honor of our children and grandchildren

Dedicated by Lisa and Chaim Abittan and family

לע״נ

הרב אשר חכם בן הרב מאיר חכם אביטאן ז״ל
חיים לייב בן מרדכי לשר ז״ל
ישעיה צבי בן הרב אשר חכם אביטאן ז״ל

תפארת גדליה

YGW

From the Desk of

RABBI AHRON LOPIANSKY

Rosh HaYeshiva

בס"ד

Kislev 5783

The mitzva of *vhigadata lvincha* obligates us to speak to our children, not merely to recite the *hagadda*. While there are many wonderful *seforim* with myriad *pirushim*, there is a tremendous benefit in having a *hagadah* that is explained succinctly, both the meaning of what we're saying and the context in which it is being said.

Rabbi Rice is putting out just such an *hagaddah*, giving over in a succinct way the halachic background to what is being said, and the clearest meaning of the words as a whole.

Iy"h this will be of extraordinary help in putting down the basics, in a way that turns the 'recital' to the testimony that it is supposed to be.

Iy"h many people will benefit greatly from this *hagaddah*.

Bivracha

אהרן שרגא לאפיאנסקי

Ahron Shraga Lopiansky

Yeshiva of Greater Washington- Tiferes Gedalya

YESHIVA OF GREATER WASHINGTON – TIFERES GEDALIAH
1216 ARCOLA AVENUE, SILVER SPRING, MD 20902 ■ 301-649-7077 ■ WWW.YESHIVA.EDU

Rabbi Hershel Schachter
24 Bennett Avenue
New York, New York 10033
(212) 795-0630

הרב צבי שכטר

ראש ישיבה וראש כולל
ישיבת רבינו יצחק אלחנן

מכתב ברכה

עברתי על כמה ענינים מבחור ההגדה שחיבר יקירי-ידידי הר"ר יצחק רייז,

נ"י, ונהניתי. כל הבאור כולו מיוסד על דברי הגמרא ושאר מקורות נאמנים,

והכל שריר וקיים, ואמת נכון הדבר, וחזקה על חבר שכל מה שמוציא מתחת

ידו מתוקן הוא.

בברכה

[חתימה]

אשר זעליג וייס

כגן 8

פעיה"ק ירושלם ת"ו

בס"ד

תאריך _____

[handwritten text]

כ"ב כסלו תשפ"ג

זה שנים שמכיר אני את יקירי הנפלא הרה"ג ר' אייזיק רייס שליט"א כרב חשוב מנהיג לעדתו
בחכמה ובתבונה ות"ח גדול, על כן שמחתי לראות את מעשה ידיו להתפאר הגדה של פסח ערוך
ומפורש על ידו מלא פנינים יקרים ופרפראות לחכמה, חידושים נפלאים ומאירי עינים. בטוחני
שהגדה זה יוסיף לשמחת החג ולמצוות ליל הסדר לרבים וטובים.

ברכתי להרה"ג שליט"א שיזכה עוד רבות בשנים לחבר ספרים יקרים, להגדיל תורה ולהאדירה
בשמחה ושלוה ונחת.

באהבה

אשר וייס

TABLE OF CONTENTS

APPENDIX
ELABORATED COMMENTARY ON HALLEL AND NIRTZAH

ACKNOWLEDGMENTS

THANK YOU, Hakadosh Baruch Hu, the *Goel Yisrael*, who has led me to this point and for giving me everything that I have.

I am the product of beautiful Pesach Sedarim that had lasting impressions. My earliest memories of Pesach begin with my grandmother in Augusta, Georgia, and then continue to the Sedarim with my grandfather joining us in Scarsdale, New York, and then jumping to Pesach in Chicago before I was blessed to lead my own Sedarim with my wife and children. Each of those magical evenings contained some of the most important lessons and memories that I have with me. Surrounded by parents, grandparents, aunts and uncles and cousins, the nights were filled with words of Torah, singing, and most importantly, an understanding that there was something special happening, and that the *emunah* and *bitachon* of one generation was being passed on to the next. It was these powerful experiences that planted the seed for this labor of love.

It is my mother and father who have supported me from the beginning with endless amounts of unconditional love and support. They have been amazing role models of *emunah* and *bitachon* for as long as I can remember. And it is their dedication to Hashem, and His Torah, that fueled the fire for me to enter into *avodas ha'kodesh*. I am eternally thankful to my parents for everything they have given me and my family. May Hashem bless them with continue health and with *nachas* from their children and grandchildren.

The place where this seed began to grow and the think-tank where this Haggadah began to come together was in the SKA High School for Girls where I have had the honor of teaching for over a decade. I initially approached Mrs. Helen Spirn, the founding head of school, with the idea of giving classes for parents before Pesach so that the parents would be able to teach their own children at the Seder. With Mrs. Spirn's support I have had the merit of sharing and learning with the parent body for a number of years, and this Haggadah is the natural culmination, and hopeful continuation, of those efforts. Helping me with project has been Mrs. Elisheva Kaminetsky, principal of Judaic studies, who has been a mentor to me and my entire family. She is the model of a master educator and I am incredibly fortunate to be able to learn from her. My thanks extend to the entire SKA and HALB family.

Thank you to Rabbi Hershel Schachter, *shlita*, from whom I have had the honor to learn from for many years. His influence on myself and my family is immeasurable.

Thank you for your Torah, guidance and the *haskamah* for this Haggadah. And thank you to Rabbi Asher Weiss, *shlita*, and to Rabbi Aharon Lopiansky, *shlita*, for your continued support and for your *haskamos* to the Haggadah.

The entire Mosaica team has been outstanding from the beginning. Thank to you Rabbi Kornbluth for agreeing to take on this project and for having the foresight to see my vision even when it wasn't clear to me. Thank you to Mrs. Sherie Gross for showing the care and concern for this project as if it were your very own. Thank you to Mrs. Rayzel Broyde for taking the scrambled thoughts of someone who is not artistic and transforming this Haggadah into a work of art that is a pleasure to learn from. Thank you to Mosaica's editors and proofreaders for your helpful comments that moved my own perspective to the perspective of my readers.

The Savitzky, Williams, Hertz, Tennenbaum, and Abittan families have been trusted supporters of myself and my family for many years. Their investment in this project is a physical manifestation of their guidance and friendship that my family and I treasure.

Thank you to my in-laws, Yitz and Gilla Stern, for their continued love and support which they show our family in so many different ways. It is very meaningful that their contribution to this Haggadah is in memory of their grandson, and our nephew, Uriel Soniker, *a"h*. But the biggest thanks I can give my in-laws is allowing me the privilege of building a home with my wife, Tamara. Hashem is truly a master *shadchan*, and in His infinite wisdom He partnered me with a remarkable wife who complements me and raises me in up in so many facets of our life.

To my children, your presence in our lives is the most wonderful and precious gift that we have. Thank you for allowing me to take time to teach Torah to others. You are all very familiar with the contents of this Haggadah, and I daven that the lessons and messages that are contained in these pages penetrate your hearts and stay with you during your journey in this world.

Thank you to our shul, Anshei Chesed, for you continued friendship, for allowing us to learn and grow together, and for your support in allowing me to create this Haggadah.

And finally, thank you, the reader, for using this Haggadah, and giving me the opportunity to learn with you on Seder night.

PROLOGUE

RETURNING THE SEDER TO ITS GLORY

The following essay was composed as part of a collection of essays on Jewish education from a mix of Jewish educators, in memory of Dannie Grajower, a"h, a talented and beloved teacher. The essay speaks to the central point of what the Seder night is meant to be.[1]

At a certain point in the history of the Jews in America, there came a time when parents who were sending their children to religious day schools started ignoring and neglecting a mitzvah in the Torah that had been practiced for over three thousand years!

The Jewish People were told after the Exodus from Egypt, "והגדת לבנך ביום ההוא לאמר: בעבור זה עשה ה׳ לי בצאתי ממצרים—On that day, you must tell your child, 'It is because of this that God acted for me when I left Egypt'" (*Shemos* 13:8). In this simple verse, we are commanded that every year on Pesach, we must sit with our children and grandchildren to relate the story of leaving Egypt specifically, as well as the story of the Jewish People in its totality, focusing on the guiding hand of Hashem's providence.

However, a great distortion has been taking place in our schools. Instead of parents sitting at the Seder and teaching their children about *yetzias Mitzrayim* and *emunah*, the children sit with binders and handmade Haggadahs and tell the story of Egypt, and much more, to their parents! The issue here is not only the negligence in ignoring a precept in the Torah. A tremendous opportunity is being wasted by parents across the world when they do not use the Seder night as it was intended.

This issue compounds itself in a different way. The morning after the first Pesach Seder, there is a jockeying of pride amongst young children to see whose Seder went longer the night before. It is true, of course, that the Haggadah tells us that it is praiseworthy to increase and magnify the content of the Haggadah. However, this statement relates to the telling of the story of Pesach and the message of *emunah*; it

---

1   Reprinted from *Alei Deshe: Thoughts on Jewish Education*, with permission of the publisher.

is not advocating more ideas that are unrelated to the goal of the evening! In fact, in the commentary on the Haggadah of the *Orchos Chaim* and the *Rashbam*, they both qualify the famous statement, "כל המרבה לספר ביציאת מצרים—All those who tell the story of the Exodus at length," as "כל המספר ביציאת מצרים אחר אכילתו הרי זה משובח—All those who tell the story of the Exodus at length after eating are praiseworthy." The *Rashbam* goes further and says that the story of the Rabbis in B'nei Brak staying up all night to learn on the night of the Seder took place after the meal was over. This is because one must speak to the children in a way in which they can appreciate the story and the message of the evening, before they are unable to stay up anymore due to exhaustion. There is a time for other ideas about Pesach and the Seder that are not related to the mitzvah of the night—but the time for that is after the meal.

In a family of elementary school–aged children, this conversation should not be taking place. The Gemara (*Pesachim* 109a) says that we give treats to the children so they should stay up for the Seder, which is assumed to be past their bedtime. If a Seder is run properly for children, there is no reason for the Seder to finish in the early hours of the morning, nor should there be any concern about eating the afikoman before *chatzos* (midnight).

Rav Reuven Leuchter, a highly respected student of Rav Shlomo Wolbe and an acclaimed and sought-after educator in his own right, made a similar point:

> In most families, the rest of the year the father speaks and the children listen, while on Seder night, the children all share what they have learned and the father listens. By me, though, it's the exact opposite. I'm conscious of fulfilling the mitzvah of והגדת לבנך, of telling over the story of the Exodus. Of course, one has to be careful to shape the story in a way that is appropriate to every age level and to encourage the children to ask. But at the end of our Seder, everybody is still awake and entranced—from age seven to eighty-seven.[2]

Rav Hershel Schachter often critiques the modern-day custom of children coming home from school for Pesach with *vortlach* and *gematrias* to share at the Seder that are irrelevant to the message and goal of the Seder night. In general, pre-Pesach lectures and talks on the Haggadah should share ideas that relate the telling of the story of *yetzias Mitzrayim* or enhance our *emunah* through the Pesach Seder.

---

2   Interview in *Mishpacha*, April 10, 2019, p. 77.

What then, should a Pesach Seder look like?

Rav Yisrael Isser of Ponevezh, a student of Rav Chaim of Volozhin, presents an important foundation:

> *Know that even if you engage with him [your child] all night with riddles in explaining the Haggadah or the verses of the Torah, you have not fulfilled your obligation. The only thing is to explain to him well all of the matters related to the depth of the miracle and the power of Hashem and His abilities to change nature with His will, His love for His nation, and how He has maintained this kindness for his beloved [nation] for generations, and elaborating on matters related to this. It is also proper to speak about why bad things happen to the righteous and good things happen to the wicked, and why we languish in this exile, but that He will be good to us in the end of days.*[3]

This is echoed by the *Chasam Sofer*:

> *I have already written that the matter of telling the story [of leaving Egypt] is not about analyzing (לפלפל) halachah...Rather, it is only for relating the miracles of Hashem and His wonders.*[4]

The goal of Seder night is to instill *emunah*, a strong connection to Hashem, in the hearts of our children. Everything else that goes on during the Seder that is not toward that goal is a wasted opportunity to connect our children to the chain of the Jewish People going back to Mount Sinai. The Seder is a time for parents to teach while children listen. It is a time for the parents to bring something to the Yom Tov table instead of the children. It is when we open our hearts and bare our souls for our children to see how important Hashem is in our lives.

The *Ohev Yisrael* explains that on the Seder night, the message of *emunah* will be engraved clearly in the child's heart and mind in a way that cannot be achieved any other day of the year. Therefore, the Mishnah (*Pesachim* 10:4) instructs, "If the child is not wise enough to ask questions, his father should teach him to ask questions." We want the child to ask questions on this night because we want to be

---

3   *Menuchah U'Kedushah*, section 2:19.
4   *Derashos Chasam Sofer*, p. 265, column 2.

obligated in the mitzvah of והגדת לבנך. We want to take advantage of the greatness of this night to teach *emunah* to our children.[5]

What I am advocating for is nothing less than a revolution in the day school and yeshiva education system. *Morahs and rebbeim should stop preparing their students for the Seder.* Cease with the handmade Haggadahs and binders full of *divrei Torah.* There is a time for children to share thoughts and insights related to Pesach and the Seder—perhaps during Shulchan Orech or during the Yom Tov meals. The schools should obviously continue teaching students the laws of Pesach and the meaning behind the holiday. But by sending students home with packets and Haggadahs, teachers inadvertently set up the family Seder to miss the mark. Because although as parents we entrust our most precious cargo to the hands of respected, talented, and warm educators, once a year, the Torah asks us to take the reins and become the teachers ourselves.

What is the parent who wants to run a proper Seder and use the Haggadah as it was intended supposed to do?

The first step, like anything important, is that the parents must prepare the Haggadah in the weeks before Pesach. Sitting with a Haggadah and making a plan of what will be said and shared at the Seder is as important, if not more, than the cooking and cleaning for Pesach. For some parents, this may take days; for others it may take hours. But no one can come to the Seder and expect to impact their children if they have not prepared for how to run the Seder and what to say at the Seder.

The leader of the Seder should be preparing the script along with the Haggadah. The Haggadah, like the siddur, is an instrument. If you pluck a few strings, the instrument will make noise, but it won't be interesting to anyone. The leader of the Seder must learn how to "play the Haggadah," to find out what kind of music the Haggadah can make. If you simply read the Haggadah without elaborating, you have missed an opportunity to make beautiful music. If you ignore the Haggadah and discuss other things, then you miss the opportunity to use this wonderful tool that was given to us by our Sages.

Part of knowing how to play the Haggadah well is knowing the people who will be at the Seder and their ages. Some Sedarim require the Haggadah and the story

---

5   See as well in the *Yesod V'Shoresh Ha'Avodah.*

to be more kid-friendly; other Sedarim need more intellectual highlights that are geared towards teenagers and young adults.

One should also be aware that the Haggadah must be understood by the participants. That means the leader of the Seder should be able to translate the different parts of the Haggadah for children to understand. And if need be—due to the limited ability of the children to focus and because of time constraints—perhaps it would be best to only use the English translation of the Haggadah.

Many Sedarim get stuck at the same juncture. There is a lot to say in the beginning about *Mah Nishtanah*, the Four Sons, the age of Rabbi Eliezer, and the Rabbis sitting in B'nei Brak, but when it comes to the central part of the Seder, many Sedarim go dark; there is nothing to say until it is time to spill the wine for the Ten Plagues. This is unfortunate, because the main part of the Seder, and what should be the highlight of the Seder, is Maggid and the four verses that the story of the evening is based on. The goal of Maggid is to use these four verses and the Midrashim based on those verses to teach and relate the high and lows of the story of Egypt, the glory of Hashem and the miracles He did for us. This is where the parent becomes a master storyteller. It is where research of Midrashim is of utmost importance. The person leading the Seder should make use of the many books, in Hebrew and in English, that collect the statements of Chazal expanding and elaborating on the events of Pesach. Any local Judaica store would be happy to recommend a volume to guide the novice Seder leader.

Gamification, tickets, and prizes can play a role at the Seder, but they shouldn't take away from the goal of the parents relating the story and *emunah* to their children. If a child leaves the Seder with tickets and cheap prizes but doesn't have a greater fascination with the story of our people and the role of Hashem in the world, then what was gained at the end of the day? Certainly, acting out the story with props and dramatic play is a welcome addition in this day and age, when many children are not satisfied with the simple telling of a story. The Seder is when a parent can become a producer, writer, director, and actor in order to put on what may be the most important show of his life.

The Seder night is also the time when families can tell their personal stories of exile and redemption. It is a safe place for parents and grandparents to relate to their descendants their personal experiences during the Holocaust, or coming to America and overcoming assimilation, or struggling behind the Iron Curtain, or escaping persecution in North Africa and Middle East. It is the perfect time to show one's children and grandchildren one's *emunah* and trust in Hashem.

Where does this place the school in the picture of preparing for Pesach? As mentioned above, the school must continue to teach the laws and customs of Pesach and the Pesach Seder. But if there is ever a time during the year for the school and home to collaborate, it is in the preparation for the Seder. It is incumbent on schools to prepare the *parents* for the Seder. Schools should open workshops and classes in the weeks before Pesach, in which teachers and educators can show, model, and teach effective methods to conduct a meaningful and impactful Seder. This can take place in one evening or over a few weeks. It can take the form of live presentations, audio recordings, or live and recorded video. Such an investment is worth the time and money of the school and parents to work toward making the Pesach Seder a foundational pedagogical moment on the yearly calendar.[6]

Pesach and the Seder are meant to be a clinic in the finest experiential education. But unfortunately, in the last century, something has taken place that has robbed parents of this important role. We have become distracted by the trees—the size of the matzah, who says the *Mah Nishtanah*, and Shulchan Orech—and we have neglected to appreciate the totality of the forest—transmitting *emunah* and *mesorah* to our children. It is my sincere hope that with proper planning and initiative, we can return the Seder to the hands of the parents and help them speak to their children in a deeper and more meaningful way.

---

6   It should go without saying, but unfortunately it must be mentioned, that the teachers and educators who spend time instructing and guiding the parents should be compensated monetarily for their efforts.

הגדה של פסח   6

ABOUT THIS HAGGADAH

What you have before you is a Haggadah that is very different from most other Haggadahs. Its purpose is to use the text itself to tell the story of *yetzias Mitzrayim*. The words of Chazal and the structure of the Haggadah itself contain everything a person needs to teach their children about the story of leaving Egypt, inspire *emunah*, and teach them how to have a relationship with Hashem. In order to highlight the potential within the Pesach Seder, there are a number of specially designed aspects of this Haggadah:

- It contains clear instructions and reasons for all the steps of the Seder so that the leader, or anyone following along, can confidently understand what exactly they are doing and why they are doing it.
- The side-by-side Hebrew-English translation is meant to make the words of the Haggadah come alive with meaning and relevance. The translation is not simply word-for-word. Rather, built into the translation is an explanation of the words, based on Chazal and the Rishonim, which is meant to clarify and bring to life the intent of the original author and editor of the Haggadah. The basis for this translation is the beautiful *Mesvita Haggadah* published by Oz V'Hadar. I have used the *Mesivta Haggadah* for a number of years, and it is their Hebrew translation that opened my eyes to the possibility of what the text of the Haggadah contains within it. I extend my deep appreciation and thanks to Rabbi Yehoshua Leifer, Nasi of Oz V'Hadar, for allowing me to borrow the styling of the elucidation along with the use of selected pieces for this Haggadah. I have added to and extensively reworked the translation based on the Midrashim and the commentaries of the Rishonim. Note: the elaborated side-by-side translation is only used when it is important for the leader of the Seder to explain the text of the Haggadah.
- The *divrei Torah* chosen for this Haggadah are focused on the essential mitzvah of explaining the story of *yetzias Mitzrayim* and highlight aspects of *emunah* and our relationship with Hakadosh Baruch Hu. Some of the *divrei Torah* may be too sophisticated for younger children, and may be more appropriate for older children and adults.
- Rav Tzvi Elimelech Shapiro in *Derech Pikudecha* and Rav Moshe Chagiz in *Eileh Hamitzvos* both note that part of the mitzvah of *sippur yetzias*

Mitzrayim is the highlighting of *ikarei ha'emunah*, principles of faith. This concept was pointed out to me by Rabbi Hershel Schachter. Therefore, the commentary will highlight where we find the Thirteen Principles of Faith within the Haggadah. Readers are encouraged to expand upon these ideas at their Seder if possible.

- I have included wide margins on the side of the Haggadah. Hopefully, this will be a canvas for parents and teachers of the Haggadah to include their own notes and ideas to be shared with their children and students for generations to come. The Haggadah, like the siddur, is a remarkable instrument capable of playing beautiful music. Part of learning to play any instrument is preparation and practice. So too, the Seder and the Haggadah require the practice and preparation of those leading and directing. In addition, every musical composition is raised to more magnificent levels when the musician includes their own emotions and adds their personal touch to the piece. Similarly, a Haggadah that is simply recited—but without the insights and experiences of the leader of the Seder—will certainly be lacking a crucial component. The leader of the Seder should prepare additional Midrashim, stories, and props (if necessary) to bring the Haggadah to life. It is my hope that the design of this Haggadah allows the space for parents and teachers to include their own thoughts and lessons.

Timing is an important ingredient for a successful Pesach Seder. Besides for the critical halachos of eating the matzah by *chatzos*, it is also important for the leader of the Seder to not lose focus on those who need to be taught and inspired. If saying *divrei Torah* will slow down the pace of the Seder and young children (and even older children and adults) will lose interest, then please skip any extra *divrei Torah*. There will be a time and place over Pesach to share other ideas of inspiration. However, on the *Leil HaSeder*, the mitzvah of teaching *sippur yetzias Mitzrayim* from the Haggadah is of primary importance. It is my hope that the text of the Haggadah will speak and teach for itself.

The *Haggadah Nishmas Kol Chai* wonders why the answer to the wise son is to teach him the law of "אין מפטירין אחר הפסח אפיקומן"—that we don't eat anything after eating the *Korban Pesach* or the afikoman? He cites Rav Dovid Cohen, the Rosh Yeshiva of Chevron, who explains as follows. The *Ramchal*, in his *Maamar Hachochmah*, explains that we eat matzah on Pesach—and not bread—because chametz represents the *yetzer hara*. On Pesach we eat matzah, a more elevated food, which represents a rejection of the *yetzer hara*. The *Ramchal* then adds:

אמנם כדי שישאר התקון לכל השנה, צריך שיאכל האפיקומן אחר כך, ושלא לאכול
אחר כך שום דבר, שכמו שאין הטעם סר מן הפה, כך אין האור סר מן הנשמה.

However, in order for this rectification to remain for the entire
year, we only eat the afikoman afterward, and we don't eat
anything else. Just like the taste of the afikoman will not leave
the mouth, so too the light will not leave the neshamah.

We are taught that a wise person is one who is "רואה את הנולד"—who can see and intuit what the future holds. When the wise son asks what these mitzvos are all about, he is asking what we gain by participating in the Seder and eating the matzah since, at some point, we will lose all the spirituality we gained from the night: we will soon go back to eating the bread of the *yetzer hara* and the regular meat we consume the rest of the year. Therefore, we tell him, "אין מפטירין אחר הפסח אפיקומן." The taste of the matzah and the spiritual sustenance can stay with the *neshamah* all year. The spiritual gains of the Seder night can remain with us—if we allow them to.

BEDIKAS CHAMETZ

On the night of the fourteenth of Nisan, a search for chametz is conducted by the light of a candle. Before the search, the following blessing is recited:

בָּרוּךְ אַתָּה יהוה אֱלֹהֵינוּ
מֶלֶךְ הָעוֹלָם, אֲשֶׁר קִדְּשָׁנוּ
בְּמִצְוֹתָיו וְצִוָּנוּ עַל בִּעוּר חָמֵץ:

Blessed are You, Hashem, our God, King of the universe, Who has sanctified us with His commandments and commanded us concerning the removal of chametz.

Conversation not relating to the search should be avoided until the search is completed. After the search, the following declaration of nullification is made:

כָּל חֲמִירָא וַחֲמִיעָא דְּאִכָּא
בִרְשׁוּתִי, דְּלָא חֲמִתֵּהּ,
וּדְלָא בְעַרְתֵּהּ, וּדְלָא יְדַעְנָא
לֵיהּ, לִבָּטֵל וְלֶהֱוֵי הֶפְקֵר
כְּעַפְרָא דְאַרְעָא:

All leaven and chametz that is in my possession, which I have not seen nor disposed of, and about which I am unaware, is hereby nullified and shall be ownerless as the dust of the earth.

BI'UR CHAMETZ

The chametz is burned on the morning of the fourteenth of Nisan, before the end of the fifth hour of daylight. After burning the chametz, the following declaration is made:

כָּל חֲמִירָא וַחֲמִיעָא דְאִכָּא בִרְשׁוּתִי, דַּחֲזִתֵּהּ וּדְלָא חֲזִתֵּהּ, דַּחֲמִתֵּהּ וּדְלָא חֲמִתֵּהּ, דְּבַעַרְתֵּהּ וּדְלָא בְעַרְתֵּהּ, לִבָּטֵל וְלֶהֱוֵי הֶפְקֵר כְּעַפְרָא דְאַרְעָא:

All leaven and chametz that is in my possession, whether I have seen it or not, whether I have disposed of it or not, is hereby nullified and shall be ownerless as the dust of the earth.

סדר אמירת קרבן פסח

Following *Minchah*, many people have the custom to recite the verses that relate to the bringing of the Pesach offering.

רִבּוֹן הָעוֹלָמִים, אַתָּה צִוִּיתָנוּ לְהַקְרִיב קָרְבַּן הַפֶּסַח בְּמוֹעֲדוֹ בְּאַרְבָּעָה עָשָׂר יוֹם לַחֹדֶשׁ הָרִאשׁוֹן, וְלִהְיוֹת כֹּהֲנִים בַּעֲבוֹדָתָם וּלְוִיִּם בְּדוּכָנָם וְיִשְׂרָאֵל בְּמַעֲמָדָם קוֹרְאִים אֶת הַהַלֵּל. וְעַתָּה בַּעֲוֹנוֹתֵינוּ חָרַב בֵּית הַמִּקְדָּשׁ וּבָטֵל קָרְבַּן הַפֶּסַח, וְאֵין לָנוּ לֹא כֹהֵן בַּעֲבוֹדָתוֹ וְלֹא לֵוִי בְּדוּכָנוֹ וְלֹא יִשְׂרָאֵל בְּמַעֲמָדוֹ, וְלֹא נוּכַל לְהַקְרִיב הַיּוֹם קָרְבַּן פֶּסַח. אֲבָל אַתָּה אָמַרְתָּ וּנְשַׁלְמָה פָרִים שְׂפָתֵינוּ. לָכֵן יְהִי רָצוֹן מִלְּפָנֶיךָ יְיָ אֱלֹהֵינוּ וֵאלֹהֵי אֲבוֹתֵינוּ שֶׁיְּהֵא שִׂיחַ שִׂפְתוֹתֵינוּ חָשׁוּב לְפָנֶיךָ כְּאִלּוּ הִקְרַבְנוּ אֶת הַפֶּסַח בְּמוֹעֲדוֹ וְעָמַדְנוּ עַל מַעֲמָדוֹ, וְדִבְּרוּ הַלְוִיִּם בְּשִׁיר וְהַלֵּל לְהוֹדוֹת לַיְיָ. וְאַתָּה תְּכוֹנֵן מִקְדָּשְׁךָ עַל מְכוֹנוֹ, וְנַעֲשֶׂה וְנַקְרִיב לְפָנֶיךָ אֶת הַפֶּסַח בְּמוֹעֲדוֹ, כְּמוֹ שֶׁכָּתַבְתָּ עָלֵינוּ בְּתוֹרָתֶךָ עַל יְדֵי מֹשֶׁה עַבְדֶּךָ כָּאָמוּר:

שמות יב:א-יא

וַיֹּאמֶר יְהֹוָה אֶל מֹשֶׁה וְאֶל אַהֲרֹן בְּאֶרֶץ מִצְרַיִם לֵאמֹר: הַחֹדֶשׁ הַזֶּה לָכֶם רֹאשׁ חֳדָשִׁים רִאשׁוֹן הוּא לָכֶם לְחָדְשֵׁי הַשָּׁנָה: דַּבְּרוּ אֶל כָּל עֲדַת יִשְׂרָאֵל לֵאמֹר בֶּעָשֹׂר לַחֹדֶשׁ הַזֶּה וְיִקְחוּ לָהֶם אִישׁ שֶׂה לְבֵית אָבֹת שֶׂה לַבָּיִת: וְאִם יִמְעַט הַבַּיִת מִהְיוֹת מִשֶּׂה וְלָקַח הוּא וּשְׁכֵנוֹ הַקָּרֹב אֶל בֵּיתוֹ בְּמִכְסַת נְפָשֹׁת אִישׁ לְפִי אָכְלוֹ תָּכֹסּוּ עַל הַשֶּׂה: שֶׂה תָמִים זָכָר בֶּן שָׁנָה יִהְיֶה לָכֶם מִן הַכְּבָשִׂים וּמִן הָעִזִּים תִּקָּחוּ: וְהָיָה לָכֶם לְמִשְׁמֶרֶת עַד אַרְבָּעָה עָשָׂר יוֹם לַחֹדֶשׁ הַזֶּה וְשָׁחֲטוּ אֹתוֹ כֹּל קְהַל עֲדַת יִשְׂרָאֵל בֵּין הָעַרְבָּיִם: וְלָקְחוּ מִן הַדָּם וְנָתְנוּ עַל שְׁתֵּי הַמְּזוּזֹת וְעַל הַמַּשְׁקוֹף עַל הַבָּתִּים אֲשֶׁר יֹאכְלוּ אֹתוֹ בָּהֶם: וְאָכְלוּ אֶת הַבָּשָׂר בַּלַּיְלָה הַזֶּה צְלִי אֵשׁ וּמַצּוֹת עַל מְרֹרִים יֹאכְלֻהוּ: אַל תֹּאכְלוּ מִמֶּנּוּ נָא וּבָשֵׁל מְבֻשָּׁל בַּמָּיִם כִּי אִם צְלִי אֵשׁ רֹאשׁוֹ עַל כְּרָעָיו וְעַל קִרְבּוֹ: וְלֹא תוֹתִירוּ מִמֶּנּוּ עַד בֹּקֶר וְהַנֹּתָר מִמֶּנּוּ עַד בֹּקֶר בָּאֵשׁ תִּשְׂרֹפוּ: וְכָכָה תֹּאכְלוּ אֹתוֹ מָתְנֵיכֶם חֲגֻרִים נַעֲלֵיכֶם בְּרַגְלֵיכֶם וּמַקֶּלְכֶם בְּיֶדְכֶם וַאֲכַלְתֶּם אֹתוֹ בְּחִפָּזוֹן פֶּסַח הוּא לַיהֹוָה:

שמות יב:כא-כח

וַיִּקְרָא מֹשֶׁה לְכָל זִקְנֵי יִשְׂרָאֵל וַיֹּאמֶר אֲלֵהֶם מִשְׁכוּ וּקְחוּ לָכֶם צֹאן לְמִשְׁפְּחֹתֵיכֶם וְשַׁחֲטוּ הַפָּסַח: וּלְקַחְתֶּם אֲגֻדַּת אֵזוֹב וּטְבַלְתֶּם בַּדָּם אֲשֶׁר בַּסַּף וְהִגַּעְתֶּם אֶל הַמַּשְׁקוֹף וְאֶל שְׁתֵּי הַמְּזוּזֹת מִן הַדָּם אֲשֶׁר בַּסָּף וְאַתֶּם לֹא תֵצְאוּ אִישׁ מִפֶּתַח בֵּיתוֹ עַד בֹּקֶר: וְעָבַר יְהֹוָה לִנְגֹּף אֶת מִצְרַיִם וְרָאָה אֶת הַדָּם עַל הַמַּשְׁקוֹף וְעַל שְׁתֵּי הַמְּזוּזֹת וּפָסַח יְהֹוָה עַל הַפֶּתַח וְלֹא יִתֵּן הַמַּשְׁחִית לָבֹא אֶל בָּתֵּיכֶם לִנְגֹּף: וּשְׁמַרְתֶּם אֶת הַדָּבָר הַזֶּה לְחָק לְךָ וּלְבָנֶיךָ עַד עוֹלָם: וְהָיָה כִּי תָבֹאוּ אֶל הָאָרֶץ אֲשֶׁר יִתֵּן יְהֹוָה לָכֶם כַּאֲשֶׁר דִּבֵּר וּשְׁמַרְתֶּם אֶת הָעֲבֹדָה הַזֹּאת: וְהָיָה כִּי יֹאמְרוּ אֲלֵיכֶם בְּנֵיכֶם מָה הָעֲבֹדָה הַזֹּאת לָכֶם: וַאֲמַרְתֶּם זֶבַח פֶּסַח הוּא לַיהֹוָה אֲשֶׁר פָּסַח עַל בָּתֵּי בְנֵי יִשְׂרָאֵל בְּמִצְרַיִם בְּנָגְפּוֹ אֶת מִצְרַיִם וְאֶת בָּתֵּינוּ הִצִּיל וַיִּקֹּד הָעָם וַיִּשְׁתַּחֲווּ: וַיֵּלְכוּ וַיַּעֲשׂוּ בְּנֵי יִשְׂרָאֵל כַּאֲשֶׁר צִוָּה יְהֹוָה אֶת מֹשֶׁה וְאַהֲרֹן כֵּן עָשׂוּ:

שמות יב:מג-נ

וַיֹּאמֶר יְהֹוָה אֶל מֹשֶׁה וְאַהֲרֹן זֹאת חֻקַּת הַפָּסַח כָּל בֶּן נֵכָר לֹא יֹאכַל בּוֹ: וְכָל עֶבֶד אִישׁ מִקְנַת כָּסֶף וּמַלְתָּה אֹתוֹ אָז יֹאכַל בּוֹ: תּוֹשָׁב וְשָׂכִיר לֹא יֹאכַל בּוֹ: בְּבַיִת אֶחָד יֵאָכֵל לֹא תוֹצִיא מִן הַבַּיִת מִן הַבָּשָׂר חוּצָה וְעֶצֶם לֹא תִשְׁבְּרוּ בוֹ: כָּל עֲדַת יִשְׂרָאֵל יַעֲשׂוּ אֹתוֹ: וְכִי יָגוּר אִתְּךָ גֵּר וְעָשָׂה פֶסַח לַיהֹוָה הִמּוֹל לוֹ כָל זָכָר וְאָז יִקְרַב לַעֲשֹׂתוֹ וְהָיָה כְּאֶזְרַח הָאָרֶץ וְכָל עָרֵל לֹא יֹאכַל בּוֹ: תּוֹרָה אַחַת יִהְיֶה לָאֶזְרָח וְלַגֵּר הַגָּר בְּתוֹכְכֶם: וַיַּעֲשׂוּ כָּל בְּנֵי יִשְׂרָאֵל כַּאֲשֶׁר צִוָּה יְהֹוָה אֶת מֹשֶׁה וְאֶת אַהֲרֹן כֵּן עָשׂוּ:

ויקרא כג:ד-ה

אֵלֶּה מוֹעֲדֵי יְהֹוָה מִקְרָאֵי קֹדֶשׁ אֲשֶׁר תִּקְרְאוּ אֹתָם בְּמוֹעֲדָם: בַּחֹדֶשׁ הָרִאשׁוֹן בְּאַרְבָּעָה עָשָׂר לַחֹדֶשׁ בֵּין הָעַרְבַּיִם פֶּסַח לַיהֹוָה:

במדבר ט:א-יד

וַיְדַבֵּר יְהֹוָה אֶל מֹשֶׁה בְמִדְבַּר סִינַי בַּשָּׁנָה הַשֵּׁנִית לְצֵאתָם מֵאֶרֶץ מִצְרַיִם בַּחֹדֶשׁ הָרִאשׁוֹן לֵאמֹר: וְיַעֲשׂוּ בְנֵי יִשְׂרָאֵל אֶת הַפָּסַח בְּמוֹעֲדוֹ: בְּאַרְבָּעָה עָשָׂר יוֹם בַּחֹדֶשׁ הַזֶּה בֵּין הָעַרְבַּיִם תַּעֲשׂוּ אֹתוֹ בְּמוֹעֲדוֹ כְּכָל חֻקֹּתָיו וּכְכָל מִשְׁפָּטָיו תַּעֲשׂוּ אֹתוֹ: וַיְדַבֵּר מֹשֶׁה אֶל בְּנֵי יִשְׂרָאֵל לַעֲשֹׂת הַפָּסַח: וַיַּעֲשׂוּ אֶת הַפֶּסַח בָּרִאשׁוֹן בְּאַרְבָּעָה עָשָׂר יוֹם לַחֹדֶשׁ בֵּין הָעַרְבַּיִם בְּמִדְבַּר סִינָי כְּכֹל אֲשֶׁר צִוָּה יְהֹוָה אֶת מֹשֶׁה כֵּן עָשׂוּ בְּנֵי יִשְׂרָאֵל: וַיְהִי אֲנָשִׁים אֲשֶׁר הָיוּ טְמֵאִים לְנֶפֶשׁ אָדָם וְלֹא יָכְלוּ לַעֲשֹׂת הַפֶּסַח בַּיּוֹם הַהוּא וַיִּקְרְבוּ לִפְנֵי מֹשֶׁה וְלִפְנֵי אַהֲרֹן בַּיּוֹם הַהוּא: וַיֹּאמְרוּ הָאֲנָשִׁים הָהֵמָּה אֵלָיו אֲנַחְנוּ טְמֵאִים לְנֶפֶשׁ אָדָם לָמָּה נִגָּרַע לְבִלְתִּי הַקְרִיב אֶת קָרְבַּן יְהֹוָה בְּמֹעֲדוֹ בְּתוֹךְ בְּנֵי יִשְׂרָאֵל: וַיֹּאמֶר אֲלֵהֶם מֹשֶׁה עִמְדוּ וְאֶשְׁמְעָה מַה יְצַוֶּה יְהֹוָה לָכֶם:

וַיְדַבֵּר יְהֹוָה אֶל מֹשֶׁה לֵּאמֹר: דַּבֵּר אֶל בְּנֵי יִשְׂרָאֵל לֵאמֹר אִישׁ אִישׁ כִּי יִהְיֶה טָמֵא לָנֶפֶשׁ אוֹ בְדֶרֶךְ רְחֹקָה לָכֶם אוֹ לְדֹרֹתֵיכֶם וְעָשָׂה פֶסַח לַיהֹוָה: בַּחֹדֶשׁ הַשֵּׁנִי בְּאַרְבָּעָה עָשָׂר יוֹם בֵּין הָעַרְבַּיִם יַעֲשׂוּ אֹתוֹ עַל מַצּוֹת וּמְרֹרִים יֹאכְלֻהוּ: לֹא יַשְׁאִירוּ מִמֶּנּוּ עַד בֹּקֶר וְעֶצֶם לֹא יִשְׁבְּרוּ בוֹ כְּכָל חֻקַּת הַפֶּסַח יַעֲשׂוּ אֹתוֹ: וְהָאִישׁ אֲשֶׁר הוּא טָהוֹר וּבְדֶרֶךְ לֹא הָיָה וְחָדַל לַעֲשׂוֹת הַפֶּסַח וְנִכְרְתָה הַנֶּפֶשׁ הַהִוא מֵעַמֶּיהָ כִּי קָרְבַּן יְהֹוָה לֹא הִקְרִיב בְּמֹעֲדוֹ חֶטְאוֹ יִשָּׂא הָאִישׁ הַהוּא: וְכִי יָגוּר אִתְּכֶם גֵּר וְעָשָׂה פֶסַח לַיהֹוָה כְּחֻקַּת הַפֶּסַח וּכְמִשְׁפָּטוֹ כֵּן יַעֲשֶׂה חֻקָּה אַחַת יִהְיֶה לָכֶם וְלַגֵּר וּלְאֶזְרַח הָאָרֶץ:

במדבר כח:טז

וּבַחֹדֶשׁ הָרִאשׁוֹן בְּאַרְבָּעָה עָשָׂר יוֹם לַחֹדֶשׁ פֶּסַח לַיהֹוָה:

דברים טז:א-ח

שָׁמוֹר אֶת חֹדֶשׁ הָאָבִיב וְעָשִׂיתָ פֶּסַח לַיהֹוָה אֱלֹהֶיךָ כִּי בְּחֹדֶשׁ הָאָבִיב הוֹצִיאֲךָ יְהֹוָה אֱלֹהֶיךָ מִמִּצְרַיִם לָיְלָה: וְזָבַחְתָּ פֶּסַח לַיהֹוָה אֱלֹהֶיךָ צֹאן וּבָקָר בַּמָּקוֹם אֲשֶׁר יִבְחַר יְהֹוָה לְשַׁכֵּן שְׁמוֹ שָׁם: לֹא תֹאכַל עָלָיו חָמֵץ שִׁבְעַת יָמִים תֹּאכַל עָלָיו מַצּוֹת לֶחֶם עֹנִי כִּי בְחִפָּזוֹן יָצָאתָ מֵאֶרֶץ מִצְרַיִם לְמַעַן תִּזְכֹּר אֶת יוֹם צֵאתְךָ מֵאֶרֶץ מִצְרַיִם כֹּל יְמֵי חַיֶּיךָ: וְלֹא יֵרָאֶה לְךָ שְׂאֹר בְּכָל גְּבֻלְךָ שִׁבְעַת יָמִים וְלֹא יָלִין מִן הַבָּשָׂר אֲשֶׁר תִּזְבַּח בָּעֶרֶב בַּיּוֹם הָרִאשׁוֹן לַבֹּקֶר: לֹא תוּכַל לִזְבֹּחַ אֶת הַפָּסַח בְּאַחַד שְׁעָרֶיךָ אֲשֶׁר יְהֹוָה אֱלֹהֶיךָ

נָתַן לָךְ: כִּי אִם אֶל הַמָּקוֹם אֲשֶׁר יִבְחַר יְהֹוָה אֱלֹהֶיךָ לְשַׁכֵּן שְׁמוֹ שָׁם תִּזְבַּח אֶת הַפֶּסַח בָּעֶרֶב כְּבוֹא הַשֶּׁמֶשׁ מוֹעֵד צֵאתְךָ מִמִּצְרָיִם: וּבִשַּׁלְתָּ וְאָכַלְתָּ בַּמָּקוֹם אֲשֶׁר יִבְחַר יְהֹוָה אֱלֹהֶיךָ בּוֹ וּפָנִיתָ בַבֹּקֶר וְהָלַכְתָּ לְאֹהָלֶיךָ: שֵׁשֶׁת יָמִים תֹּאכַל מַצּוֹת וּבַיּוֹם הַשְּׁבִיעִי עֲצֶרֶת לַיהֹוָה אֱלֹהֶיךָ לֹא תַעֲשֶׂה מְלָאכָה:

יהושע ה: י-יא

וַיַּחֲנוּ בְנֵי יִשְׂרָאֵל בַּגִּלְגָּל וַיַּעֲשׂוּ אֶת הַפֶּסַח בְּאַרְבָּעָה עָשָׂר יוֹם לַחֹדֶשׁ בָּעֶרֶב בְּעַרְבוֹת יְרִיחוֹ: וַיֹּאכְלוּ מֵעֲבוּר הָאָרֶץ מִמָּחֳרַת הַפֶּסַח מַצּוֹת וְקָלוּי בְּעֶצֶם הַיּוֹם הַזֶּה:

מלכים ב כג:כא-כג

וַיְצַו הַמֶּלֶךְ אֶת כָּל הָעָם לֵאמֹר עֲשׂוּ פֶסַח לַיהֹוָה אֱלֹהֵיכֶם כַּכָּתוּב עַל סֵפֶר הַבְּרִית הַזֶּה: כִּי לֹא נַעֲשָׂה כַּפֶּסַח הַזֶּה מִימֵי הַשֹּׁפְטִים אֲשֶׁר שָׁפְטוּ אֶת יִשְׂרָאֵל וְכֹל יְמֵי מַלְכֵי יִשְׂרָאֵל וּמַלְכֵי יְהוּדָה: כִּי אִם בִּשְׁמֹנֶה עֶשְׂרֵה שָׁנָה לַמֶּלֶךְ יֹאשִׁיָּהוּ נַעֲשָׂה הַפֶּסַח הַזֶּה לַיהֹוָה בִּירוּשָׁלָיִם:

דברי הימים ב ל:א-כ

וַיִּשְׁלַח יְחִזְקִיָּהוּ עַל כָּל יִשְׂרָאֵל וִיהוּדָה וְגַם אִגְּרוֹת כָּתַב עַל אֶפְרַיִם וּמְנַשֶּׁה לָבוֹא לְבֵית יְהֹוָה בִּירוּשָׁלַיִם לַעֲשׂוֹת פֶּסַח לַיהֹוָה אֱלֹהֵי יִשְׂרָאֵל: וַיִּוָּעַץ הַמֶּלֶךְ וְשָׂרָיו וְכָל הַקָּהָל בִּירוּשָׁלָיִם לַעֲשׂוֹת הַפֶּסַח בַּחֹדֶשׁ הַשֵּׁנִי: כִּי לֹא יָכְלוּ לַעֲשֹׂתוֹ בָּעֵת הַהִיא כִּי הַכֹּהֲנִים לֹא הִתְקַדְּשׁוּ לְמַדַּי וְהָעָם לֹא נֶאֶסְפוּ לִירוּשָׁלָיִם: וַיִּישַׁר הַדָּבָר בְּעֵינֵי הַמֶּלֶךְ וּבְעֵינֵי כָּל הַקָּהָל: וַיַּעֲמִידוּ דָבָר לְהַעֲבִיר קוֹל בְּכָל יִשְׂרָאֵל מִבְּאֵר שֶׁבַע וְעַד דָּן לָבוֹא לַעֲשׂוֹת פֶּסַח לַיהֹוָה אֱלֹהֵי יִשְׂרָאֵל בִּירוּשָׁלָיִם כִּי לֹא לָרֹב עָשׂוּ כַּכָּתוּב: וַיֵּלְכוּ הָרָצִים בָּאִגְּרוֹת מִיַּד הַמֶּלֶךְ וְשָׂרָיו בְּכָל יִשְׂרָאֵל וִיהוּדָה וּכְמִצְוַת הַמֶּלֶךְ לֵאמֹר בְּנֵי יִשְׂרָאֵל שׁוּבוּ אֶל יְהֹוָה אֱלֹהֵי אַבְרָהָם יִצְחָק וְיִשְׂרָאֵל וְיָשֹׁב אֶל הַפְּלֵיטָה הַנִּשְׁאֶרֶת לָכֶם מִכַּף מַלְכֵי אַשּׁוּר: וְאַל תִּהְיוּ כַּאֲבוֹתֵיכֶם וְכַאֲחֵיכֶם אֲשֶׁר מָעֲלוּ בַּיהֹוָה אֱלֹהֵי אֲבוֹתֵיהֶם וַיִּתְּנֵם לְשַׁמָּה כַּאֲשֶׁר אַתֶּם רֹאִים: עַתָּה אַל תַּקְשׁוּ עָרְפְּכֶם כַּאֲבוֹתֵיכֶם תְּנוּ יָד לַיהֹוָה וּבֹאוּ לְמִקְדָּשׁוֹ אֲשֶׁר הִקְדִּישׁ לְעוֹלָם וְעִבְדוּ אֶת יְהֹוָה אֱלֹהֵיכֶם וְיָשֹׁב מִכֶּם חֲרוֹן אַפּוֹ: כִּי בְשׁוּבְכֶם עַל יְהֹוָה אֲחֵיכֶם וּבְנֵיכֶם לְרַחֲמִים לִפְנֵי שׁוֹבֵיהֶם וְלָשׁוּב לָאָרֶץ הַזֹּאת כִּי חַנּוּן וְרַחוּם יְהֹוָה אֱלֹהֵיכֶם וְלֹא יָסִיר פָּנִים מִכֶּם אִם תָּשׁוּבוּ אֵלָיו: וַיִּהְיוּ הָרָצִים עֹבְרִים מֵעִיר לָעִיר בְּאֶרֶץ אֶפְרַיִם וּמְנַשֶּׁה וְעַד זְבֻלוּן וַיִּהְיוּ מַשְׂחִיקִים עֲלֵיהֶם וּמַלְעִגִים בָּם: אַךְ אֲנָשִׁים מֵאָשֵׁר וּמְנַשֶּׁה וּמִזְּבֻלוּן נִכְנְעוּ וַיָּבֹאוּ לִירוּשָׁלָיִם: גַּם בִּיהוּדָה הָיְתָה יַד הָאֱלֹהִים לָתֵת לָהֶם לֵב אֶחָד לַעֲשׂוֹת מִצְוַת הַמֶּלֶךְ וְהַשָּׂרִים בִּדְבַר יְהֹוָה: וַיֵּאָסְפוּ יְרוּשָׁלַםִ עַם רָב לַעֲשׂוֹת אֶת חַג הַמַּצּוֹת בַּחֹדֶשׁ הַשֵּׁנִי קָהָל לָרֹב מְאֹד: וַיָּקֻמוּ וַיָּסִירוּ אֶת הַמִּזְבְּחוֹת אֲשֶׁר בִּירוּשָׁלָיִם וְאֵת כָּל הַמְקַטְּרוֹת הֵסִירוּ וַיַּשְׁלִיכוּ לְנַחַל קִדְרוֹן: וַיִּשְׁחֲטוּ הַפֶּסַח בְּאַרְבָּעָה עָשָׂר לַחֹדֶשׁ הַשֵּׁנִי וְהַכֹּהֲנִים וְהַלְוִיִּם נִכְלְמוּ וַיִּתְקַדְּשׁוּ וַיָּבִיאוּ עֹלוֹת בֵּית יְהֹוָה: וַיַּעַמְדוּ עַל עָמְדָם כְּמִשְׁפָּטָם כְּתוֹרַת מֹשֶׁה אִישׁ הָאֱלֹהִים הַכֹּהֲנִים זֹרְקִים אֶת הַדָּם מִיַּד הַלְוִיִּם: כִּי רַבַּת בַּקָּהָל אֲשֶׁר לֹא הִתְקַדָּשׁוּ וְהַלְוִיִּם עַל שְׁחִיטַת הַפְּסָחִים לְכֹל לֹא טָהוֹר לְהַקְדִּישׁ לַיהֹוָה: כִּי מַרְבִּית הָעָם רַבַּת מֵאֶפְרַיִם וּמְנַשֶּׁה יִשָּׂשכָר וּזְבֻלוּן לֹא הִטֶּהָרוּ כִּי אָכְלוּ אֶת הַפֶּסַח בְּלֹא כַכָּתוּב כִּי הִתְפַּלֵּל יְחִזְקִיָּהוּ עֲלֵיהֶם לֵאמֹר יְהֹוָה הַטּוֹב יְכַפֵּר בְּעַד: כָּל לְבָבוֹ הֵכִין לִדְרוֹשׁ הָאֱלֹהִים יְהֹוָה אֱלֹהֵי אֲבוֹתָיו וְלֹא כְּטָהֳרַת הַקֹּדֶשׁ: וַיִּשְׁמַע יְהֹוָה אֶל יְחִזְקִיָּהוּ וַיִּרְפָּא אֶת הָעָם:

וַיַּעַשׂ יֹאשִׁיָּהוּ בִירוּשָׁלַ͏ִם פֶּסַח לַיהוָה וַיִּשְׁחֲטוּ הַפֶּסַח בְּאַרְבָּעָה עָשָׂר לַחֹדֶשׁ הָרִאשׁוֹן: וַיַּעֲמֵד הַכֹּהֲנִים עַל מִשְׁמְרוֹתָם וַיְחַזְּקֵם לַעֲבוֹדַת בֵּית יְהוָה: וַיֹּאמֶר לַלְוִיִּם הַמְּבִינִים לְכָל יִשְׂרָאֵל הַקְּדוֹשִׁים לַיהוָה תְּנוּ אֶת אֲרוֹן הַקֹּדֶשׁ בַּבַּיִת אֲשֶׁר בָּנָה שְׁלֹמֹה בֶן דָּוִיד מֶלֶךְ יִשְׂרָאֵל אֵין לָכֶם מַשָּׂא בַּכָּתֵף עַתָּה עִבְדוּ אֶת יְהוָה אֱלֹהֵיכֶם וְאֵת עַמּוֹ יִשְׂרָאֵל: וְהָכִינוּ לְבֵית אֲבוֹתֵיכֶם כְּמַחְלְקוֹתֵיכֶם בִּכְתָב דָּוִיד מֶלֶךְ יִשְׂרָאֵל וּבְמִכְתַּב שְׁלֹמֹה בְנוֹ: וְעִמְדוּ בַקֹּדֶשׁ לִפְלֻגּוֹת בֵּית הָאָבוֹת לַאֲחֵיכֶם בְּנֵי הָעָם וַחֲלֻקַּת בֵּית אָב לַלְוִיִּם: וְשַׁחֲטוּ הַפָּסַח וְהִתְקַדְּשׁוּ וְהָכִינוּ לַאֲחֵיכֶם לַעֲשׂוֹת כִּדְבַר יְהוָה בְּיַד מֹשֶׁה: וַיָּרֶם יֹאשִׁיָּהוּ לִבְנֵי הָעָם צֹאן כְּבָשִׂים וּבְנֵי עִזִּים הַכֹּל לַפְּסָחִים לְכָל הַנִּמְצָא לְמִסְפַּר שְׁלֹשִׁים אֶלֶף וּבָקָר שְׁלֹשֶׁת אֲלָפִים אֵלֶּה מֵרְכוּשׁ הַמֶּלֶךְ: וְשָׂרָיו לִנְדָבָה לָעָם לַכֹּהֲנִים וְלַלְוִיִּם הֵרִימוּ חִלְקִיָּה וּזְכַרְיָהוּ וִיחִיאֵל נְגִידֵי בֵּית הָאֱלֹהִים לַכֹּהֲנִים נָתְנוּ לַפְּסָחִים אַלְפַּיִם וְשֵׁשׁ מֵאוֹת וּבָקָר שְׁלֹשׁ מֵאוֹת: וְכָנַנְיָהוּ וּשְׁמַעְיָהוּ וּנְתַנְאֵל אֶחָיו וַחֲשַׁבְיָהוּ וִיעִיאֵל וְיוֹזָבָד שָׂרֵי הַלְוִיִּם הֵרִימוּ לַלְוִיִּם לַפְּסָחִים חֲמֵשֶׁת אֲלָפִים וּבָקָר חֲמֵשׁ מֵאוֹת: וַתִּכּוֹן הָעֲבוֹדָה וַיַּעַמְדוּ הַכֹּהֲנִים עַל עָמְדָם וְהַלְוִיִּם עַל מַחְלְקוֹתָם כְּמִצְוַת הַמֶּלֶךְ: וַיִּשְׁחֲטוּ הַפָּסַח וַיִּזְרְקוּ הַכֹּהֲנִים מִיָּדָם וְהַלְוִיִּם מַפְשִׁיטִים: וַיָּסִירוּ הָעֹלָה לְתִתָּם לְמִפְלַגּוֹת לְבֵית אָבוֹת לִבְנֵי הָעָם לְהַקְרִיב לַיהוָה כַּכָּתוּב בְּסֵפֶר מֹשֶׁה וְכֵן לַבָּקָר: וַיְבַשְּׁלוּ הַפֶּסַח בָּאֵשׁ כַּמִּשְׁפָּט וְהַקֳּדָשִׁים בִּשְּׁלוּ בַּסִּירוֹת וּבַדְּוָדִים וּבַצֵּלָחוֹת וַיָּרִיצוּ לְכָל בְּנֵי הָעָם: וְאַחַר הֵכִינוּ לָהֶם וְלַכֹּהֲנִים כִּי הַכֹּהֲנִים בְּנֵי אַהֲרֹן בְּהַעֲלוֹת הָעוֹלָה וְהַחֲלָבִים עַד לָיְלָה וְהַלְוִיִּם הֵכִינוּ לָהֶם וְלַכֹּהֲנִים בְּנֵי אַהֲרֹן: וְהַמְשֹׁרְרִים בְּנֵי אָסָף עַל מַעֲמָדָם כְּמִצְוַת דָּוִיד וְאָסָף וְהֵימָן וִידֻתוּן חֹזֵה הַמֶּלֶךְ וְהַשֹּׁעֲרִים לְשַׁעַר וָשָׁעַר אֵין לָהֶם לָסוּר מֵעַל עֲבֹדָתָם כִּי אֲחֵיהֶם הַלְוִיִּם הֵכִינוּ לָהֶם: וַתִּכּוֹן כָּל עֲבוֹדַת יְהוָה בַּיּוֹם הַהוּא לַעֲשׂוֹת הַפֶּסַח וְהַעֲלוֹת עֹלוֹת עַל מִזְבַּח יְהוָה כְּמִצְוַת הַמֶּלֶךְ יֹאשִׁיָּהוּ: וַיַּעֲשׂוּ בְנֵי יִשְׂרָאֵל הַנִּמְצְאִים אֶת הַפֶּסַח בָּעֵת הַהִיא וְאֶת חַג הַמַּצּוֹת שִׁבְעַת יָמִים: וְלֹא נַעֲשָׂה פֶסַח כָּמֹהוּ בְּיִשְׂרָאֵל מִימֵי שְׁמוּאֵל הַנָּבִיא וְכָל מַלְכֵי יִשְׂרָאֵל לֹא עָשׂוּ כַּפֶּסַח אֲשֶׁר עָשָׂה יֹאשִׁיָּהוּ וְהַכֹּהֲנִים וְהַלְוִיִּם וְכָל יְהוּדָה וְיִשְׂרָאֵל הַנִּמְצָא וְיוֹשְׁבֵי יְרוּשָׁלָ͏ִם: בִּשְׁמוֹנֶה עֶשְׂרֵה שָׁנָה לְמַלְכוּת יֹאשִׁיָּהוּ נַעֲשָׂה הַפֶּסַח הַזֶּה:

ERUV TAVSHILIN

When Pesach (or any festival) occurs on a Friday, an *eruv tavshilin* must be made in order to allow cooking (and other preparations) for Shabbos on that Friday. The *eruv* consists of a whole piece of matzah and at least a *k'zayis* (approximately the volume of half an egg) of a cooked food, which are set aside (before the festival begins) and kept intact until Shabbos preparations are completed. The *eruv* is held in the hand, and the following blessing is recited:

בָּרוּךְ אַתָּה יהוה אֱלֹהֵינוּ מֶלֶךְ הָעוֹלָם, אֲשֶׁר קִדְּשָׁנוּ בְּמִצְוֹתָיו וְצִוָּנוּ עַל מִצְוַת עֵרוּב:

Blessed are You, Hashem, our God, King of the universe, Who has sanctified us through His commandments and commanded us concerning the precept of the *eruv*.

Say the following declaration of intent:

בַּהֲדֵין עֵירוּבָא יְהֵא שָׁרֵא לָנָא לַאֲפוּיֵי וּלְבַשּׁוּלֵי וּלְאַטְמוּנֵי וּלְאַדְלוּקֵי שְׁרָגָא וּלְאַפּוּקֵי וּלְמֶעְבַּד כָּל צָרְכָנָא מִיּוֹמָא טָבָא לְשַׁבַּתָּא:

By this *eruv*, it shall be permitted for us to bake, to cook, to insulate pots of hot food, to light candles, and to do all [permissible acts] that are necessary on the festival in preparation for the Sabbath.

HALACHOS
AND PREPARATION
BEFORE THE SEDER

Before the Seder—perhaps in the afternoon of Erev Pesach—the leader should take the children and sit with them around the box of *shemurah matzah* and select the three special matzos that will be placed by the Seder plate. Discuss with the children what the matzos represent, the time and effort that goes into making them, and how excited you are about eating them later on that evening.

It is the custom of many Jewish communities, excluding Chabad and Sephardim, for the leader of the Seder to wear a *kittel*. There are numerous reasons given for this beautiful custom, and certainly, the impression of the leader of the Seder, resplendent in his *kittel*, adds an aura of majesty and holiness to the evening.

HADLAKAS NEIROS

The following are the blessings over the lighting of the holiday candles.
On Shabbos, the words in parentheses are added.

בָּרוּךְ אַתָּה יהוה אֱלֹהֵינוּ
מֶלֶךְ הָעוֹלָם, אֲשֶׁר קִדְּשָׁנוּ
בְּמִצְוֹתָיו וְצִוָּנוּ לְהַדְלִיק נֵר
שֶׁל (שַׁבָּת וְשֶׁל) יוֹם טוֹב:

Blessed are You, Hashem, our God, King of the universe, Who has sanctified us through His commandments and commanded us to kindle the candle of (the Sabbath and) the festival.

בָּרוּךְ אַתָּה יהוה אֱלֹהֵינוּ
מֶלֶךְ הָעוֹלָם, שֶׁהֶחֱיָנוּ וְקִיְּמָנוּ
וְהִגִּיעָנוּ לַזְּמַן הַזֶּה:

Blessed are You, Hashem, our God, King of the universe, Who has granted us life and sustained us and allowed us to reach this occasion.

SEDER PLATE

The Gemara has no mention of a *ke'arah*, the Seder plate. The *Tur* and *Shulchan Aruch* (473) simply list many of the items we put on our Seder plate and note that they are placed together on the table. The *Biur HaGra* notes that the earliest source for the *ke'arah* is in *Tosafos* (*Pesachim* 115b), who mention that in their time, they removed the Seder plate from in front of the guests instead of removing the small personal tables that were commonly used in the days of the Talmud.

There are three popular customs as to how the Seder plate should be set up:

- The *Rama* cites the *Maharil*, who says the Seder plate should be set up in the order in which the items are used during the Seder, so that the mitzvos that come first are positioned at the front of the plate. This is based on the principle that one doesn't pass up a mitzvah that is right in front of them. Therefore, at the front of the plate is the saltwater and *karpas*. Behind them is the maror and *charoses*, and at the back is the *beitzah* and the *zeroa*.
- According to the *Maaseh Rav* (191), the *Vilna Gaon* held that only two matzos are used. Behind them are the maror and *charoses*, and at the front of the plate is the *zeroa* and the *beitzah*. There is no *karpas* since the Seder plate is only used after the stage of *karpas* has been completed.
- The *Be'er Heitev* (473:8) cites the most common custom, which is that of the *Arizal*. There are ten items on the plate, including the three matzos and the plate itself, which correspond to the ten *Sefiros*. The placement of each item corresponds to the location of its corresponding *Sefirah*.

We will now give the simple explanation of the different items on the Seder plate.[7]

MATZOS

Why three matzos? Because the Seder is also a Yom Tov meal, it requires *lechem mishneh* (a double portion of bread). However, during the Seder we break the middle matzah (Yachatz). This is because we are supposed to have poor man's bread over which to recite the Haggadah—and the poor only eat part of their bread and save the rest for later. To accommodate having a broken matzah and still having

---

7   For a Kabbalistic approach, see the Haggadah of Rav Shimshon Pincus.

two complete ones for *Hamotzi*, we use a third matzah. The number three also hints to other significant concepts like the sections of Tanach, the three Avos, and the division of the Jewish People into Kohen, Levi, and Yisrael.

ZEROA

This is to remind us of the *Korban Pesach*. The *Korban Pesach* cannot be eaten on an empty stomach. Therefore, in the days of the Beis Hamikdash, they would eat a *Korban Chagigah* beforehand. The Mishnah says that we should have two cooked foods at the Seder table to remember the *Korban Chagigah* and the *Korban Pesach*. Any two cooked foods can be used to accomplish this. However, our custom is to remember to *Korban Pesach* using the *zeroa* as a reference to the "זרוע נטויה—outstretched arm" of Hashem, Who took us out of Egypt.

BEITZAH

This is to remind us of the *Korban Chagigah*. We use an egg as our cooked food because the first night of Pesach always falls on the same day of the week as Tishah B'Av. Before Tishah B'Av we eat eggs as a sign of our mourning and on Pesach we remind ourselves that as wonderful as our Sedarim are, we are still missing the real thing—the Beis Hamikdash.[8]

KARPAS

This is eaten so the children will ask questions, remain interested in the Seder, and stay awake. They will wonder—why we are dipping and eating vegetables after *Kiddush* but before the meal? We make a berachah on something that is a *Pri Ha'adamah* to cover the maror eaten later on. This is because there is a doubt about whether maror, which is eaten after the matzah and therefore during the meal, should have a berachah recited over it.

MAROR

This is eaten to remind us of the Torah's description, "וימררו את חייהם בעבודה קשה—The Egyptians embittered our lives." The Gemara in *Pesachim* 39a lists five species

---

8   For a deeper connection between Tishah B'Av and Pesach, see *The Seder Night: An Exalted Evening* (OU Press, 2009), based on the teachings of Rabbi Joseph B. Soloveitchik, pp. 12–13.

of bitter herbs. The first on the list is romaine lettuce, which has a bitter taste when left in the ground. It is also first because its name, *chasa* (חסא), is a hint that Hashem was *chas*, merciful, on the Jewish People. In Europe, they did not have lettuce, so they relied on horseradish. There is no great mitzvah in causing oneself pain by eating horseradish, especially since romaine lettuce is the preferred maror of the Gemara.

CHAROSES

The Gemara says that the maror is bitter, and it is placed in the *charoses* to curb its sharpness. Rabbeinu Chananel says that the *charoses* contains all the ingredients the Jewish People are compared to in *Shir Hashirim*, such as apples or citrus, wine, nuts, etc. We don't place *charoses* on the maror like a spread; rather, the maror is dipped into the *charoses*.

> It is a wonderful idea to have the children help in preparing the *charoses* for the Seder. There are so many different recipes from different types of Jewish communities that can be used.

CHAZERES

This is additional maror for Korech.

Rav Yisroel Harfenes, in his *Mikdash Yisrael* (*Pesach*, p. 234), asks why we don't have larger spaces for the items that go on the Seder plate. Is the plate not meant to be used? Many people mistakenly think the Seder plate is just for show, when it should, in fact, be used by the leader of the Seder throughout the proceedings. The proper amounts of each item should therefore be placed on the Seder plate.

SALTWATER

The Gemara (*Pesachim* 114a) says that before we eat matzah, we dip a vegetable. This is a reference to *karpas*. The Gemara doesn't define what the dipping liquid is, but the opinions in the Rishonim include *charoses*, vinegar, lemon juice, and salt-water. The *Seder Ha'aruch* (chap. 121) brings a number of reasons for the custom of dipping in saltwater:

- The Gemara (*Berachos* 5a) says that salt softens meat, just like trials and difficulties in life soften a person's transgressions. *Karpas* (כרפס) has the letters פרך, difficult work. This is a reference to our slavery in Egypt, which softened our sins and allowed us to be more receptive to accepting the Torah.

- Water and salt are integral parts of the world. So too, going through the difficulties of Egypt were integral prerequisites for receiving the Torah.
- Sodom was overturned on the night of Pesach through the means of salt. The wife of Lot had gone out under the guise of asking for salt and informed on her husband's charitable act of inviting guests. This triggered the outrage of the cruel and merciless Sodomites who abhorred charity. The city of Sodom and Lot's wife were therefore both punished with salt—and we counteract their lack of *hachnasas orchim* by having extra salt and inviting guests to our Seder. We use salt for acts of righteousness, in contrast to those who used it for evil.

Many contemporary Haggadahs suggest that the saltwater represents the tears of the Jewish People suffering under the slavery of Egypt. Despite the popularity of this explanation, I am not aware of such an idea appearing in the works of the Rishonim or Acharonim.

There is a debate as to whether or not the saltwater should go on the Seder plate. The *Rama* says that it should sit on the Seder plate. However, Rav Yaakov Emden, the *Kaf Hachaim*, the *Chayei Adam*, and the *Aruch Hashulchan* all say it should be placed separately from the plate. This is the popular custom.

> The importance of a beautiful Seder plate cannot be understated, whether a family heirloom or something the family spent a little extra on in honor of Yom Tov. A beautiful plate brings a sense of honor and sanctity to the Seder. A child remembers the beauty of a special Seder plate and is excited to see their family's traditional plate each year, placed majestically at the head of the table. It evokes the feeling that this is a very special item for a very special evening.

SIMANEI HASEDER — STEPS OF THE SEDER

There are fifteen stages to the Seder.[9] The number fifteen is not accidental. Fifteen is the *gematria* of the name of Hashem that is spelled *Yud-Hei* (י-ה). There are fifteen *Shirei Hamaalos*, Songs of Ascent, that are sung on the fifteen steps of the Beis Hamikdash. Each step brings one closer to a greater level of holiness in the Beis Hamikdash. Similarly, each step of the Seder is meant to bring us closer to greater levels of personal holiness.

> The singing of the fifteen steps of the Seder at the start of the proceedings is not simply a formality or a cute way to get our children to sing before the Seder. Rather, it is like looking at a map before going on a journey. (You can explain what a map is to the younger people at the table — and perhaps even prepare one beforehand.) Before we begin the glorious experience of marching our way to Hallel and Nirtzah, we first map out for ourselves a picture of what we are trying to accomplish this evening. Tonight is a *leil shimurim*, a night of protection, and by reviewing the map of where we are headed, it gives us a feeling of safety and security.
>
> One should not skip this part or simply mumble through it. Rather, we should understand that this list is the start of the Seder. Therefore, it should be treated as an important opening to our journey this evening. The one leading the Seder should encourage young and old to sing along and join in with whichever popular tune is known by those at the table.

---

9   Some make the mistake of counting Motzi and Matzah as one step, when they are, in fact, two separate steps.

קַדֵּשׁ KADDESH

וּרְחַץ URCHATZ

כַּרְפַּס KARPAS

יַחַץ YACHATZ

מַגִּיד MAGGID

רָחְצָה RACHTZAH

מוֹצִיא MOTZI

מַצָּה MATZAH

מָרוֹר MAROR

כּוֹרֵךְ KORECH

שֻׁלְחָן עוֹרֵךְ SHULCHAN ORECH

צָפוּן TZAFUN

בָּרֵךְ BARECH

הַלֵּל HALLEL

נִרְצָה NIRTZAH

Before beginning each of the fifteen steps, the leader of the Seder should announce it by name.

KADDESH

According to the Torah, we must sanctify Shabbos by speaking about the *kedushas ha'yom*, the holiness of the day. In order to enhance this sanctification, Chazal instituted that it should be done while holding a cup of wine. On Shabbos, the mitzvah of *Kiddush* in general is from the Torah, while the obligation to recite it over wine is Rabbinic. On Yom Tov, however, there is a debate as to whether the mitzvah of reciting *Kiddush* in general is from the Torah or if it is Rabbinic.

On Shabbos, we have the custom of adding the paragraph of *Va'yechulu Ha'shamayim* to *Kiddush* so that those who were not in shul have the opportunity to hear it. In addition, there is an idea that *Va'yechulu* should be recited three times on Shabbos (in the private *Amidah*, after the *Amidah*, and later in *Kiddush*) to correspond to the three special Shabbosos in Jewish history: the first Shabbos after the world was created, the Shabbos at Marah before the giving of the Torah, and the Shabbos of the days of Mashiach.

On Yom Tov, we also recite the berachah of *Shehecheyanu* to thank Hashem for the opportunity to experience and enjoy another Yom Tov.

YAKNEHAZ (יקנה"ז)

*When Yom Tov begins on Motzaei Shabbos there is both the mitzvah to make Havdalah and the mitzvah to make Kiddush. The Gemara (Pesachim 103a) wonders what the order of the various berachos of these mitzvos should be. Several different opinions are cited and the Gemara labels each option with roshei teivos, an abbreviation. At the conclusion of this list, the Gemara brings the opinion of Rava, who says that when Yom Tov falls on Motzaei Shabbos, we should perform "**Yaknehaz**" (יקנה"ז). What does this mean?*

- *Yayin*—*The berachah of Hagafen always comes first in Kiddush or Havdalah. This follows Beis Hillel (Berachos 51b), who say that the presence of the wine is what enables Kiddush to be said. In addition, there is the principle of "תדיר ושאינו תדיר תדיר קודם," when there is a competition between two events and one is more common, the more common one comes first. The berachah on wine is the most common of all the berachos recited during Kiddush and Havdalah.*

Rav Shlomo Zalman Auerbach, in Shemiras Shabbos K'Hilchasah (62, note 25) is quoted as saying that we don't overflow the cup for a Kiddush Yaknehaz like we do during a regular Havdalah. This is because the overflowing cup is intended as a good omen for monetary success. It is a disgrace to the sanctity of Yom Tov to make mention of physical and monetary success.

- **Kiddush**—The berachah on kedushas ha'yom, the sanctity of the day, is said next because it is more important than Havdalah. In addition, if you recited Havdalah before kedushas ha'yom, it would appear as if you were trying to run away from Shabbos.
- **Ner**—Now we can move on to say Havdalah. This begins with a candle for Motzaei Shabbos. The custom is that for this Havdalah, we do not look at our nails.
- **Havdalah**—Then the berachah on Havdalah itself. Concluding, according to the Rambam, with the words "המבדיל בין קודש לקודש."
- **Z'man**—The berachah of Shehecheyanu should come last because it is always recited last during Kiddush. This is because it is not specifically connected to Kiddush; it is said on many other occasions without a cup of wine.

Pour the first of the four cups.

Even if one usually follows the *minhag* of washing for *Hamotzi* before *Kiddush*, it is not done on the night of the Seder. Before beginning *Kiddush*, one should have in mind to fulfill the mitzvah of *Kiddush* and the four cups of wine. Remind those participating that when listening to the berachah of *Shehecheyanu*, they should have in mind for it to cover all of the mitzvos of the night that we are about to fulfill.

One should make sure to not begin *Kiddush* until after *tzeis ha'kochavim*.

On Friday night begin here:

וַיְהִי עֶרֶב וַיְהִי בֹקֶר

יוֹם הַשִּׁשִּׁי: וַיְכֻלּוּ הַשָּׁמַיִם וְהָאָרֶץ וְכָל צְבָאָם:
וַיְכַל אֱלֹהִים בַּיּוֹם הַשְּׁבִיעִי מְלַאכְתּוֹ אֲשֶׁר
עָשָׂה, וַיִּשְׁבֹּת בַּיּוֹם הַשְּׁבִיעִי מִכָּל מְלַאכְתּוֹ
אֲשֶׁר עָשָׂה: וַיְבָרֶךְ אֱלֹהִים אֶת יוֹם הַשְּׁבִיעִי
וַיְקַדֵּשׁ אֹתוֹ, כִּי בוֹ שָׁבַת מִכָּל מְלַאכְתּוֹ אֲשֶׁר
בָּרָא אֱלֹהִים לַעֲשׂוֹת:

And it was evening and it was morning, the sixth day. The heavens and the earth and all their hosts were completed. God completed on the seventh day His work that He had done, and He rested on the seventh day from all His work that He had done. God blessed the seventh day and sanctified it, for on it He rested from all His work that God had created to fulfill its purpose.

On a weekday begin here:

סַבְרִי מָרָנָן וְרַבָּנָן וְרַבּוֹתַי:

בָּרוּךְ אַתָּה יהוה
אֱלֹהֵינוּ מֶלֶךְ הָעוֹלָם,
בּוֹרֵא פְּרִי הַגָּפֶן:

With your permission, my masters:

Blessed are You, Hashem, our God, King of the universe, Who creates the fruit of the vine.

בָּרוּךְ אַתָּה יהוה אֱלֹהֵינוּ מֶלֶךְ הָעוֹלָם,
אֲשֶׁר בָּחַר בָּנוּ מִכָּל עָם, וְרוֹמְמָנוּ מִכָּל לָשׁוֹן,
וְקִדְּשָׁנוּ בְּמִצְוֹתָיו, וַתִּתֶּן לָנוּ יהוה אֱלֹהֵינוּ
בְּאַהֲבָה (לשבת: שַׁבָּתוֹת לִמְנוּחָה וּ) מוֹעֲדִים
לְשִׂמְחָה, חַגִּים וּזְמַנִּים לְשָׂשׂוֹן (לשבת: אֶת יוֹם
הַשַּׁבָּת הַזֶּה וְ) אֶת יוֹם חַג הַמַּצּוֹת הַזֶּה
זְמַן חֵרוּתֵנוּ (לשבת: בְּאַהֲבָה) מִקְרָא קֹדֶשׁ,

Blessed are You, Hashem, our God, King of the universe, Who has chosen us from all the nations, raised us above all nationalities, and made us holy through His commandments. You, Hashem, our God, gave us, with love (Sabbaths

זֵכֶר לִיצִיאַת מִצְרָיִם. כִּי בָנוּ בָחַרְתָּ וְאוֹתָנוּ קִדַּשְׁתָּ מִכָּל הָעַמִּים, (לשבת: וְשַׁבָּת) וּמוֹעֲדֵי קָדְשֶׁךָ (לשבת: בְּאַהֲבָה וּבְרָצוֹן) בְּשִׂמְחָה וּבְשָׂשׂוֹן הִנְחַלְתָּנוּ. בָּרוּךְ אַתָּה יהוה, מְקַדֵּשׁ (לשבת: הַשַּׁבָּת וְ) יִשְׂרָאֵל וְהַזְּמַנִּים:

for rest and) holidays for rejoicing, festivals and festive seasons for gladness, (this Sabbath day and) this day of the Festival of Matzos, the time of our freedom (with love), a holy convocation, in commemoration of the Exodus from Egypt. For You have chosen us and sanctified us from all the nations, and You have bestowed upon us Your holy (Sabbath and) festivals (with love and favor), with happiness and joy. Blessed are You, Hashem, Who sanctifies (the Sabbath and) Israel and the festive seasons.

On Motzaei Shabbos add this paragraph:

בָּרוּךְ אַתָּה יהוה אֱלֹהֵינוּ מֶלֶךְ הָעוֹלָם, בּוֹרֵא מְאוֹרֵי הָאֵשׁ: בָּרוּךְ אַתָּה יהוה אֱלֹהֵינוּ מֶלֶךְ הָעוֹלָם, הַמַּבְדִּיל בֵּין קֹדֶשׁ לְחֹל, בֵּין אוֹר לְחוֹשֶׁךְ, בֵּין יִשְׂרָאֵל לָעַמִּים, בֵּין יוֹם הַשְּׁבִיעִי לְשֵׁשֶׁת יְמֵי הַמַּעֲשֶׂה, בֵּין קְדוּשַׁת שַׁבָּת לִקְדוּשַׁת יוֹם טוֹב הִבְדַּלְתָּ, וְאֶת יוֹם הַשְּׁבִיעִי מִשֵּׁשֶׁת יְמֵי הַמַּעֲשֶׂה קִדַּשְׁתָּ, הִבְדַּלְתָּ וְקִדַּשְׁתָּ אֶת עַמְּךָ יִשְׂרָאֵל בִּקְדוּשָׁתֶךָ: בָּרוּךְ אַתָּה יהוה, הַמַּבְדִּיל בֵּין קֹדֶשׁ לְקֹדֶשׁ:

Blessed are You, Hashem, our God, King of the universe, Who creates the radiances of fire. Blessed are You, Hashem, our God, King of the universe, Who distinguishes between the sacred and the profane, between light and darkness, between Israel and the nations, and between the seventh day and the six workdays. You distinguished between the holiness of the Sabbath and the holiness of the festivals, and You have sanctified the seventh day above the six workdays. You have distinguished and sanctified Your people Israel through Your holiness. Blessed are You, Hashem, Who distinguishes between [one level of] holiness and [another level of] holiness.

On all nights, conclude with the following blessing:

בָּרוּךְ אַתָּה יהוה אֱלֹהֵינוּ
מֶלֶךְ הָעוֹלָם, שֶׁהֶחֱיָנוּ וְקִיְּמָנוּ
וְהִגִּיעָנוּ לַזְּמַן הַזֶּה:

Blessed are You, Hashem, our God, King of the universe, Who has granted us life, sustained us, and allowed us to reach this occasion.

Drink the first cup while leaning to the left.

Chazal enacted that when we eat or drink on Seder night, we should do so while reclining to the side. This was the manner in which royalty used to eat and it is a way to recall our freedom from slavery. It is also an important part of viewing ourselves as if we ourselves left Egypt.

All leaning should be toward the left and should be done on something (such as a chair or the table); it is not considered proper reclining to just tilt the body into the air. The *minhag* of women is not to recline during the Seder.

URCHATZ

The leader of the Seder should ask the children—or prompt the children to ask—why we are washing our hands at this point. We are not up to eating the matzah yet!

The answer is that we are about to eat a food that is dipped in a liquid. In the days of the Beis Hamikdash, when we observed many of the laws of *tumah* and *taharah*, the Chachamim made a rule to protect certain foods (like *terumah*) from becoming *tamei*. Because *tumah* can only transfer to produce if the receiving item is wet or has been wet, the Chachamim made a rule that anyone touching a wet food should wash their hands first so that if their hands were *tamei*, the *tumah* wouldn't transfer to the food and make it *tamei*. There is a major debate among the

Rishonim about whether this Rabbinic law applies nowadays, so the *Shulchan Aruch* (*Orach Chaim* 158:4) rules that we should wash our hands, but without a berachah. The *Magen Avraham* later noted that the custom of most Jews is to not wash hands before eating a food that is wet.

The *Taz* (473:6) asks why people are careful to wash their hands before eating wet food at the Seder but not during the rest of the year. In the introduction to his *Haggadah Imrei Shefer*, the *Netziv* explains that on this night we wash before eating dipped foods because Chazal constructed the Seder to mimic the Seder during the times of the Beis Hamikdash and the *Korban Pesach*. We are reenacting the story of leaving Egypt and what it would have been like to eat the *Korban Pesach* in the days of the Beis Hamikdash.

Wash hands in preparation for Karpas and do not make a berachah.

The opinion of the *Vilna Gaon* is that we do recite a berachah when washing hands for a food dipped in liquid. However, the *Mishnah Berurah* (158:20) says that this is not our custom. Even those who do follow the *Vilna Gaon* don't make a berachah if they eat less than a *k'zayis* of *karpas*, which is the recommended amount for the Seder.

KARPAS

What is the purpose of Karpas at the Seder? As always, the answer is so that the children will ask questions. But what are the answers to those questions?

- At the time of *yetzias Mitzrayim* and the days of the Beis Hamikdash, it was considered very regal and a sign of nobility to dip one's food before eating. Therefore, in the spirit of being free from slavery and like royalty on this night, we also dip our food before eating it.

- According to the laws of berachos, when eating and making a berachah on bread, the berachah of *Hamotzi* covers the remaining foods of the meal. However, if the food eaten after *Hamotzi* is not part of the main meal, it needs its own berachah. This, for example, is why we make a new berachah before eating dessert. On the night of the Seder, we make the berachah of *Hamotzi* on the matzah, but not long after, before the main meal we eat maror. This placement of maror—after *Hamotzi* but before Shulchan Orech—creates a *hilchos berachos* dilemma. Is the maror considered part of the meal and covered by the *Hamotzi* or is it separate from the meal and therefore requires its own berachah? In order to alleviate this doubt, we make a berachah of *Ha'adamah* on another food earlier in the Seder so that the berachah will cover the maror as well.

Because of the issue of *hilchos berachos*, some recommend not eating more than a *k'zayis* of *karpas*. Eating more than a *k'zayis* could raise the possibility of having to make a *berachah acharonah* on the Karpas. Making a *berachah acharonah* before eating the maror would undermine the whole point of eating the *karpas*, as described above. However, there are other *poskim* who rule that one should eat a *k'zayis* because *karpas* is a mitzvah—and when performing a mitzvah of eating, one should eat a *k'zayis*.

- Rav Shlomo Kluger explains that at our Pesach Seder we talk at great length about the evils of Pharaoh, the hardships forced upon us by the Egyptians, and the glorious redemption by Hashem. Although we do review the pre-Egyptian history of our people, we never seem to address the fundamental cause of our enslavement: *Why* did Hashem subject us to such brutal slavery in Egypt? We were made slaves because we sold our brother Yosef into slavery to the Arabs. What triggers this memory? After Kaddesh, we wash our hands before eating a vegetable, which is referred to as *karpas*. Why do we call it *karpas* when it would seem that *yerek* (vegetable), would be a more appropriate and accurate name for what we are eating? In the beginning of *Parashas Vayeishev*, the Torah records that Yaakov made a coat of "*pasim*" for Yosef. *Rashi* explains that the word *pasim* means fine wool and adds that it is similar to the term "*karpas*," which is used in *Esther* (1:5) to describe the fancy decor at the party of Achashveirosh. He certainly wasn't hanging vegetables from his walls; he was hanging decorations made of fine wool. What does fine wool have to do with dipping a vegetable into saltwater at the beginning of the Seder? Rabbeinu Manoach, commenting on the *Rambam* (*Hilchos Chametz U'Matzah* 8:2), writes that the word *karpas* hints to the words "כְּתֹנֶת פַּסִּים." This was the extra cloak Yaakov gave Yosef, which was the basis for the brothers' hatred of Yosef and subsequently drove them to sell him. The *Ben Ish Chai* explains that the dipping of the *karpas* in saltwater symbolizes the brothers dipping Yosef's coat into goat's blood. In light of all this, we now understand that *karpas* means fine wool, not vegetables, and the term is being used to remind us of the brothers selling Yosef into slavery. Why bring this up now? Because as we ponder leaving Egypt, we must remember how and why we descended there in the first place. It is not a question we enjoy discussing, because the shameful answer is that we descended there because of the disunity and fighting among the twelve brothers.

Anything that has the berachah of *Ha'adamah* can be used for *karpas*. It can range from the classic potato, celery, or radish to the more exotic banana, pineapple, or watermelon.

Since the goal is to keep the children engaged, try to mix things up to keep it interesting.

Remind those present to have in mind that the berachah of *Ha'adamah* should cover the maror that will be eaten later.
There is a debate as to whether one should lean for Karpas. One should follow their family's custom.

בָּרוּךְ אַתָּה יהוה אֱלֹהֵינוּ מֶלֶךְ הָעוֹלָם, בּוֹרֵא פְּרִי הָאֲדָמָה:

Blessed are You, Hashem, our God, King of the universe, Who creates the produce of the ground.

YACHATZ

Ask the children why we are breaking the matzah at this point.

The name the Torah gives for matzah is *lechem oni*, the bread of the poor. One of the ways we show this is by breaking it in half and saving some of it for later. A person who doesn't know where their next meal will come from takes whatever food they have and portions it so there will be more for later. Our breaking of the matzah is part of reenacting the lives of slaves in Egypt.

Why do we do this now and not before eating the matzah? Because another way to explain *lechem oni* is as the bread on which we are *oneh*, answering, the questions of the night. This is the bread that will be uncovered and discussed discuss how Hashem took us out of Egypt. Therefore, we prepare the matzah to be broken *lechem oni* before we begin the story of *yetzias Mitzrayim*.

Take the middle matzah and break it into two pieces.

The larger piece should be hidden away for the afikoman and the smaller piece should be returned to its location in between the top and bottom matzos.

Hiding the afikoman is an old and popular *minhag* to keep the children engaged and awake, although it shouldn't become the focus of the evening. There are two popular customs. One is for the children to try and take the afikoman and hide it from the leader of the Seder. In some homes, the children will then hold on to the afikoman as a ransom for an afikoman present. The other custom is for the adult to hide the afikoman and for the children to search for it before Tzafun. Whichever child finds the afikoman is given a present as a prize. The concept of giving a present is not as old as the hiding of the afikoman, and parents should not feel pressured to give elaborate presents as a reward for finding the afikoman.

MAGGID

We now begin the central mitzvah of the night, Maggid—teaching the story of how Hashem took us out of Egypt. Before beginning, those present should have in mind or express verbally that they are about to fulfill the mitzvah of *sippur yetzias Mitzrayim*. This is a very important mitzvah that demands our full attention. Because of this, we do not lean during Maggid.

It is imperative that the Haggadah be understood by everyone present. It should be read by the leader of the Seder out loud and in a clear voice. The translation that accompanies this Haggadah is meant to be clear and highlight the central messages of the night. Maggid should be accessible to the learning levels of all present at the table. All the participants should be following along during Maggid, and it is the responsibility of the leader of the Seder to make sure that everyone is engaged in the story. It should not be so fast that those listening cannot follow, but it should also not be so slow that people will lose interest. Women and children must be present in order to hear and follow along with the story.

> Gently and respectfully encourage people at the Seder not to leave toward the end of Maggid to prepare for the meal. Everyone should try and stay and participate in this special mitzvah. Staying through the end of Maggid will have an impact on ourselves and on the children. The story is told of an ignorant man who was running his Seder and it came time for the Ten Plagues. His wife wanted to go to the kitchen and get ready for the meal, but she didn't want to miss this part of the Seder. The husband assured her it wasn't a problem because he would do it for her. She agreed, and so he began, "*Dam* for me and *dam* for my wife, *tzefardei'a* for me and *tzefardei'a* for my wife, etc." Obviously, this is not the way we want our Sedarim to be experienced.

The rule for the raising of the cup and the covering of the matzah throughout Maggid is that whenever the cup is raised, the matzah is covered and whenever the cup is lowered, the matzah is uncovered. The cup of wine represents freedom, and the matzah represents slavery. It is incompatible for both to be put on display at the same time.

Uncover the matzah and raise up the Seder plate.

The following is an introduction to tell those present that we are going to eat matzah. This will then cause them to ask "*Mah Nishtanah*"—why is this night different than other nights?

הָא לַחְמָא עַנְיָא דִּי אֲכַלוּ אַבְהָתָנָא
בְּאַרְעָא דְמִצְרָיִם.

This is the matzah, the poor man's bread, that our fathers ate while in Egypt.

The foods required for the Seder night are expensive, so we now invite anyone who cannot afford them to come and join us.

כָּל דִּכְפִין יֵיתֵי וְיֵכוֹל. כָּל דִּצְרִיךְ יֵיתֵי וְיִפְסַח.

Whoever is hungry and doesn't have what to eat, come and eat with us. Whoever needs and doesn't have the necessary items for Pesach, like matzah, *charoses*, maror, and wine for the four cups **should come and have Pesach with us.**

הָשַׁתָּא הָכָא, לְשָׁנָה הַבָּאָה
בְּאַרְעָא דְיִשְׂרָאֵל.

An introductory prayer to Hashem: **This year we are here** in *galus*, and we hope that **the next year** Mashiach will come and we will be **in Eretz Yisrael.**

הָשַׁתָּא עַבְדֵי,
לְשָׁנָה הַבָּאָה בְּנֵי חוֹרִין:

This year we are slaves, and it should be the will of Hashem **that next year we will be free.**

Cover the matzah.

The cup does not need to be washed out before refilling. The second cup should now be poured. The goal of this is that the children will ask why we are pouring more wine before the meal.

Mah Nishtanah is more than a place in the Seder for children to show what they have learned in school. The Gemara (Pesachim 116a) says that this is an integral part of the Seder. The Torah instructs us that we must fulfill the mitzvah of sippur yetzias Mitzrayim at the Seder by telling the story through a question-and-answer dialogue.

All children who show interest should be allowed to recite the Mah Nishtanah. If a child is not interested or very shy, don't put the spotlight on them and force them to perform. Some coaxing and bribery are certainly welcome, but there is no need to make the child anxious and uncomfortable for the sake of making the parents and grandparents happy. In order to keep the Seder moving at a pace that will be engaging for all ages, there is no need for the various children to recite the Mah Nishtanah in many different languages. It should be kept to one recitation per child, in the language of their choice.

מַה נִּשְׁתַּנָּה הַלַּיְלָה הַזֶּה מִכָּל הַלֵּילוֹת:

שֶׁבְּכָל הַלֵּילוֹת אָנוּ אוֹכְלִין חָמֵץ וּמַצָּה, הַלַּיְלָה הַזֶּה כֻּלּוֹ מַצָּה:

שֶׁבְּכָל הַלֵּילוֹת אָנוּ אוֹכְלִין שְׁאָר יְרָקוֹת, הַלַּיְלָה הַזֶּה מָרוֹר:

שֶׁבְּכָל הַלֵּילוֹת אֵין אָנוּ מַטְבִּילִין אֲפִילוּ פַּעַם אֶחָת, הַלַּיְלָה הַזֶּה שְׁתֵּי פְעָמִים:

שֶׁבְּכָל הַלֵּילוֹת אָנוּ אוֹכְלִין בֵּין יוֹשְׁבִין וּבֵין מְסֻבִּין, הַלַּיְלָה הַזֶּה כֻּלָּנוּ מְסֻבִּין:

Why is this night different from all other nights? For on all nights we eat chametz and matzah; on this night only matzah! For on all nights we eat other vegetables; on this night bitter herbs! For on all nights we do not dip our food even once; on this night we do it twice! For on all nights we eat either sitting upright or reclining; on this night we all recline!

We will now answer those who asked why this night is different by using the verses from the Torah. In doing so, we will also elaborate on the mitzvah of the night.

עֲבָדִים הָיִינוּ לְפַרְעֹה בְּמִצְרָיִם, וַיּוֹצִיאֵנוּ יהוה אֱלֹהֵינוּ מִשָּׁם

We were slaves to Pharaoh in Egypt, and it was so bad that the only One who could get us out was **Hashem our God** Who **took us out from there**, not like slaves who ran away from their master, but rather

בְּיָד חֲזָקָה וּבִזְרוֹעַ נְטוּיָה.

with a strong hand against the will of the Egyptians **and an outstretched arm** in front of the entire world to see.

וְאִלּוּ לֹא הוֹצִיא הַקָּדוֹשׁ בָּרוּךְ הוּא אֶת אֲבוֹתֵינוּ מִמִּצְרַיִם, הֲרֵי אָנוּ וּבָנֵינוּ וּבְנֵי בָנֵינוּ מְשֻׁעְבָּדִים הָיִינוּ לְפַרְעֹה בְּמִצְרָיִם.

And what does that have to do with you? **Because if Hakadosh Baruch Hu hadn't taken our ancestors out of Egypt, we, our children, and our children's children,** and all future generations **would still be enslaved to Pharaoh in Egypt.** There is no hope for any people that are under the control of another people. Therefore, we began, "We were slaves."

וַאֲפִילוּ כֻּלָּנוּ חֲכָמִים, כֻּלָּנוּ נְבוֹנִים, כֻּלָּנוּ זְקֵנִים, כֻּלָּנוּ יוֹדְעִים אֶת הַתּוֹרָה

Because of this, Hashem commanded **that even if we were all knowledgeable** and we heard this story from our parents, **we were all smart** and could figure things out on our own, **and we were all older** and had heard this for many years, **or we all knew the Torah** and when learning Torah every day constantly speak about *yetzias Mitzrayim*, nevertheless

מִצְוָה עָלֵינוּ לְסַפֵּר בִּיצִיאַת מִצְרָיִם. **there is a mitzvah for us to tell the story of leaving Egypt** on this night, with joy and thanks. The Gemara tells us that even if two *talmidei chachamim* were having a Pesach Seder together, they would still have to ask each other about *sippur yetzias Mitzrayim* in order to fulfill the mitzvah.

וְכָל הַמַּרְבֶּה לְסַפֵּר בִּיצִיאַת מִצְרַיִם, הֲרֵי זֶה [10] מְשׁוּבָּח. **And whoever speaks at length about what occurred during** *yetzias Mitzrayim*, **this is praiseworthy** because it gives honor to Hashem.

A proof to the idea that (1) even great *talmidei chachamim* need to tell the story of leaving Egypt on the night of Pesach, and that (2) it is a good thing to spend a lot of time discussing the story, is found in the following event.

מַעֲשֶׂה בְּרַבִּי אֱלִיעֶזֶר וְרַבִּי יְהוֹשֻׁעַ וְרַבִּי אֶלְעָזָר בֶּן עֲזַרְיָה וְרַבִּי עֲקִיבָא וְרַבִּי טַרְפוֹן שֶׁהָיוּ מְסוּבִּין בִּבְנֵי בְרַק, וְהָיוּ מְסַפְּרִים בִּיצִיאַת מִצְרַיִם כָּל אוֹתוֹ הַלַּיְלָה, **It once happened that Rabbi Eliezer, Rabbi Yehoshua, Rabbi Elazar ben Azaryah, Rabbi Akiva, and Rabbi Tarfon were reclining in B'nei Brak and they were relating the story of leaving Egypt the entire night** of Pesach.[11] After they had finished the mitzvos of the Seder, they began to tell the story and explain the *pesukim* in the Torah. They ended up getting so involved in their discussion that they didn't notice that the entire evening had flown by.

---

10 Rav Gershon Stern, in his *Yalkut Hagershuni* (*Osios*, vol. 2, *os yud*) explains that the purpose of *sippur yetzias Mitzrayim* is to awaken our *emunah* and give us the strength to not give up on the *geulah*. The more we speak about the slavery of Egypt and how Hashem took us out, the more we will come to understand that the *geulah* can happen at any time, no matter how long the wait.

11 The Lubavitcher Rebbe explains that this section is a proof for the previous paragraph that everyone must participate in the Haggadah and *sippur yetzias*

עַד שֶׁבָּאוּ תַלְמִידֵיהֶם וְאָמְרוּ לָהֶם רַבּוֹתֵינוּ הִגִּיעַ זְמַן קְרִיאַת שְׁמַע שֶׁל שַׁחֲרִית. **Until their students came and said to them, "Our Rabbis, it is time for the morning Shema."** It is already *alos ha'shachar* and it is soon time to say *Shema* just before *ha'neitz ha'chamah*.

Ask those present: When else do we remember *yetzias Mitzrayim*? Not only do we have a mitzvah to **speak** about *yetzias Mitzrayim* on the night of the Seder, but on all the nights of the year there is a mitzvah to **remember** that Hashem took us out of Egypt.

אָמַר רַבִּי אֶלְעָזָר בֶּן עֲזַרְיָה **Rabbi Elazar ben Azaryah said** when he was eighteen years old and he was appointed to be the Nasi of the Jewish People:

הֲרֵי אֲנִי כְּבֶן שִׁבְעִים שָׁנָה, וְלֹא זָכִיתִי **It appears as if I am seventy years old,[12] and nevertheless I have never been successful** in convincing the other *chachamim* of my opinion

---

Mitzrayim. Rabbi Eliezer and Rabbi Yehoshua were Leviim. Rabbi Eliezer ben Azaryah and Rabbi Tarfon were Kohanim. Rabbi Akiva descended from converts to Judaism. Therefore, none of their ancestors were subjugated to slavery in Egypt—but still they sat and participated in the mitzvah of *sippur yetzias Mitzrayim.*

Rabbi Refael Bloom, in *Tal Hashamayim* (499), asks why it is important to know that they were in B'nei Brak. A person may think to themselves: How can I sing and praise God when *galus* is so painful, and times can be dark and difficult? The answer is that these rabbis had seen the glory of the Beis Hamikdash and Yerushalayim in its heyday, but now they were sitting in B'nei Brak and not Yerushalayim—a clear indication that the *churban* had just occurred. Yet these rabbis found the ability and wherewithal to speak about the exodus from Egypt all night long.

12 Although it is popular to talk about how Rabbi Elazar ben Azaryah was eighteen and his beard turned white, or that he was a *gilgul* of Shmuel HaNavi, it is not relevant at all to the story of *yetzias Mitzrayim* we are teaching our

שֶׁתֵּאָמֵר יְצִיאַת מִצְרַיִם בַּלֵּילוֹת **that** *yetzias Mitzrayim* **should be discussed at**

night in the third section of *Shema*, which mentions tzitzis and *yetzias Mitzrayim*,

עַד שֶׁדְּרָשָׁהּ בֶּן זוֹמָא, שֶׁנֶּאֱמַר, **until Ben Zoma showed,** on the day that I was

appointed Nasi, that one must read this paragraph at night, **as it says:**

לְמַעַן תִּזְכֹּר אֶת יוֹם צֵאתְךָ מֵאֶרֶץ מִצְרַיִם כֹּל יְמֵי חַיֶּיךָ. **"You will then remember the day you left Egypt all the days of your life."**

יְמֵי חַיֶּיךָ הַיָּמִים, כֹּל יְמֵי חַיֶּיךָ הַלֵּילוֹת. If it would have said **"the days of your life,"** alone,

we would have learned that during the day there is a mitzvah to mention leaving Egypt. Now that the *pasuk* says **"all the days of your life,"** this comes to teach us that there is a mitzvah to mention leaving Egypt in **the nighttime** as well.

וַחֲכָמִים אוֹמְרִים יְמֵי חַיֶּיךָ הָעוֹלָם הַזֶּה, כֹּל יְמֵי חַיֶּיךָ לְהָבִיא לִימוֹת הַמָּשִׁיחַ: **The Chachamim say:** If it would have said **"the days of your life,"** we would

understand that we need to mention *yetzias Mitzrayim* **in this world.** This is because "your days" refers to the limited years of a person's life. Now that it says **"all the days of your life,"** this teaches us **that it includes** a mitzvah to mention *yetzias Mitzrayim* in **the days of Mashiach.** Even in those times we must mention *yetzias Mitzrayim*.[13]

---

children and those at the table. Perhaps it is relevant for *mekubalim*, but for most people, it will detract from the story and the lessons of *emunah*. It is better to not mention these ideas here.

13   This refers to the twelfth principle of faith, the coming of Mashiach. The *Tiferes Shlomo* asks why we are learning about the laws of *Shema* at the Seder. He explains that the holiness of the night of the Seder should impact how we refer to *yetzias Mitzrayim* and our recitation of *Shema* for the rest of the year. We should understand that it is important to reflect on *yetzias Mitzrayim* during Seder night and throughout all of Pesach. But this is not sufficient.

Before we begin actually telling the story of *yetzias Mitzrayim*, we make a special *birkas haTorah* on the special type of Torah learning we will be doing this evening.

בָּרוּךְ הַמָּקוֹם, בָּרוּךְ הוּא. בָּרוּךְ שֶׁנָּתַן תּוֹרָה לְעַמּוֹ יִשְׂרָאֵל, בָּרוּךְ הוּא.

Blessed is Hashem that He gave the Torah to the Jewish People!

As another form of introduction for the night, we should be aware that there are different types of children, and each learns in a different way. Not everyone is the same, and each person needs to be taught in a way that relates to them. There are different explanations of *yetzias Mitzrayim* given in the Torah, and each is designed for a different type of child:

כְּנֶגֶד אַרְבָּעָה בָנִים דִּבְּרָה תוֹרָה: אֶחָד חָכָם, וְאֶחָד רָשָׁע, וְאֶחָד תָּם, וְאֶחָד שֶׁאֵינוֹ יוֹדֵעַ לִשְׁאוֹל.

The Torah speaks in a way that corresponds to four different types of sons: One who is wise, one who is rebellious, one who is simple, and one who doesn't know how to ask.

חָכָם מָה הוּא אוֹמֵר? מָה הָעֵדֹת וְהַחֻקִּים וְהַמִּשְׁפָּטִים אֲשֶׁר צִוָּה יהוה אֱלֹהֵינוּ אֶתְכֶם.

The son who is wise and interested in learning, **what does he say?**

"What are the rituals, rules, and laws that Hashem our God has commanded you?" Meaning, what are the different laws of Pesach that we are observing on this night?

וְאַף אַתָּה אֱמָר לוֹ כְּהִלְכוֹת הַפֶּסַח, אֵין מַפְטִירִין אַחַר הַפֶּסַח אֲפִיקוֹמָן:

You should explain to him all the laws of Pesach, even those from the

Rabbis such as **that it is forbidden to eat dessert after eating the *Korban Pesach*,** so that the taste of the *Korban Pesach* remains in your mouth.

רָשָׁע מָה הוּא אוֹמֵר? מָה הָעֲבֹדָה הַזֹּאת לָכֶם. לָכֶם וְלֹא לוֹ. וּלְפִי שֶׁהוֹצִיא אֶת עַצְמוֹ מִן הַכְּלָל כָּפַר בְּעִקָּר.

The rebellious son, who asks as if Pesach isn't relevant to him, **what does he say? "What is this service to you?"** What is all this burden that you put on us each year with these laws? His use of the words **"to you,"** implies that the mitzvos are **not for him. Because he removes himself from the Jewish community** that keeps mitzvos and acts as if he is not part of the Jewish People, **he is denying a foundation of our faith** that he is responsible to serve Hashem.[14]

וְאַף אַתָּה הַקְהֵה אֶת שִׁנָּיו וֶאֱמָר לוֹ: "בַּעֲבוּר זֶה עָשָׂה יהוה לִי בְּצֵאתִי מִמִּצְרָיִם." לִי וְלֹא לוֹ. אִלּוּ הָיָה שָׁם לֹא הָיָה נִגְאָל.

In response, **you should speak sharply to him and say** that the Torah speaks to you as well when it says: **"It is because of this that Hashem acted for me when I left Egypt."** It was **"for me"** that He did all of those miracles **and not for you,** the rebellious child. **If you,** the rebellious child, **would have been there, you wouldn't have been taken out.**

תָּם מָה הוּא אוֹמֵר? מַה זֹּאת?

The simple child, who doesn't ask deep questions and doesn't want to attack the Torah, but simply wants to understand, **what does he say? "What is this** that we are doing on Pesach that we don't do the rest of the year?"

The holiness should accompany us throughout the entire year and change the way we say *Shema* all year long.

14 In the notes to the *Haggadah Olas Haraayah*, Rav Tzvi Yehudah Kook cites a comment from his father, Rav Avraham Yitzchak Kook, about the rebellious son. When the Haggadah says that the *rasha* is a *kofer b'ikar*, one who denies a central pillar of Judaism, it means that this person separated himself from the holiness of the Jewish People, and this was the greatest heresy.

וְאָמַרְתָּ אֵלָיו "בְּחֹזֶק יָד הוֹצִיאָנוּ יהוה מִמִּצְרַיִם מִבֵּית עֲבָדִים." You should **tell him** the entire story in the Torah, where it relates: **"With a show of power, God brought us out of Egypt, the place of slavery…"** and the mitzvos we are doing are to remember the miracles.

וְשֶׁאֵינוֹ יוֹדֵעַ לִשְׁאוֹל—אַתְּ פְּתַח לוֹ, And the son **who doesn't know how to ask** even the most basic question, **you should draw him out** and explain the Haggadah and publicize the miracles.

שֶׁנֶּאֱמַר, וְהִגַּדְתָּ לְבִנְךָ בַּיּוֹם הַהוּא לֵאמֹר בַּעֲבוּר זֶה עָשָׂה יהוה לִי בְּצֵאתִי מִמִּצְרָיִם. As it says: **"On that day, you must tell your child: It is because of this that God acted for me when I left Egypt."**

Because we just discussed the *pasuk* of "וְהִגַּדְתָּ לְבִנְךָ בַּיּוֹם הַהוּא," let us relate how we know there is a mitzvah to retell the story of *yetzias Mitzrayim* tonight:

יָכוֹל מֵרֹאשׁ חוֹדֶשׁ? **I would have thought** to say that one must relate the story of *yetzias Mitzrayim* to the children **on Rosh Chodesh** Nissan, because this was the day that Moshe taught B'nei Yisrael about Pesach in Mitzrayim.

תַּלְמוּד לוֹמַר בַּיּוֹם הַהוּא. However, **the verse teaches: "On that day,"** the day we were taken out, and not on Rosh Chodesh.

אִי בַּיּוֹם הַהוּא יָכוֹל מִבְּעוֹד יוֹם? If the mitzvah to tell the story is **"on that day"** and not from Rosh Chodesh, **I would have thought** that one must begin teaching the story **on Erev Pesach**, which is when the *Korban Pesach* is offered.

תַּלְמוּד לוֹמַר בַּעֲבוּר זֶה However, **the verse teaches: "It is because of this,"** and "this" must refer to something you are able point to.

בַּעֲבוּר זֶה לֹא אָמַרְתִּי אֶלָּא בְּשָׁעָה שֶׁיֵּשׁ מַצָּה וּמָרוֹר מוּנָּחִים לְפָנֶיךָ. Therefore, we explain the expression **"because of this"** to mean that I, **Hashem, didn't tell you** to teach the story **unless it is the time when matzah and** maror **are placed before you** on the table, and you can point to them with your finger. This is on the night of Pesach and not beforehand.

This concludes the section of the children's questions and the short answers to them.

We will now begin telling the story of *yetzias Mitzrayim* in full. The story begins with Hashem's selection of Avraham Avinu, who descended from worshippers of *avodah zarah*. This is certainly not the most flattering way to describe the beginning of the Jewish People. However, in order to for a person to fully express their *hakaras hatov*, it is important to acknowledge how difficult and challenging things were before they were helped.[15]

---

15 The Gemara says that the Haggadah follows the format of "מתחיל בגנות ומסיים בשבח," beginning with negativity and concluding with praise. Why is this format so important? Rav Shlomo Brevda, in his *Leil Shimurim* (p. 115), explains with the following story: Having survived the Holocaust, Moshe was left completely alone, with no family or friends. He was very weak as a result of the ordeal he had endured and was suffering from several illnesses. He was penniless and totally destitute. Moshe had an uncle in America who discovered that his nephew had survived the Holocaust. He immediately arranged, at great cost, to bring him to the US. He greeted him with tremendous joy and boundless love. The uncle brought him home and started nursing him back to health. Moshe became a part of his newfound family. The uncle bought him a complete wardrobe and dressed him from head to toe. He took him to the top doctors until he was nursed back to health, and all this at a very great expense. The uncle taught him English and trained him in business. He bought Moshe his own business enterprise and found him a suitable wife. He purchased a house for him and proceeded to fully furnish it with all the trimmings. Moshe and his wife embarked on their new life and raised a wonderful family. The day arrived. Moshe's oldest son was getting married. Of course, the uncle was at the top of the invitation list. He was seated at the head table. During one of

מִתְּחִלָּה עוֹבְדֵי עֲבוֹדָה זָרָה הָיוּ אֲבוֹתֵינוּ,

In the beginning, our forefathers Terach and his family **were idol worshippers.**

וְעַכְשָׁיו קֵרְבָנוּ הַמָּקוֹם לַעֲבוֹדָתוֹ,

And now with the redemption from Egypt, **Hashem has brought us close** by separating us from the nations of the world **to serve Him** and to do mitzvos.[16]

שֶׁנֶּאֱמַר:

As it says when Yehoshua spoke to the people about trusting in Hashem:

וַיֹּאמֶר יְהוֹשֻׁעַ אֶל כָּל הָעָם כֹּה אָמַר יהוה אֱלֹהֵי יִשְׂרָאֵל:

"Yehoshua said to the entire nation: So said Hashem, the God of Israel:

---

the dances around the groom, Moshe danced with Uncle and whispered in his ear, "Dear Uncle. Thank you for everything you did for me!" The uncle reacted immediately with a stern look and forcefully pulled Moshe into a corner of the wedding hall. "That's the thanks I get from you for the multitude of *chessed* I did for you?" Moshe was shocked. He looked at his uncle and asked, "Uncle, how can I thank you properly?" Uncle replied, "This is what you should have said. 'My dear Uncle. I was left with no family, all alone in the world. I was weak, sick, and destitute. I had nothing: no clothes or money, I was barefoot and homeless. And you in your great mercy brought me to your country at great expense. You fed me and dressed me from head to foot. You took me to the best doctors and nursed me back to health. You set me up in business and helped me build a family and a life of prosperity for myself. Everything I have until this very day, came from you. If I live a thousand years, I won't be able to thank you enough.' That is how you express thanks!"

16 This is the answer as to why this night is special. We are learning that we became servants of Hashem only because we were first servants to Pharaoh.

בְּעֵבֶר הַנָּהָר יָשְׁבוּ אֲבוֹתֵיכֶם מֵעוֹלָם, תֶּרַח אֲבִי אַבְרָהָם וַאֲבִי נָחוֹר,

Your forefathers, Terach, the father of Avraham and the father of Nachor, always dwelled beyond the Euphrates River

וַיַּעַבְדוּ אֱלֹהִים אֲחֵרִים.

and they served other gods.

וָאֶקַּח אֶת אֲבִיכֶם אֶת אַבְרָהָם מֵעֵבֶר הַנָּהָר

But I took your forefather Avraham from beyond the river from the people who worshipped idols

וָאוֹלֵךְ אוֹתוֹ בְּכָל אֶרֶץ כְּנַעַן,

and I led him throughout all the land of Canaan;

וָאַרְבֶּה אֶת זַרְעוֹ, וָאֶתֵּן לוֹ אֶת יִצְחָק,

I gave him children, Yishmael, and I also gave him Yitzchak.

וָאֶתֵּן לְיִצְחָק אֶת יַעֲקֹב וְאֶת עֵשָׂו.

To Yitzchak I gave Yaakov and Eisav so that in the womb Eisav would take away the negative attributes of Yaakov and Yaakov would come out pure.

וָאֶתֵּן לְעֵשָׂו אֶת הַר שֵׂעִיר לָרֶשֶׁת אוֹתוֹ,

To Eisav I gave Mount Se'ir to inherit because he didn't want to deal with the slavery of Egypt,

וְיַעֲקֹב וּבָנָיו יָרְדוּ מִצְרָיִם.

and Yaakov and his sons went down to Egypt" to fulfill the prophecy about the descendants of Avraham, declared by Hashem at the Bris Bein Habesarim. Because of all of this the Jewish People were able to inherit Eretz Yisrael.

Now that we are about to go through the *pesukim* and Midrashim that describe how we were slaves in Mitzrayim and how Hashem took us out, we first thank Hashem for having kept His promises:

בָּרוּךְ שׁוֹמֵר הַבְטָחָתוֹ לְיִשְׂרָאֵל, בָּרוּךְ הוּא.

Blessed is Hashem, **Who kept His promise** to Avraham Avinu **regarding Klal Yisrael** to bring them out of Egypt and, **blessed is Hashem** that He fulfilled the promise that we would leave with great wealth.

שֶׁהַקָּדוֹשׁ בָּרוּךְ הוּא חִשַּׁב אֶת הַקֵּץ, לַעֲשׂוֹת כְּמָה שֶׁאָמַר לְאַבְרָהָם אָבִינוּ בִּבְרִית בֵּין הַבְּתָרִים, שֶׁנֶּאֱמַר:

For Hakadosh Baruch Hu planned the end of the slavery, **in order to do as He had said to Avraham Avinu at the** *Bris Bein Habesarim*.[17] **As it says:**

וַיֹּאמֶר לְאַבְרָם,

"**And He said to Avram:**

יָדֹעַ תֵּדַע כִּי גֵר יִהְיֶה זַרְעֲךָ בְּאֶרֶץ לֹא לָהֶם,

'**You should know for certain that your children will be strangers** after the birth of Yitzchak **in a land that is not theirs** since Avraham and Yitzchak were strangers already in Eretz Yisrael,

---

17 What were the events of the *Bris Bein Habesarim*? After Avraham's miraculous victory over the four kings, he was concerned that the miracles Hashem had performed for him may have come at the expense of his merits. Hashem, therefore, reaffirmed His promise to Avraham that his descendants would be as numerous as the stars, that a son would be born to him, and that the Land of Israel would belong to Avraham and his children. In order to show this promise (*bris*) to Avraham, Hashem told him to take different animals and cut them in half. It then got very dark and when birds tried to attack the animal flesh, Avraham chased them away. The animal pieces and the birds represent different concepts, but the essential message of the *Bris Bein Habesarim* is that

וַעֲבָדוּם וְעִנּוּ אֹתָם אַרְבַּע מֵאוֹת שָׁנָה. **and they will serve the Egyptians, and the** Egyptians **will treat them harshly, for four hundred years;**

וְגַם אֶת הַגּוֹי אֲשֶׁר יַעֲבֹדוּ דָּן אָנֹכִי, וְאַחֲרֵי כֵן יֵצְאוּ בִּרְכֻשׁ גָּדוֹל. **but** even though Hashem was the one who decreed that this would happen **I will also judge the nation** Egypt **that they will serve, and after** I take revenge on Egypt, **the** Jewish People **will come out** of Egypt **with great wealth.'"**

Because we have just mentioned the promise of the *Bris Bein Habesarim*, let's take a moment to reflect on the promise of Hashem to protect us in all generations:

Pick up the cup and cover the matzah.[18]

There are a number of popular tunes for this paragraph. You can sing one of the tunes together, and then go back to read and explain.

וְהִיא שֶׁעָמְדָה לַאֲבוֹתֵינוּ וְלָנוּ. **And it is this** promise from the *Bris Bein Habesarim* **that has stood by our fathers** in Egypt **and us** in all other exiles;

שֶׁלֹּא אֶחָד בִּלְבָד עָמַד עָלֵינוּ לְכַלּוֹתֵינוּ, **for not only did one** of the nations **rise up against us to destroy us,**

---

the Jewish People will face harsh and trying times, but at the end of it all, they will remain steadfast and strong. It is Hashem's promise that the Jewish People will inherit the entire Land of Israel.

18 The grandson of Rav Menachem Mendel of Vorka came to visit Rav Yissachar Dov of Belz during Pesach. The Belzer Rebbe asked him to say something over from his grandfather. The grandson said he had heard his grandfather ask why we cover the matzah and lift up the cup of wine before *V'Hi She'amdah*. The reason is that we want to highlight that in *galus*, it is our commitment to the words of Chazal that has left us intact. We therefore cover the matzah, which

הגדה של פסח **50**

אֶלָּא שֶׁבְּכָל דּוֹר וָדוֹר עוֹמְדִים עָלֵינוּ לְכַלּוֹתֵינוּ,

but in all generations, they rise up against us to destroy us;

וְהַקָדוֹשׁ בָּרוּךְ הוּא מַצִּילֵנוּ מִיָּדָם.

and Hakadosh Baruch Hu rescues us from their hands as He promised.[19]

---

is a Torah commandment, and lift up the cup of wine, which is a Rabbinic commandment, and we say that it is the laws and fences built by our Sages that have enabled us to last in exile. When the Belzer Rebbe heard this, he told his son to write it down, even though it was Chol Hamoed (when writing is forbidden except in cases of great need), because not writing this down and possibly forgetting it would be a "דבר האבד ממש," a substantial loss.

19 The *Vilna Gaon* explains that "destroying" us can come in the form of the sword and physical annihilation, and it can also come in the form of spiritual destruction when our non-Jewish neighbors befriend us and try to lead us toward assimilation. Why do we lift up the cup of wine? Rav Gedaliah Silverstone was the rabbi in Belfast, Ireland, and then Washington D.C., USA. He writes in his *Korban Pesach* that Chazal forbade us from drinking the wine of non-Jews because of the possibility of intermarriage. If we would have intermarried with the non-Jews and given up our Torah, it would have stopped the non-Jews' hatred toward us as we would have been absorbed into their culture. Therefore, we hold up this cup and say that all of this pain and suffering we have gone through is because we refuse to mix in with the non-Jews around us. It is because of this cup of wine that all these difficulties happened. In response to this idea, we put the cup down and respond with "צא ולמד"—go and see what Yaakov did. He ate and drank and intermarried with Lavan—and still Lavan wanted to destroy him. There is only one path, and that is to have a relationship with Hashem and His Torah and to follow the path of the Avos. We should not even think twice about mixing too intimately with the non-Jewish world. The more we stick to our Torah and the more we refrain from following their ways, the better we will be protected and the better off we will be.

Put down the cup of wine and uncover the matzah.

Already in the days of Yaakov, Hashem began keeping his promise of the *Bris Bein Habesarim*:

צֵא וּלְמַד מַה בִּקֵּשׁ לָבָן הָאֲרַמִּי
לַעֲשׂוֹת לְיַעֲקֹב אָבִינוּ:

Go and learn what Lavan of Aram planned to do to our father Yaakov when he chased after him;

שֶׁפַּרְעֹה לֹא גָזַר אֶלָּא עַל הַזְּכָרִים,
וְלָבָן בִּקֵּשׁ לַעֲקוֹר אֶת הַכֹּל.

because Pharaoh decreed only that the male children should be put to death, but Lavan wanted to uproot everything.

We now begin with the central part of the Haggadah, which consists of an in-depth analysis of the *yetzias Mitzrayim* story. The following four *pesukim* come from the section of the Torah that describes what a person says when thanking Hashem while bringing *bikkurim* to the Beis Hamikdash. Each of the different parts of the *pesukim* will be explained with *Torah She'baal Peh*. The *Rambam* tells us it is best to spend most of our time during the Seder on these *d'rashos*.

שֶׁנֶּאֱמַר:

As it says:

אֲרַמִּי אֹבֵד אָבִי,

"Lavan **the Arami wanted to destroy my father** Yaakov,

וַיֵּרֶד מִצְרַיְמָה
וַיָּגָר שָׁם בִּמְתֵי מְעָט,

later, others planned to destroy us when **he** [Yaakov] **went down to Mitzrayim and stayed their temporarily, with** a family **few in number,**

וַיְהִי שָׁם לְגוֹי גָּדוֹל עָצוּם וָרָב.

and there he became a nation, great, mighty, and numerous."

Let's explain:

וַיֵּרֶד מִצְרַיְמָה—אָנוּס עַל פִּי הַדִּבּוּר "And he went down to Mitzrayim"—compelled

against his will, because Yaakov knew that eventually, this would lead to the slavery of his children, **by the Divine decree** from the *Bris Bein Habesarim.*

וַיָּגָר שָׁם—מְלַמֵּד שֶׁלֹּא יָרַד יַעֲקֹב אָבִינוּ לְהִשְׁתַּקֵּעַ בְּמִצְרַיִם אֶלָּא לָגוּר שָׁם, "And he sojourned there"—which teaches us that our father Yaakov did not go to Egypt to

settle there permanently and to gain power and success,[20] **but merely to stay there for a time** until the famine had passed,

שֶׁנֶּאֱמַר, וַיֹּאמְרוּ אֶל פַּרְעֹה לָגוּר בָּאָרֶץ בָּאנוּ, כִּי אֵין מִרְעֶה לַצֹּאן אֲשֶׁר לַעֲבָדֶיךָ, כִּי כָבֵד הָרָעָב בְּאֶרֶץ כְּנָעַן, וְעַתָּה יֵשְׁבוּ נָא עֲבָדֶיךָ בְּאֶרֶץ גֹּשֶׁן. as it says: "They [Yaakov's sons] explained to Pharaoh, 'We have come to stay a while in your land, because there is no grazing for our

flocks in Canaan. If there would have been food for grazing we wouldn't have come, **because the famine is so severe in Canaan** but in Egypt there was food for grazing because of the Nile River. **If you allow us, we will settle in the Goshen district'"** which was closer to Eretz Yisrael.

בִּמְתֵי מְעָט—כְּמָה שֶׁנֶּאֱמַר: "Few in number" when they went down to Egypt—as it says:

בְּשִׁבְעִים נֶפֶשׁ יָרְדוּ אֲבֹתֶיךָ מִצְרַיְמָה, "Your ancestors went down to Egypt with only

seventy people but afterward, there were millions of Jews,

---

20 Our role in *galus* is to remain strangers and not assimilate, while continuing to be a light to the nations of the world, as role models of beautiful *middos* and *emunah.*

וְעַתָּה שָׂמְךָ יהוה אֱלֹהֶיךָ כְּכוֹכְבֵי הַשָּׁמַיִם לָרֹב.

and now Hashem your God has made you as numerous as the stars of the sky."

וַיְהִי שָׁם לְגוֹי—

"And there he became a nation"—

מְלַמֵּד שֶׁהָיוּ יִשְׂרָאֵל מְצֻיָּנִים שָׁם.

which teaches us that the Jews were distinctive **there.** They were noticeable because they lived in their own community and they didn't scatter amongst the Egyptian communities.

גָּדוֹל עָצוּם כְּמָה שֶׁנֶּאֱמַר: וּבְנֵי יִשְׂרָאֵל

"Great, mighty"—as it says: "The Jews were:

פָּרוּ

fruitful (1)

וַיִּשְׁרְצוּ

and increased a lot (2)

וַיִּרְבּוּ

and multiplied (3)

וַיַּעַצְמוּ בִּמְאֹד מְאֹד,

and became very very mighty (4–6)

וַתִּמָּלֵא הָאָרֶץ אֹתָם.

and the land was filled with them"

because the Jewish mothers gave birth to six babies at a time.[21]

---

21 Imagine how many children were in the house—six babies at a time needing to be fed, changed, and put to sleep. Imagine packing lunches, carpools, laundry, etc. And these were not healthy women enjoying the benefits of modern medicine; they were slaves, working while expecting, in harsh conditions and without proper nutrition.

וָרָב—כְּמָה שֶׁנֶּאֱמַר: "And numerous"—
as it says:

רְבָבָה כְּצֶמַח הַשָּׂדֶה נְתַתִּיךְ, "I made you thrive
like the plants of the
field, the Jews multiplied and grew quickly like grass in the field without any difficulty or pain,

וַתִּרְבִּי וַתִּגְדְּלִי וַתָּבֹאִי בַּעֲדִי עֲדָיִים, and you grew big and tall,
and you came to be of
great charm, the Jewish People grew to the stage where it was time to leave *galus,*

שָׁדַיִם נָכֹנוּ וּשְׂעָרֵךְ צִמֵּחַ, beautiful form, and your
hair was grown long, like
a mature person;

וְאַתְּ עֵרֹם וְעֶרְיָה. but you were naked of
mitzvos **and bare"** without
bris milah. You did not have the merits needed to leave Egypt.

וָאֶעֱבֹר עָלַיִךְ וָאֶרְאֵךְ מִתְבּוֹסֶסֶת בְּדָמָיִךְ, "And I passed over
you and I saw you
downtrodden, covered in mud, and depressed with no time to take care of yourselves[22] **in your blood.** So I, Hashem, helped you. And when it was time to leave, I gave you mitzvos relating to blood, the *Korban Pesach* and *bris milah* on the fourteenth of Nissan.

וָאֹמַר לָךְ בְּדָמַיִךְ חֲיִי, וָאֹמַר לָךְ בְּדָמַיִךְ חֲיִי. And I said to you:
'Through your blood you
shall live,' and I said to you: 'Through your blood you shall live.'" Repeated once for each mitzvah.

The next *pasuk* from the *bikkurim* declaration continues the story:

---

22 Ask the children which mitzvos involving blood Hashem gave the Jewish People before they left Egypt.
The *Derech Sichah* (p. 244) cites Rav Leib Fein of Slonim who noted that מתבוססת

וַיָּרֵעוּ אֹתָנוּ הַמִּצְרִים וַיְעַנּוּנוּ, וַיִּתְּנוּ עָלֵינוּ עֲבֹדָה קָשָׁה.

"The Egyptians treated us badly, oppressed us and placed hard labor upon us."

וַיָּרֵעוּ אֹתָנוּ הַמִּצְרִים—כְּמָה שֶׁנֶּאֱמַר:

"The Egyptians treated us badly"[23]—as it says:

הָבָה נִתְחַכְּמָה לוֹ פֶּן יִרְבֶּה,

"We must deal wisely with them to prevent them from multiplying.[24]

וְהָיָה כִּי תִקְרֶאנָה מִלְחָמָה וְנוֹסַף גַּם הוּא עַל שֹׂנְאֵינוּ וְנִלְחַם בָּנוּ,

Otherwise, they may increase so much, that if there is war, they will join our enemies and fight against us,

---

is from the word בסיס, a basis. The blood of the *bris milah* and the blood of the *Korban Pesach* are the בסיס, the basis of our Judaism; meaning, the dedication and sacrifice of the Jewish People to kill the god of the Egyptians—a sheep—and to give themselves a *bris milah* became the basis for the future dedication and self-sacrifice of the Jewish People.

23 This can also mean that the Egyptians made us out to be evil. They spread ideas about how the Jews were the root of all the problems in Egypt. This is a common first step in anti-Semitism: those who resent us begin by spreading lies about how we are subhuman, like animals. These ideas habituate the population to the concept that it is OK to harm and attack Jews because they are less than human.

24 The *Ramban* explains that the Egyptians needed to be smart about their evil plans because they couldn't kill the Jewish people right away. Normal people wouldn't be able to accept the reality of simply killing others for no reason. Every society has a basic moral compass that prevents the average person from carrying out crimes against innocent people. Therefore, the Egyptian leadership began with creative propaganda and spreading lies to slowly convince the Egyptian people over time that it was OK to wipe out the Jews.

וְעָלָה מִן הָאָרֶץ. | driving us from the land"
or they will leave the land.

וַיְעַנּוּנוּ—כְּמָה שֶׁנֶּאֱמַר: | "Oppressed us"—
as it says:

וַיָּשִׂימוּ עָלָיו שָׂרֵי מִסִּים לְמַעַן עַנֹּתוֹ בְּסִבְלֹתָם. | "The Egyptians appointed
tax collectors over the

Jews **to oppress them in their suffering** and make them poor,

וַיִּבֶן עָרֵי מִסְכְּנוֹת לְפַרְעֹה. | Then, because the Jews
had no money, they gave

them hard labor to pay for the taxes they owed. And in this way **they**, that is,
the Jewish People, **built storage cities for Pharaoh;**

אֶת פִּתֹם וְאֶת רַעַמְסֵס. | of Pisom and Raamses."[25]

וַיִּתְּנוּ עָלֵינוּ עֲבֹדָה קָשָׁה—כְּמָה שֶׁנֶּאֱמַר: | "And put upon us hard
labor"—as it says:

---

25   The issue with these cities is that they stood on unstable ground and after they
would finish construction, or even during the construction, the cities would
collapse. The cruelty was threefold: (1) The very act of building weakened the
Jews. (2) The collapse of the building having spent months and years con-
structing it was demoralizing after investing all that time and backbreaking
effort. Imagine putting all your energies into a project and then seeing it
crumble before your eyes; it can make a person depressed and want to give up
on life. (3) Finally, there were many Jews who were killed under the collapse
the buildings. (If possible, an effective tool to prepare for the Seder is to build
some miniature buildings out of toy blocks or magnetic tiles and then have
them collapse at the table. This can bring to life the feeling of working on
something and then having it collapse. A child can appreciate the frustration
of building with toys and then to have someone knock it down.)

"The Egyptians started to make the Jews do labor designed to break their bodies."[26] וַיַּעֲבִדוּ מִצְרַיִם אֶת בְּנֵי יִשְׂרָאֵל בְּפָרֶךְ.

26　At first, Pharaoh led his fellow Egyptians to assist in building the cities. Over time, the Egyptians were promoted to taskmasters while the Jews remained laborers. Soon the shovels of the Egyptians were replaced with whips and the Jews didn't realize what was happening. By the time the Jews understood that they had been turned into slaves, the Egyptians were already in control. (The group of Jews who never participated in the building project, and therefore were never tricked into slavery, were the tribe of Levi.) Every Jewish laborer was commanded to make a certain quota of bricks, in addition to the building work they had to do. If the bricks and the building quotas weren't completed, the slave would be beaten.

The Jews were given no breaks during the day and no days off, and it made no difference what the weather was or how difficult the conditions were. No one was spared from slavery in Egypt: men, women, and children all had to work in these terrible conditions. Imagine having to wake up while it is still dark, rushing out of bed exhausted because there wasn't enough time to sleep and your body is in pain from the slavery. There is no time to grab something to eat. Immediately, you are thrown into a pit of mud while someone is screaming at you to make bricks. After a full day of doing this in the burning hot sun, you collapse in your house—and after only a few hours of sleep, you are awakened to do the exact same thing all over again. There are no breaks and no vacations. Soon the Egyptians appointed Jewish policemen to be in charge of their fellow Jews, one policeman for every ten Jews. Each policeman needed to make sure that his group produced six hundred bricks a day. If the quota of bricks wasn't completed by the end of the day, the Jewish policeman would be beaten. Nevertheless, we are told that the Jewish policemen never took out their frustrations on their fellow Jews; instead, they suffered and took the beatings from their Egyptian taskmasters. Later they would be rewarded by being appointed the original seventy elders in the desert.

The slavery was constant and without any breaks. Sixty seconds of every minute. Sixty minutes of every hour. Twenty-four hours of every day. All seven days of the week. All fifty-two weeks of the year. For one hundred and twenty

הגדה של פסח　**58**

The third *pasuk* from the *bikkurim* declaration:

וַנִּצְעַק אֶל יהוה אֱלֹהֵי אֲבֹתֵינוּ
וַיִּשְׁמַע יהוה אֶת קֹלֵנוּ
וַיַּרְא אֶת עָנְיֵנוּ וְאֶת עֲמָלֵנוּ
וְאֶת לַחֲצֵנוּ.

"We cried out to Hashem, God of our ancestors, and Hashem heard our voice, saw our suffering, our harsh labor, and our distress."

וַנִּצְעַק אֶל יהוה אֱלֹהֵי אֲבֹתֵינוּ—
כְּמָה שֶׁנֶּאֱמַר:

"We cried out to Hashem"—as it says:

וַיְהִי בַיָּמִים הָרַבִּים הָהֵם וַיָּמָת מֶלֶךְ מִצְרַיִם,

"A long time then passed, and the king of Egypt died,** meaning he got *tzaraas*, which is like death. To try and cure his *tzaraas* he had 150 Jewish children slaughtered and used their blood to bathe in,[27] therefore,

וַיֵּאָנְחוּ בְנֵי יִשְׂרָאֵל מִן הָעֲבֹדָה וַיִּזְעָקוּ,

the Jews were still groaning because of their subjugation to the Egyptians. **And they cried out** because of their slavery,

וַתַּעַל שַׁוְעָתָם אֶל הָאֱלֹהִים מִן הָעֲבֹדָה.

and their pleas went up before God from their work," but their prayers weren't accepted because the Jews lacked the proper merits.

וַיִּשְׁמַע יהוה אֶת קֹלֵנוּ—כְּמָה שֶׁנֶּאֱמַר:

"And Hashem heard our voice"—as it says:

---

years. And it wasn't only forced labor; the Jews were also at the beck and call of the Egyptians. Whatever task or job the Egyptians wanted to be done, the Jews were compelled to do it for them.

The difficulty of the slavery was so severe that by the time the Jews left Egypt, they were mostly blinded, lame, and crippled by their physical injuries.

27   He would slaughter 150 in the morning and 150 at night.

וַיִּשְׁמַע אֱלֹהִים אֶת נַאֲקָתָם, "Hashem heard their cries but this was not enough of a *zechus*, rather:

וַיִּזְכֹּר אֱלֹהִים אֶת בְּרִיתוֹ אֶת אַבְרָהָם אֶת יִצְחָק וְאֶת יַעֲקֹב. And He remembered His promise with Avraham, Yitzchak, and Yaakov."

וַיַּרְא אֶת עָנְיֵנוּ— "Seeing our suffering"—

זוֹ פְּרִישׁוּת דֶּרֶךְ אֶרֶץ, this refers to the breaking up of their **family life** so mothers and fathers couldn't live together,[28]

כְּמָה שֶׁנֶּאֱמַר: וַיַּרְא אֱלֹהִים אֶת בְּנֵי יִשְׂרָאֵל וַיֵּדַע אֱלֹהִים. as it says: "God saw the Jewish People, and He was concerned."

וְאֶת עֲמָלֵנוּ—אֵלּוּ הַבָּנִים, "And our harsh labor"—this refers to the **children** because raising children is our main job. And the Egyptians threw the babies into the Nile,[29]

---

28 Pharaoh wanted to break up the fathers and mothers so there wouldn't be Jewish families. However, it was in the merit of the righteous Jewish women who worked very hard to keep the families together that Hashem would eventually take the Jews out of Egypt.

29 The Torah records that the Jewish boys were also saved by Shifrah and Puah, better known as Yocheved and Miriam, the mother and sister of Moshe Rabbeinu. Shifrah and Puah were midwives, and they helped the Jewish mothers deliver their babies. Pharaoh offered them a lot of money to kill the babies as they were being born, but Shifrah and Puah had *yiras Hashem* and deep *emunah*. Not only did they not kill the Jewish babies, they saved as many as they could and were even given special *siyata d'Shmaya* to cure Jewish babies who were born sick. When Pharaoh found out that the Jewish baby boys were not dying at birth, he called Shifrah and Puah to his palace to find out

what was going on. However, these two brave women were not scared. They explained to Pharaoh that the Jewish women gave birth to the baby boys even before they arrived, so they could never reach the children before they were in their mother's arms. The reward for these two *tzidkaniyos* was that their descendants became great leaders of the Jewish People. Pharaoh, however, was not pleased, and he looked for another solution to stop the Jewish People from multiplying. The plan he adopted was to throw all the Jewish baby boys into the Nile River. This law lasted for more than three years, and was enacted based on the advice of Bilaam HaRasha. He felt that the boys should be killed because they were more likely to grow up and physically fight back. In addition, the magicians and fortune-tellers of Pharaoh predicted that the future redeemer of the Jews would be stopped by means of water. Therefore, the best way to prevent this prophecy from becoming reality was to drown the boys in water. The Egyptian soldiers would march from house to house and grab Jewish baby boys away from their mothers. The Egyptians even sent little children to hang out near the Jewish homes to spy on who was pregnant and was expecting a new child. When the Jewish babies were born, they would be hidden right away by their families in order to avoid being found and taken away. (Imagine the immense distress of having to give birth to a child without making a sound because otherwise the Egyptians would come and discover them!) The Egyptian mothers would bring their own babies into the Jewish neighborhoods and have their babies cry. When one baby cries it makes other babies nearby cry as well, and this would alert the soldiers as to where the Jewish babies were hiding.

The Midrash tells us that the Nile river wouldn't swallow up the Jews' babies and let them drown. Instead, it would carry them and spit them out in the desert. Hashem would then nourish them from a rock that fed them milk and honey. When the Jewish families arrived in the desert, the boys were reunited with their families.

Other women escaped to the fields and gave birth to their babies there. They would leave them in the fields and daven to Hashem saying, "I have done my part; now You do Yours and take care of my child." Hashem then proceeded to take care of those children born in the fields and to watch over them and protect them. Imagine this picture of all these children being raised by Hashem and then being reunited with their families later on.

כְּמָה שֶׁנֶּאֱמַר: כָּל הַבֵּן הַיִּלּוֹד הַיְאֹרָה תַּשְׁלִיכֻהוּ וְכָל הַבַּת תְּחַיּוּן.

as it says: "Every boy—even Egyptian—**who is born must be cast into the Nile, but every girl shall be allowed to live** and forced to be wives to the Egyptians."

וְאֶת לַחֲצֵנוּ—זוֹ הַדְּחַק,

"And our distress"— this refers to the pressure that the Egyptians placed upon the Jews to make bricks and to produce a certain amount each and every day,

כְּמָה שֶׁנֶּאֱמַר: וְגַם רָאִיתִי אֶת הַלַּחַץ אֲשֶׁר מִצְרַיִם לֹחֲצִים אֹתָם.

as it says: "I have also seen the pressure which Egypt is subjecting them to."

We now will learn the last *pasuk* from the *bikkurim* declaration:

וַיּוֹצִאֵנוּ יהוה מִמִּצְרַיִם בְּיָד חֲזָקָה וּבִזְרֹעַ נְטוּיָה וּבְמֹרָא גָּדֹל וּבְאֹתוֹת וּבְמֹפְתִים.

"Hashem then brought us out of Egypt with a strong hand and an outstretched arm, with great visions and with signs and miracles."

וַיּוֹצִאֵנוּ יהוה מִמִּצְרַיִם—לֹא עַל יְדֵי מַלְאָךְ וְלֹא עַל יְדֵי שָׂרָף וְלֹא עַל יְדֵי שָׁלִיחַ, אֶלָּא הַקָּדוֹשׁ בָּרוּךְ הוּא בִּכְבוֹדוֹ וּבְעַצְמוֹ.

"Hashem then brought us out of Egypt"— not with an angel, not through a *saraf*, an angel of fire, **and not through a messenger, but Hakadosh Baruch Hu, alone in His glory** took us out.

שֶׁנֶּאֱמַר:

As it says:

וְעָבַרְתִּי בְאֶרֶץ מִצְרַיִם בַּלַּיְלָה הַזֶּה, וְהִכֵּיתִי כָל בְּכוֹר בְּאֶרֶץ מִצְרַיִם מֵאָדָם וְעַד בְּהֵמָה וּבְכָל אֱלֹהֵי מִצְרַיִם אֶעֱשֶׂה שְׁפָטִים אֲנִי יהוה.

"I will pass through Egypt on that night, and I will kill every firstborn in Egypt, man and beast.

I will perform acts of judgment against all the gods of Egypt. I am God."[30]
We learn from this *pasuk* that Hashem Himself took us out because it is Hashem speaking about what He did.

וְעָבַרְתִּי בְאֶרֶץ מִצְרַיִם בַּלַּיְלָה הַזֶּה — אֲנִי וְלֹא מַלְאָךְ;

"I alone **will pass through Egypt on that night"—Me and not a messenger**

וְהִכֵּיתִי כָל בְּכוֹר בְּאֶרֶץ מִצְרַיִם — אֲנִי וְלֹא שָׂרָף;

"**and I will kill every firstborn in Egypt"—I and not a** *saraf*, an angel of fire.[31]

וּבְכָל אֱלֹהֵי מִצְרַיִם אֶעֱשֶׂה שְׁפָטִים — אֲנִי וְלֹא הַשָּׁלִיחַ;

"I will perform acts of judgment against all the gods of Egypt"—

I, and not a messenger or any other angel that normally carries out the will of Hashem

אֲנִי יהוה — אֲנִי הוּא וְלֹא אַחֵר.

"I am Hashem"— It is I and no other.

בְּיָד חֲזָקָה —

"With a strong hand"—

זוּ הַדֶּבֶר,

this refers to an epidemic of illness that accompanied every one of the ten plagues,

---

30 This is the first principle of faith, that there is a God. And it is the fifth principle as well, that there should be no other gods.

31 There are three opinions about what exactly Hashem used to kill the firstborn: (1) Some sort of poisonous gas. (2) A loud clap of thunder, the sound of which caused them to die. (3) The very words of Hashem caused them to die.

כְּמָה שֶׁנֶּאֱמַר: הִנֵּה יַד יהוה הוֹיָה בְּמִקְנְךָ אֲשֶׁר בַּשָּׂדֶה בַּסוּסִים בַּחֲמֹרִים בַּגְּמַלִּים בַּבָּקָר וּבַצֹּאן, דֶּבֶר כָּבֵד מְאֹד.

as it says: "God's hand will be directed against your livestock in the field. The horses, donkeys, camels, cattle, and sheep will die from a very serious epidemic."[32]

וּבִזְרֹעַ נְטוּיָה—זוּ הַחֶרֶב,

"And an outstretched arm"—this refers to the sword that the Egyptian firstborn picked up to attack their parents. The firstborn Egyptians heard they were going to die because the Jews weren't allowed to leave. So they approached their parents and said that so far, everything Moshe promised had come true. They asked why it was fair that they should die because the older Egyptians refused to let the Jews go? When their parents and Pharaoh wouldn't listen to them and their cries, the firstborn children picked up weapons and began rebelling and attacking their fellow citizens in a fit of rage.

כְּמָה שֶׁנֶּאֱמַר: וְחַרְבּוֹ שְׁלוּפָה בְּיָדוֹ נְטוּיָה עַל יְרוּשָׁלָיִם.

We know that the word "stretched" can refer to a sword as it says: "His drawn sword in his hand, stretched out over Yerushalayim." This happened when the *malach* of Hashem came to punish the Jewish People after David HaMelech made the mistake of counting them.

וּבְמֹרָא גָּדֹל—זוּ גִּילוּי שְׁכִינָה.

"And with great visions"—this refers to the revelation of the Shechinah that occurred during *Makkas Bechoros* when Hashem carried out the plague himself,

---

32 The mention of God's hand is also a reference to the fifth plague of *Dever*, because five fingers make up one hand, a *yad ha'chazakah*. By this point, the Egyptians began to understand the power of Hashem.
The *Netziv*, in his Haggadah, suggests that "plague" here refers to the Jews who died during *Choshech*, darkness. Those Jews who didn't want to be redeemed and didn't want to go to Eretz Yisrael were judged unworthy of leaving.

כְּמָה שֶׁנֶּאֱמַר, אוֹ הֲנִסָּה אֱלֹהִים לָבוֹא לָקַחַת לוֹ גוֹי מִקֶּרֶב גּוֹי בְּמַסֹּת בְּאֹתֹת וּבְמוֹפְתִים וּבְמִלְחָמָה וּבְיָד חֲזָקָה וּבִזְרוֹעַ נְטוּיָה וּבְמוֹרָאִים גְּדֹלִים כְּכֹל אֲשֶׁר עָשָׂה לָכֶם יהוה אֱלֹהֵיכֶם בְּמִצְרַיִם לְעֵינֶיךָ.

as it says: "Has another god ever done miracles, bringing one nation out of another nation with such tremendous miracles, **signs** like the staff turning into a snake, **wonders** like the ten plagues, **war** at the splitting of the Yam Suf, **a mighty hand and an outstretched arm, and terrifying phenomena, as God did for you in Egypt before your very eyes?"**

וּבְאֹתוֹת—זֶה הַמַּטֶּה,

"And with signs"— this refers to the **staff** of Moshe,

כְּמָה שֶׁנֶּאֱמַר: וְאֶת הַמַּטֶּה הַזֶּה תִּקַּח בְּיָדֶךָ אֲשֶׁר תַּעֲשֶׂה בּוֹ אֶת הָאֹתֹת.

as it is says: Hashem told Moshe, **"Take this staff in your hand. With it, you will perform the signs"** for Pharaoh by turning it into a snake.[33]

Therefore, in order to not embarrass them and their families, their *neshamos* were taken from them during *Choshech* when the Egyptians couldn't see what was happening to the Jews. This is an important lesson in understanding that we should not be too comfortable in *galus*: we should not find ourselves preferring life without Mashiach or preferring life outside of Eretz Yisrael.

33   In fact, Moshe was shown three signs at the burning bush. The staff turned into a snake; his hand turned white with *tzaraas*; and he poured water on the ground that turned to blood. However, when Moshe came to Pharaoh, he and Aharon only performed the first sign—turning the staff into a snake. Pharaoh was unimpressed and brought out his wife and children, who were able to reproduce the sign using magic. In response, Aharon's staff was able to go and swallow the other live snakes. This impressed everyone in the palace of Pharaoh.

A nice addition to this part of the Seder is to prepare a staff and hold it when speaking about it. It can be made from any item you have around the house. Bonus points if you can set up the staff so it appears to turn into a snake or have a snake come out of it.

The *Maharil* cites the *minhag* of dripping wine out of the cup using one's finger when mentioning דָּם, אֵשׁ, and תִּמְרוֹת עָשָׁן, the ten plagues themselves, and דְּצַ״ךְ עַדַ״שׁ בְּאַחַ״ב, which comes to a total of sixteen times. There are different customs for removing the wine, including using specific fingers to remove the wine, or pouring drops of wine from the cup without using a finger. Regardless, when one does remove the wine, they should have in mind that Hashem should save the Jewish People from such terrible events, which should instead be brought upon those who try and harm the Jewish People. After you have finished removing all sixteen drops of wine, the wine should not be returned to your cup; it should be disposed of.

וּבְמוֹפְתִים—זֶה הַדָּם,

"And miracles"— this refers to the blood of the first plague,

כְּמָה שֶׁנֶּאֱמַר: וְנָתַתִּי מוֹפְתִים בַּשָּׁמַיִם וּבָאָרֶץ.

as it says: "I will show miracles in the heaven and on earth."

The miracle of the staff turning into a snake is also a reference to the thirteenth principle of faith, that Hashem can and will resurrect the dead, *techiyas hameisim.*

A little bit about the staff itself: The staff was either made of sapphire (a beautiful blue stone) or out of wood. It was given to Adam HaRishon by Hashem on the Sixth Day of Creation. It was then passed down from generation to generation until it came to Yaakov Avinu. Yaakov then gave it to his son Yosef, and it was then taken by Pharaoh. When Yisro refused to participate in the planned destruction of the Jewish People and had to flee the palace of Pharaoh, he took the staff with him. He then planted the staff in the ground, and it miraculously grew into a tree. He established a contest that whoever could pull the staff from the ground would marry his daughter Tziporah. It was Moshe Rabbeinu who succeeded in pulling the staff from the ground. He married Tziporah and took the staff as his own. On the staff, a series of mysterious *roshei teivos*, acronyms, were inscribed—דְּצַ״ךְ עַדַ״שׁ בְּאַחַ״ב—along with the name of Hashem.

Spill out of your cup while reciting the following:

דָּם   **Blood**

וָאֵשׁ   **Fire**

וְתִימְרוֹת עָשָׁן.   **And Pillars of Smoke**

We see in this *pasuk* that the word "miracles" (*mofsim*) is referring to blood, including the plague of blood.

דָּבָר אַחֵר: **Another explanation**

which demonstrates in a different way that the final *pasuk* of the *bikkurim* declaration is referring to the ten plagues:

בְּיָד חֲזָקָה—שְׁתַּיִם,   **With a strong hand—is two**

וּבִזְרֹעַ נְטוּיָה—שְׁתַּיִם,   **And an outstretched arm—is two**

וּבְמֹרָא גָּדֹל—שְׁתַּיִם,   **With great visions—is two**

וּבְאֹתוֹת—שְׁתַּיִם,   **And with signs—is two**

וּבְמֹפְתִים—שְׁתַּיִם.   **And miracles—is two.**

אֵלּוּ עֶשֶׂר מַכּוֹת שֶׁהֵבִיא הַקָּדוֹשׁ בָּרוּךְ הוּא עַל הַמִּצְרִים בְּמִצְרַיִם,   **These are the ten plagues that Hakadosh Baruch Hu brought upon the Egyptians in Egypt**

וְאֵלּוּ הֵן: **And they are as follows:**

After mentioning each plague, spill some wine from your cup.

דָם Blood

צְפַרְדֵּעַ Frogs

כִּנִּים Lice

עָרוֹב Wild Animals

דֶּבֶר Pestilence

שְׁחִין Boils

בָּרָד Hail

אַרְבֶּה Locusts

חוֹשֶׁךְ Darkness

מַכַּת בְּכוֹרוֹת Death of the Firstborn

At this point, the leader of the Seder should spend time describing in detail the events of the ten plagues. The retelling of the plagues is based on the fourth principle of faith, that Hashem controls every aspect of the physical world. It is time to bring the words of the Chumash and Chazal to life. Those leading the Seder should find their inner storyteller, and with much excitement and interest, try and bring the plagues to life by painting a vivid picture with words, and even some props if necessary. The following are some ideas from Chazal that elaborate on what went on during the ten plagues.

Once the plagues began in Egypt, the slavery and subjugation of the Jewish People began to lighten. On Rosh Hashanah of that year, the physical labor stopped, even though they were still slaves to the Egyptians. There are many different opinions about which day on the calendar the plagues began.

Each plague, except for darkness, lasted between twenty-three to thirty days, with a seven-day break between one plague and the next. There is also a debate regarding whether Moshe would come to warn Pharaoh before each plague or if this was only before *Kinnim*, *Shechin*, and *Choshech*. Nevertheless, when Moshe did come to warn Pharaoh, it was always in a time or place where Pharaoh would be caught off guard or embarrassed.

A more in-depth explanation and description of the plagues can be found in the *Matamei Hashulchan* of Rav Moshe Lewis and *Let My People Go* by Yosef Deutsch. These works are based on Midrashim, and most of the items here are not explicitly stated in the Torah. However, they are part of *Torah She'baal Peh* and our understanding of the events of *yetzias Mitzrayim*.

DAM

- This plague began with Aharon hitting the Nile River with his staff.
- It was an attack on the water, which the Egyptians worshipped as a god.
- Blood was everywhere, in their drinking water and bathing water. It was everywhere except for Goshen where the Jewish People lived.[34]
- The fish and all the water animals died.
- The smell of blood was all over Egypt, and it was impossible to hide from it.
- Blood even oozed out of the walls.
- The waters of Goshen remained clean, and so the Egyptians came to drink there. But when they drank, it turned to blood. It only remained water if they paid for it.

TZEFARDEI'A

- This plague began by Aharon hitting the water.
- A giant single frog emerged from the water. The guards attacked the frog, and it started spitting out frogs everywhere.

---

34 This highlights the eleventh principle of faith—that Hashem punishes those who sin and rewards those who act properly.

- The croaking was deafening. The Egyptians could not hear one another.
- The frogs bit people.
- They crawled inside the mouths of the Egyptians.
- They had remarkable strength and could knock down doors.
- Wherever there was mud, frogs would spontaneously grow.

KINNIM

- This plague began by Aharon hitting the ground.
- The dust of Egypt turned into lice.
- There were fourteen different types of lice, from the size of a chicken egg to that of a goose egg.
- There were so many lice that the pile of lice was two *amos* deep.
- The lice climbed on the clothes, hair, and skin of the Egyptians and into their noses and ears. The people couldn't see where they were going.
- The lice bit the Egyptians and caused a lot of pain.

AROV

- This plague was performed by Hashem.
- Animals came to Egypt from all over the world. Lions, bears, leopards, panthers, hyenas, wolves, pigs, donkeys, kangaroos, foxes, goats, cats, rats, mice, lizards, turtles, and all kinds of birds. Even the frogs came back. Bugs were everywhere.
- Sea monsters even came out of the Nile to attack the Egyptians.

DEVER

- Performed by Hashem Himself.
- All Egyptian animals died, even very healthy ones.
- The animals were like cars and trucks for the Egyptians. Imagine riding your horse in the street or working with an ox in the field and suddenly, the animal drops dead.
- This was a tremendous financial loss for the Egyptians.

SHECHIN

- Performed by Moshe taking the soot from an oven and throwing it in the air. The air became foggy, spread across Egypt, and landed on humans and animals. Wherever it landed, boils began to grow.

- These were infectious blisters that made the skin of the Egyptians burn, and be aggravated by bleeding and swelling.
- The skin would start to fall off.
- The Egyptians couldn't stop rubbing and scratching.
- The boils hurt so much that the Egyptians couldn't lie down on them or sit on them. They couldn't stand either because the boils were on the bottom of their feet too. They would stand on tiptoes, but not for long because of the boils on their toes. The Egyptians were hopping back and forth on their toes trying to get comfortable.

BARAD

- Performed by Moshe.
- The hail that fell was composed of a mixture of fire and ice. There was lightning and thunder. The earth shook.
- When the hailstones hit the ground, the fire spread everywhere.
- The hail was the size of bricks. It knocked down trees and plants.
- The noise from the crashing hail was deafening.
- The hail damaged people and property.

ARBEH

- Performed by Moshe.
- The wind blew all night and carried the locusts to Egypt.
- Instantly, Egypt was covered with seven different types of locusts.
- They created a dense cloud that blocked out the sun.
- They had teeth like iron, claws like a lion, and a horn that could hurt like an ox. It was as if they had armor and could not be harmed.
- The locusts carried a poisonous saliva that killed the Egyptians.
- They destroyed the trees until there was nothing left.
- They also ate inedible things like clothing.
- They crawled inside the Egyptians' bodies, clothes, and houses.

CHOSHECH

- Performed by Moshe.
- This plague started during the day so the people would understand that it was a miracle.

- The Jewish area of Goshen remained lit up.
- The Egyptians couldn't see anything in front of their faces.
- The darkness lasted three days.
- The Egyptians couldn't even light fires because the darkness smothered the fire.
- It had toxic fumes that made the Egyptians sick.
- In the next three days, the darkness worsened. It was a much thicker darkness, and it froze the Egyptians in place. They couldn't change the position they were in. (Imagine having to sit still for three days!)
- The Jews were able to enter Egyptian homes and see their belongings.

MAKKAS BECHOROS

- Performed by Hashem Himself. At exactly midnight, all of the Egyptian firstborns began to die. (This highlights the third principle of faith: that Hashem has no body and is not bound by physical constraints. A physical being would not be able to be in multiple places across an entire country in the same instance.)
- At the exact moment of midnight, all of Egypt lit up as if it were the middle of the day.
- Thunder, lightning, and poisonous gas filled the air and killed the firstborn Egyptians. Others were killed from the sound of the thunder. Another group died simply from the word of Hashem.
- Not all the firstborns died right away. Some suffered for one to three days before finally dying.
- Animals dug up the corpses of firstborn Egyptians who had already died and ripped them to pieces.
- If a firstborn Egyptian left the country, he also died. And if there was a firstborn visiting from another country, he died as well, so that the Egyptians wouldn't think the gods of another nation were attacking them.
- The only surviving firstborns were Pharaoh and his daughter Basyah, who had saved Moshe in the water. In the end, they both came running to Moshe in the middle of the night, begging him to end the plague.

רַבִּי יְהוּדָה הָיָה **Rabbi Yehudah devised**
נוֹתֵן בָּהֶם סִמָּנִים **an easy way to remember the ten plagues:**

As you say each of the next three words,
spill some wine from your cup.

[35] דְּצַ"ךְ עֲדַ"שׁ בְּאַחַ"ב *D'tzach, adash, b'achav*

Now refill the cups back to the top.

Because we have just discussed the plagues Hashem brought upon the Egyptians, let us elaborate on this and describe how many different plagues and punishments Hashem brought upon the Egyptians. There is a debate among Chazal regarding this number, based on the *pesukim*. Regardless of the final number, we can still appreciate how harsh Hashem was in punishing those who harmed us.

---

35 The plagues are divided into three categories: (1) דצ"ך are plagues that showed that Hashem is real. The first two plagues, which took place on the water, showed that Hashem is God and not the Nile. During the third plague of *Kinnim*, the Egyptians sorcerers had to admit, "אצבע אלוקים היא—This is an act of God." (2) עד"ש speaks to the fact that Hashem is in charge of every detail in the world and doesn't simply sit back and let things happen on their own. In these plagues, Hashem clearly distinguished between groups: the Jews of Goshen weren't affected by the wild animals, and the animals of the Egyptians died while those of the Jews did not. During *Shechin*, the dust landed all over Egypt, but only the Egyptians were affected. (3) In באח"ב we see that there is only one power in the world that controls everything, and that is the Ribbono Shel Olam. The last plagues blotted out the sun or occurred at night. The Egyptians mistakenly thought the sun had an independent power of its own—but these plagues showed that there is no power in the world that does not depend on Hashem.

רַבִּי יוֹסֵי הַגְּלִילִי אוֹמֵר: Rabbi Yosi HaGelili said:

מִנַּיִן אַתָּה אוֹמֵר שֶׁלָּקוּ הַמִּצְרִים בְּמִצְרַיִם עֶשֶׂר מַכּוֹת וְעַל הַיָּם לָקוּ חֲמִשִּׁים מַכּוֹת? How can you come to say that the Egyptians were struck with ten plagues in Egypt, but with fifty plagues at the Yam Suf?

בְּמִצְרַיִם מַה הוּא אוֹמֵר? Of the plagues in Egypt, what does it say?

וַיֹּאמְרוּ הַחַרְטֻמִּים אֶל פַּרְעֹה: אֶצְבַּע אֱלֹהִים הִוא, "The magicians said to Pharaoh: 'It [i.e., the ten plagues] is the finger of God.'"[36]

וְעַל הַיָּם מָה הוּא אוֹמֵר? And of the Sea what does it say?

וַיַּרְא יִשְׂרָאֵל אֶת הַיָּד הַגְּדֹלָה אֲשֶׁר עָשָׂה יהוה בְּמִצְרַיִם, וַיִּירְאוּ הָעָם אֶת יהוה, וַיַּאֲמִינוּ בַּיהוה וּבְמֹשֶׁה עַבְדּוֹ. "The Jews saw the great power that Hashem had unleashed against Egypt, and the people were in awe of Hashem. They believed in Hashem and in his servant Moshe."[37]

---

36 In *Shemos* (3:19), it says that Hashem told Moshe that Pharaoh was not going to let B'nei Yisrael leave Egypt, even before Moshe spoke with Pharaoh. This is the tenth principle of faith, that Hashem knows what every creature is thinking and plans to do.

37 Note that this is the only mention of Moshe in the entire Haggadah. But it is still an important instance because it highlights the sixth and seventh principles of faith, that there are prophets who relate the message of Hashem to the Jewish People and that the greatest of those prophets was Moshe Rabbeinu.

כַּמָה לָקוּ בְאֶצְבַּע?

How many plagues did they receive with the "finger" in Egypt?

עֶשֶׂר מַכּוֹת.

Ten.

אֱמֹר מֵעַתָּה:

Therefore, it follows

בְּמִצְרַיִם לָקוּ עֶשֶׂר מַכּוֹת וְעַל הַיָּם לָקוּ חֲמִשִּׁים מַכּוֹת.

that since there were ten plagues in Egypt, there were fifty at the sea where they were hit with the whole hand.

רַבִּי אֱלִיעֶזֶר אוֹמֵר:

Rabbi Eliezer said:

מִנַּיִן שֶׁכָּל מַכָּה וּמַכָּה שֶׁהֵבִיא הַקָדוֹשׁ בָּרוּךְ הוּא עַל הַמִּצְרִים בְּמִצְרַיִם הָיְתָה שֶׁל אַרְבַּע מַכּוֹת?

How do we know that each plague that Hakadosh Baruch Hu brought upon the Egyptians in Egypt consisted of four plagues?

שֶׁנֶּאֱמַר: יְשַׁלַּח בָּם חֲרוֹן אַפּוֹ, עֶבְרָה וָזַעַם וְצָרָה, מִשְׁלַחַת מַלְאֲכֵי רָעִים.

For it says: "He sent forth upon them Egypt His burning anger; wrath, affliction and trouble, troops of messengers of evil."

עֶבְרָה—אַחַת,

"Wrath" was one plague

וָזַעַם—שְׁתַּיִם,

"affliction" was a second,

וְצָרָה—שָׁלשׁ,

"trouble" a third,

מִשְׁלַחַת מַלְאֲכֵי רָעִים—אַרְבַּע.

and "troops of messengers of evil"

a fourth. What emerges is that each one of the ten plagues was actually four plagues happening at the same time.

אֱמֹר מֵעַתָּה:

בְּמִצְרַיִם לָקוּ אַרְבָּעִים מַכּוֹת
וְעַל הַיָּם לָקוּ מָאתַיִם מַכּוֹת.

Therefore, it follows,

they were struck by forty plagues in Egypt and two hundred at the Sea.

רַבִּי עֲקִיבָא אוֹמֵר:

Rabbi Akiva said:

מִנַּיִן שֶׁכָּל מַכָּה וּמַכָּה שֶׁהֵבִיא
הַקָּדוֹשׁ בָּרוּךְ הוּא עַל הַמִּצְרִים בְּמִצְרַיִם
הָיְתָה שֶׁל חָמֵשׁ מַכּוֹת?

How do we know that each plague that Hakadosh Baruch Hu brought upon the Egyptians in Egypt consisted of five plagues?

שֶׁנֶּאֱמַר: יְשַׁלַּח בָּם חֲרוֹן אַפּוֹ
עֶבְרָה וָזַעַם וְצָרָה
מִשְׁלַחַת מַלְאֲכֵי רָעִים.

For it says: "He sent forth upon them His burning anger; wrath, affliction and trouble, troops of messengers of evil."

חֲרוֹן אַפּוֹ—אַחַת,

"His burning anger" was one plague.

עֶבְרָה—שְׁתַּיִם,

"Wrath" was a second plague,

וָזַעַם—שָׁלֹשׁ,

"affliction" was a third,

וְצָרָה—אַרְבַּע,

"trouble" a fourth,

מִשְׁלַחַת מַלְאֲכֵי רָעִים—חָמֵשׁ.

and "troops of messengers of evil"

a fifth. What emerges is that each one of the ten plagues was actually five plagues happening at the same time.

אֱמֹר מֵעַתָּה:

בְּמִצְרַיִם לָקוּ חֲמִשִּׁים מַכּוֹת
וְעַל הַיָּם לָקוּ חֲמִשִּׁים וּמָאתַיִם מַכּוֹת.

Therefore, it follows,

they were struck by fifty plagues in Egypt and two hundred and fifty at the Sea.

This rhyming and scaled translation of *Dayeinu* is from Rabbi Dovid Yankelowitz, a very talented and dedicated *rebbi* in Yeshiva Darchei Torah. It is being used here with his permission.

כַּמָּה מַעֲלוֹת טוֹבוֹת לַמָּקוֹם עָלֵינוּ!

How many favors do we owe thanks to Hashem!

אִלּוּ הוֹצִיאָנוּ מִמִּצְרַיִם וְלֹא עָשָׂה בָהֶם שְׁפָטִים, **דַּיֵּנוּ.**

If from Mitzrayim we were taken out, and none of the *makkos* came about...for us it would be enough![38]

אִלּוּ עָשָׂה בָהֶם שְׁפָטִים וְלֹא עָשָׂה בֵאלֹהֵיהֶם, **דַּיֵּנוּ.**

If the *makkos*, the Mitzrim annoyed, but their idols weren't destroyed...for us it would be enough!

אִלּוּ עָשָׂה בֵאלֹהֵיהֶם וְלֹא הָרַג אֶת בְּכוֹרֵיהֶם, **דַּיֵּנוּ.**

If the idols Hashem did deprive, but their firstborn had stayed alive...for us it would be enough!

אִלּוּ הָרַג אֶת בְּכוֹרֵיהֶם וְלֹא נָתַן לָנוּ אֶת מָמוֹנָם, **דַּיֵּנוּ.**

If the firstborn He made not live, but their money to us He didn't give... for us it would be enough!

---

38 Rav Yerucham Levovitz explains that it would be enough for us to serve Hashem for each particular reason on its own.

אִלּוּ נָתַן לָנוּ אֶת מָמוֹנָם
וְלֹא קָרַע לָנוּ אֶת הַיָּם, **דַּיֵּנוּ.**

If to give us their money
Hashem saw fit, but the
Sea for us He did not
split...for us it would
be enough!

אִלּוּ קָרַע לָנוּ אֶת הַיָּם
וְלֹא הֶעֱבִירָנוּ בְּתוֹכוֹ בֶּחָרָבָה, **דַּיֵּנוּ.**

If the Sea He split for
us, too, but through the
dryness He didn't pass us
through...for us it would
be enough!

אִלּוּ הֶעֱבִירָנוּ בְּתוֹכוֹ בֶּחָרָבָה
וְלֹא שִׁקַּע צָרֵינוּ בְּתוֹכוֹ, **דַּיֵּנוּ.**

If through the dry Sea
He let us cross, but the
Mitzrim in it He did not
toss...for us it would
be enough!

אִלּוּ שִׁקַּע צָרֵינוּ בְּתוֹכוֹ
וְלֹא סִפֵּק צָרְכֵּנוּ בַּמִּדְבָּר
אַרְבָּעִים שָׁנָה, **דַּיֵּנוּ.**

If the Mitzrim He had
sunk and calmed our
fears, but didn't care for
us in the desert for forty
years...for us it would
be enough!

אִלּוּ סִפֵּק צָרְכֵּנוּ בַּמִּדְבָּר אַרְבָּעִים שָׁנָה
וְלֹא הֶאֱכִילָנוּ אֶת הַמָּן, **דַּיֵּנוּ.**

If He cared in the desert
forty years for us, the
mann He didn't give us
as a plus...for us it would
be enough!

אִלּוּ הֶאֱכִילָנוּ אֶת הַמָּן
וְלֹא נָתַן לָנוּ אֶת הַשַּׁבָּת, **דַּיֵּנוּ.**

If the *mann* He did give
us to be our food, but the
great Shabbos He did not
include...for us it would
be enough!

אִלּוּ נָתַן לָנוּ אֶת הַשַּׁבָּת
וְלֹא קֵרְבָנוּ לִפְנֵי הַר סִינַי, דַּיֵּנוּ.

If the Shabbos for us He did not deny, but had not brought us close before Har Sinai...for us it would be enough!

אִלּוּ קֵרְבָנוּ לִפְנֵי הַר סִינַי
וְלֹא נָתַן לָנוּ אֶת הַתּוֹרָה, דַּיֵּנוּ.

If it to Har Sinai He did bring us near, but didn't give us the holy Torah so dear...for us it would be enough!

אִלּוּ נָתַן לָנוּ אֶת הַתּוֹרָה
וְלֹא הִכְנִיסָנוּ לְאֶרֶץ יִשְׂרָאֵל, דַּיֵּנוּ.

If the Torah He had given us without fail, but not brought us to Eretz Yisrael...for us it would be enough!

אִלּוּ הִכְנִיסָנוּ לְאֶרֶץ יִשְׂרָאֵל
וְלֹא בָנָה לָנוּ אֶת בֵּית הַבְּחִירָה, דַּיֵּנוּ.

If to Eretz Yisrael, He did bring us, But did not build for us the Beis Hamikdash...for us it would be enough!

עַל אַחַת כַּמָּה וְכַמָּה טוֹבָה כְּפוּלָה וּמְכֻפֶּלֶת לַמָּקוֹם עָלֵינוּ:

Therefore, how much more so do we owe thanks to Hashem for all of His many favors.

שֶׁהוֹצִיאָנוּ מִמִּצְרַיִם,

He brought us from Egypt,

וְעָשָׂה בָהֶם שְׁפָטִים,

And judged the Egyptians

וְעָשָׂה בֵאלֹהֵיהֶם, | and their gods during *Makkas Bechoros*,

וְהָרַג אֶת בְּכוֹרֵיהֶם, | And slew their firstborn,

וְנָתַן לָנוּ אֶת מָמוֹנָם, | And gave us their wealth when we left Egypt,

וְקָרַע לָנוּ אֶת הַיָּם, | And divided the sea for us,

וְהֶעֱבִירָנוּ בְתוֹכוֹ בֶּחָרָבָה, | And led us through it on dry land

וְשִׁקַּע צָרֵינוּ בְּתוֹכוֹ, | And drowned our oppressors in it,

וְסִפֵּק צָרְכֵּנוּ בַּמִּדְבָּר אַרְבָּעִים שָׁנָה, | And supplied our needs in the wilderness for forty years

וְהֶאֱכִילָנוּ אֶת הַמָּן, | And fed us the *mann*,

וְנָתַן לָנוּ אֶת הַשַּׁבָּת, | And gave us the Shabbos,

וְקֵרְבָנוּ לִפְנֵי הַר סִינַי, | And led us before Har Sinai to see the greatness of Hashem,[39]

---

39 The eighth principle of faith is that Hashem gave us the Torah in the revelation at Har Sinai.

וְנָתַן לָנוּ אֶת הַתּוֹרָה,[40]

And gave us the Torah,[40]

וְהִכְנִיסָנוּ לְאֶרֶץ יִשְׂרָאֵל,

And brought us into Eretz Yisrael

וּבָנָה לָנוּ אֶת בֵּית הַבְּחִירָה לְכַפֵּר עַל כָּל עֲוֹנוֹתֵינוּ.

And built us a Beis Hamikdash to atone for all of our sins so we wouldn't have to go into *galus*.

We have now concluded telling the story of *yetzias Mitzrayim*. We will now explain the other central mitzvos of the night and their connection the Jewish People leaving Egypt. We will explain why we ate the *Korban Pesach* during the days of the Beis Hamikdash, and why we continue to eat matzah and maror nowadays.

רַבָּן גַּמְלִיאֵל הָיָה אוֹמֵר:

Rabban Gamliel used to say:

כָּל שֶׁלֹּא אָמַר שְׁלֹשָׁה דְבָרִים אֵלּוּ בַּפֶּסַח,

Whoever doesn't explain these three things on Pesach

לֹא יָצָא יְדֵי חוֹבָתוֹ,

has not fulfilled his responsibility in the ideal way.

וְאֵלּוּ הֵן: פֶּסַח, מַצָּה, וּמָרוֹר.

And they are: Pesach, Matzah, and Maror.

---

40 The ninth principle of faith is that the Torah that Hashem gave us does not change and it is relevant forever.

When talking about the *Korban Pesach*, we do not raise up or point to the *zeroa* on the Seder plate so as not to mistakenly give the impression that we have *korbanos* outside of Yerushalayim. Instead, we look at it.

פֶּסַח שֶׁהָיוּ אֲבוֹתֵינוּ אוֹכְלִים בִּזְמַן שֶׁבֵּית הַמִּקְדָּשׁ הָיָה קַיָּם, עַל שׁוּם מָה?

The *Korban Pesach* that our parents ate at the time when the Beis Hamikdash was still standing—What is the reason for it?

עַל שׁוּם שֶׁפָּסַח הַקָּדוֹשׁ בָּרוּךְ הוּא עַל בָּתֵּי אֲבוֹתֵינוּ בְּמִצְרַיִם,

Because Hakadosh Baruch Hu passed over the houses of our parents in Egypt.

שֶׁנֶּאֱמַר:

As it says:

וַאֲמַרְתֶּם זֶבַח פֶּסַח הוּא לַיהוה,

"You must answer your children that the reason for **the *Korban Pesach*** is that it is **a service to Hashem**,

אֲשֶׁר פָּסַח עַל בָּתֵּי בְּנֵי יִשְׂרָאֵל בְּמִצְרַיִם בְּנָגְפּוֹ אֶת מִצְרַיִם,

Who passed over (*pasach*) the houses of the Israelites in Egypt when He struck the Egyptians,

וְאֶת בָּתֵּינוּ הִצִּיל.

sparing our homes,

וַיִּקֹּד הָעָם וַיִּשְׁתַּחֲווּ.

and the people bent their heads and bowed" over the good news.

When we read about the matzah, we should lift up the matzah from the plate and show it to everyone present in order to create feelings of love for the mitzvah. We should also make sure to lift the broken matzah, which is the *lechem oni*, the poor man's bread.

מַצָּה זוֹ שֶׁאָנוּ אוֹכְלִים, This matzah that we eat—

עַל שׁוּם מָה? What is the reason for it?[41]

עַל שׁוּם שֶׁלֹּא הִסְפִּיק בְּצֵקָם שֶׁל אֲבוֹתֵינוּ לְהַחֲמִיץ, עַד שֶׁנִּגְלָה עֲלֵיהֶם מֶלֶךְ מַלְכֵי הַמְּלָכִים הַקָּדוֹשׁ בָּרוּךְ הוּא וּגְאָלָם, Because the dough of our parents didn't have time to become leavened before the King of Kings, Hakadosh Baruch Hu, revealed Himself to them and redeemed them,

שֶׁנֶּאֱמַר: as it says:

וַיֹּאפוּ אֶת הַבָּצֵק אֲשֶׁר הוֹצִיאוּ מִמִּצְרַיִם עֻגֹת מַצּוֹת כִּי לֹא חָמֵץ, "The Jews baked the dough they had brought out of Egypt into unleavened matzah cakes, since it had not risen.

---

41   The introduction to the *Birkas HaPesach* cites the *Maharam Schiff*, who asks why the question is in this backward form of מַצָּה זוֹ שֶׁאָנוּ אוֹכְלִים עַל שׁוּם מה. Why is it not written in the more conventional fashion of עַל שׁוּם מה אנו אוכלים מצה זו— for what reason do we eat this matzah? He answers that we want to show our *emunah* in that we eat the matzah because of our deep relationship with Hashem. We eat the matzah without reason and without questioning, and only later do we ask *why* we are eating the matzah. Our desire to do the mitzvos should be no different than that of a child who wants to kiss his parent. The child can't explain why or what the reason is, but this is simply his innate desire. He doesn't need to give a reason as to why he wants to kiss his parent.

כִּי גֹרְשׁוּ מִמִּצְרַיִם
וְלֹא יָכְלוּ לְהִתְמַהְמֵהַּ,

The reason is that **they had been driven out of Egypt and could not delay,**

וְגַם צֵדָה לֹא עָשׂוּ לָהֶם.

and they had not prepared any other provisions."

When we read about the maror, we should lift up the maror from the plate and show it to everyone present.

מָרוֹר זֶה שֶׁאָנוּ אוֹכְלִים,

This maror that we eat—

עַל שׁוּם מָה?

What is the reason for it?

עַל שׁוּם שֶׁמֵּרְרוּ הַמִּצְרִים אֶת חַיֵּי אֲבוֹתֵינוּ בְּמִצְרָיִם,

Because the Egyptians embittered the lives of our fathers in Egypt,

שֶׁנֶּאֱמַר:

as it says:

וַיְמָרְרוּ אֶת חַיֵּיהֶם בַּעֲבֹדָה קָשָׁה,

"They made the lives of the Jews **miserable with harsh labor**

בְּחֹמֶר וּבִלְבֵנִים וּבְכָל עֲבֹדָה בַּשָּׂדֶה

involving mortar and bricks for building,[42]

as well as all kinds of work in the field, i.e., digging and planting.[43]

אֵת כָּל עֲבֹדָתָם אֲשֶׁר עָבְדוּ בָהֶם בְּפָרֶךְ.

All the work they made them do was intended to break them."

---

42 Originally, the Jews were given bricks with which to build. Then, in order to make the work more difficult, the Egyptians stopped giving the Jews bricks

There is one other mitzvah that we have encountered this evening: telling the story of *yetzias Mitzrayim*. Now that we have gone through Maggid and recalled, imagined, and reenacted the story, we can appreciate the following:

בְּכָל דּוֹר וָדוֹר חַיָּב אָדָם לִרְאוֹת אֶת עַצְמוֹ כְּאִלּוּ הוּא יָצָא מִמִּצְרַיִם,

In every generation, one is obligated to view himself as though he himself were a slave and had gone out from Egypt,

שֶׁנֶּאֱמַר:

as the Torah says:

וְהִגַּדְתָּ לְבִנְךָ בַּיּוֹם הַהוּא לֵאמֹר,

"On that day, you must tell your child:

בַּעֲבוּר זֶה עָשָׂה יהוה לִי בְּצֵאתִי מִמִּצְרַיִם.

'It is because of this that God acted for me when I left Egypt.'"[44]

and made them gather the mud themselves. The only ingredient they were given was the straw. Later, even the straw was not provided and the Jews had to spend time gathering the mud and straw in order to make the bricks. All this had to be done while still being required to produce the same number of bricks.

43 The Jews were forced to shepherd the Egyptians' animals. The Egyptians would make the Jews travel great distances to feed the animals so that the fathers would be separated from their homes for a long time. The fathers who were shepherding would be lonely and miss their families, while their families would worry about where their fathers were. The Egyptians would send their Jewish slaves out into the field to capture animals—sometimes dangerous ones—for the Egyptians to eat. Obviously, the Jews wouldn't be given any of the food.

44 A Jew must believe that he was in Egypt. He must say to himself, "The Jewish People were there, and I am part of the Jewish People. Therefore, I was literally there." Don't be afraid to express this with passion and excitement.

We see that we, on a literal level, left Egypt based on the following:

Not only our parents did Hakadosh Baruch Hu redeem, לֹא אֶת אֲבוֹתֵינוּ בִּלְבָד גָּאַל הַקָּדוֹשׁ בָּרוּךְ הוּא,

but He also redeemed us with אֶלָּא אַף אוֹתָנוּ גָּאַל עִמָּהֶם,

them because if they had not been taken out, we would still be there,

as it says: שֶׁנֶּאֱמַר:

"We are the ones He brought out of there, וְאוֹתָנוּ הוֹצִיא מִשָּׁם,

to bring us to the land לְמַעַן הָבִיא אוֹתָנוּ,

to give us the land that He promised to our fathers." לָתֶת לָנוּ אֶת הָאָרֶץ אֲשֶׁר נִשְׁבַּע לַאֲבוֹתֵינוּ.

Because we see ourselves as if we had left Egypt, we will now sing Hallel in order to praise Hashem for all the good He has given us. This is our introduction to the first part of Hallel. It is in the place of a berachah on Hallel or the berachah of *She'asah Nissim*.

We will raise the cup of wine in order to sing praises of Hashem over a cup of wine, and then cover the matzah.

Therefore, לְפִיכָךְ

because we see ourselves as if we left Egypt **we must thank,** אֲנַחְנוּ חַיָּבִים לְהוֹדוֹת,

לְהַלֵּל,   praise,

לְשַׁבֵּחַ,   laud,

לְפָאֵר,   glorify,

לְרוֹמֵם,   exalt,

לְהַדֵּר,   honor,

לְבָרֵךְ,   bless,

לְעַלֵּה   extol,

וּלְקַלֵּס   and give respect

לְמִי שֶׁעָשָׂה לַאֲבוֹתֵינוּ וְלָנוּ אֶת כָּל הַנִּסִּים הָאֵלֶּה: to Hashem who performed all these miracles for our fathers and for us.

הוֹצִיאָנוּ מֵעַבְדוּת לְחֵרוּת   He has brought us out of slavery in Egypt to freedom,

מִיָּגוֹן לְשִׂמְחָה,   from brokenness to joy,

וּמֵאֵבֶל לְיוֹם טוֹב,   from mourning to festivity,

וּמֵאֲפֵלָה לְאוֹר גָּדוֹל,   from spiritual darkness to the bright light of Torah

וּמִשִּׁעְבּוּד לִגְאֻלָּה.   and from the bondage of Mitzrayim to redemption.

וְנֹאמַר לְפָנָיו
שִׁירָה חֲדָשָׁה:

Therefore, let us say
before Him a new song
for our *geulah*.

הַלְלוּיָהּ.

Halleluyah!

We now begin the first half of the Hallel by reading sections of
Tehillim. The careful translation and explanation we did during
Maggid is not necessary at this point. Instead, the leader should
choose tunes that will draw the children and those present into
the singing so that the first part of the Seder can end with joyful
singing. Ask the children what songs they sing in school so that
they can join in with confidence.

The reason Hallel is split into two sections is so that the song can be recited over
the second cup. The second cup of Maggid, the telling of the story, is not complete
with only words and stories. The complete mitzvah of recounting *yetzias Mitzrayim*
should include songs of praise to Hashem for taking us out of Egypt. We recite
these particular sections of Hallel at this point because they discuss the Exodus
from Egypt.

The cup of wine should be held until the conclusion of the berachah of *Gaal
Yisrael*. The matzah should be covered.

הַלְלוּיָהּ, הַלְלוּ עַבְדֵי יהוה, הַלְלוּ אֶת שֵׁם
יהוה: יְהִי שֵׁם יהוה מְבֹרָךְ, מֵעַתָּה וְעַד
עוֹלָם: מִמִּזְרַח שֶׁמֶשׁ עַד מְבוֹאוֹ, מְהֻלָּל שֵׁם
יהוה: רָם עַל כָּל גּוֹיִם יהוה, עַל הַשָּׁמַיִם
כְּבוֹדוֹ: מִי כַּיהוה אֱלֹהֵינוּ, הַמַּגְבִּיהִי לָשָׁבֶת:
הַמַּשְׁפִּילִי לִרְאוֹת, בַּשָּׁמַיִם וּבָאָרֶץ: מְקִימִי
מֵעָפָר דָּל, מֵאַשְׁפֹּת יָרִים אֶבְיוֹן:

Halleluyah! Praise, you
servants of Hashem,
praise the Name of
Hashem! May Hashem's
Name be blessed from now
to eternity. From the place
of the rising of the sun
to the place of its setting,
Hashem's Name is praised.
Hashem is raised above all

לְהוֹשִׁיבִי עִם נְדִיבִים, עִם נְדִיבֵי עַמּוֹ: עֲקֶרֶת הַבַּיִת, אֵם הַבָּנִים שְׂמֵחָה, הַלְלוּיָהּ.

nations, His glory is over the heavens. Who is like Hashem our God, Who dwells on high, and lowers Himself to look upon heaven and earth! He raises up the poor from the dust, He lifts the needy from the trash heaps—to seat them with nobles, with the nobles of His people. He causes the barren woman to be established with a family, a joyful mother of children. Halleluyah! (*Tehillim* 113)

בְּצֵאת יִשְׂרָאֵל מִמִּצְרָיִם, בֵּית יַעֲקֹב מֵעַם לֹעֵז: הָיְתָה יְהוּדָה לְקָדְשׁוֹ יִשְׂרָאֵל מַמְשְׁלוֹתָיו: הַיָּם רָאָה וַיָּנֹס, הַיַּרְדֵּן יִסֹּב לְאָחוֹר: הֶהָרִים רָקְדוּ כְאֵילִים, גְּבָעוֹת כִּבְנֵי צֹאן: מַה לְּךָ הַיָּם כִּי תָנוּס, הַיַּרְדֵּן תִּסֹּב לְאָחוֹר: הֶהָרִים תִּרְקְדוּ כְאֵילִים, גְּבָעוֹת כִּבְנֵי צֹאן: מִלִּפְנֵי אָדוֹן חוּלִי אָרֶץ מִלִּפְנֵי אֱלוֹהַּ יַעֲקֹב: הַהֹפְכִי הַצּוּר אֲגַם מָיִם, חַלָּמִישׁ לְמַעְיְנוֹ מָיִם.

When Israel went out of Egypt, the House of Yaakov from a people of a foreign language, Yehuda became His sanctifier, Israel His dominions. The sea saw and fled, the Jordan turned back. The mountains skipped like rams, the hills like young sheep. What is with you, O sea, that you flee, O Jordan, that you turn back? You mountains, why do you skip like rams; you hills, like young sheep? Tremble, O earth, from before Hashem, from before the God of Yaakov, Who transforms a rock into a pool of water, a hard stone into a spring of water! (*Tehillim* 114)

The following concluding berachah fulfills multiple purposes: It is a berachah on the second cup of wine, it is a berachah thanking Hashem for the miracle of taking us out of Egypt, and it is also a berachah on the mitzvah of reciting the Haggadah. When reciting the berachah, one should think of thanking Hashem for the miraculous *geulah* from Egypt and imagine that he himself is being redeemed on the night of the Exodus.

בָּרוּךְ אַתָּה יהוה אֱלֹהֵינוּ מֶלֶךְ הָעוֹלָם,
אֲשֶׁר גְּאָלָנוּ וְגָאַל אֶת אֲבוֹתֵינוּ מִמִּצְרַיִם,
וְהִגִּיעָנוּ הַלַּיְלָה הַזֶּה לֶאֱכָל בּוֹ מַצָּה וּמָרוֹר.
כֵּן יהוה אֱלֹהֵינוּ וֵאלֹהֵי אֲבוֹתֵינוּ יַגִּיעֵנוּ
לְמוֹעֲדִים וְלִרְגָלִים אֲחֵרִים הַבָּאִים לִקְרָאתֵנוּ
לְשָׁלוֹם, שְׂמֵחִים בְּבִנְיַן עִירֶךָ, וְשָׂשִׂים
בַּעֲבוֹדָתֶךָ. וְנֹאכַל שָׁם מִן הַזְּבָחִים וּמִן
הַפְּסָחִים (במוצ״ש: מִן הַפְּסָחִים וּמִן הַזְּבָחִים)
אֲשֶׁר יַגִּיעַ דָּמָם עַל קִיר מִזְבַּחֲךָ לְרָצוֹן וְנוֹדֶה
לְךָ שִׁיר חָדָשׁ עַל גְּאֻלָּתֵנוּ וְעַל פְּדוּת נַפְשֵׁנוּ:
בָּרוּךְ אַתָּה יהוה גָּאַל יִשְׂרָאֵל.

Blessed are You, Hashem, our God, King of the universe, Who has redeemed us and redeemed our ancestors from Egypt, and allowed us to reach this night, to eat matzah and maror on it. So too, Hashem, our God and the God of our fathers, allow us to reach in peace other holidays and festivals in the future, happy in the rebuilding of Your city, and joyful in Your Temple service. And there we will partake of sacrifices and Pesach offerings (on Saturday night reverse the order: of Pesach offerings and sacrifices), whose blood will be poured on the wall of Your altar for Your acceptance, and we will give thanks to You with a new song over our redemption and the salvation of our souls. Blessed are You, Hashem, Who redeemed Israel.

בָּרוּךְ אַתָּה יהוה אֱלֹהֵינוּ
מֶלֶךְ הָעוֹלָם, בּוֹרֵא פְּרִי הַגָּפֶן.

Blessed are You, Hashem, our God, King of the universe, Who creates the fruit of the vine.

If you drank without leaning you should drink another cup while leaning, but without a berachah.

RACHTZAH

When announcing the steps of the Seder one should announce both Rachtzah and Motzi Matzah now, because soon we will refrain from talking.

One should remind those who are able to remain quiet to not talk about things unrelated to performing the upcoming mitzvos. Ideally, going forward, the participants should understand that there shouldn't be any talking (aside for the necessary berachos) between washing the hands and eating Korech. If a child is unable to keep quiet for so long, that is fine.

This is a good place to tell a story about the *mesirus nefesh* and dedication the Jewish People had for eating matzah. There are many such stories from the Spanish Inquisition, the Holocaust, or Communist Russia that one can find and retell.

We already washed our hands earlier in the Seder for Karpas. However, because we were reciting the Haggadah, we weren't paying attention to where we were placing our hands, and they may have touched something that would require us to wash them again.

בָּרוּךְ אַתָּה יהוה אֱלֹהֵינוּ מֶלֶךְ הָעוֹלָם, אֲשֶׁר קִדְּשָׁנוּ בְּמִצְוֹתָיו וְצִוָּנוּ עַל נְטִילַת יָדַיִם.

Blessed are You, Hashem, our God, King of the universe, Who has sanctified us through His commandments and commanded us concerning the washing of the hands.

MOTZI

We are now arriving at one of the highlights of Pesach and of the Seder itself. Many of us have waited all year to eat matzah on Pesach. The leader of the Seder should make sure to build up the excitement of this moment by uncovering the matzah in a dramatic fashion and expressing a feeling of excitement over the special mitzvah we are about to engage in. (Matzah is the only food item (*cheftza shel mitzvah*) there is a mitzvah to eat even when there is no Beis Hamikdash.)

Pick up all three matzos and recite the berachah for eating bread:

בָּרוּךְ אַתָּה יהוה אֱלֹהֵינוּ מֶלֶךְ הָעוֹלָם, הַמּוֹצִיא לֶחֶם מִן הָאָרֶץ.

Blessed are You, Hashem, our God, King of the universe, Who brings forth bread from the earth.

MATZAH

Put down the bottom matzah. While holding the top and the broken middle matzah, recite the berachah for the mitzvah:

בָּרוּךְ אַתָּה יהוה אֱלֹהֵינוּ מֶלֶךְ הָעוֹלָם, אֲשֶׁר קִדְּשָׁנוּ בְּמִצְוֹתָיו וְצִוָּנוּ עַל אֲכִילַת מַצָּה.

Blessed are You, Hashem, our God, King of the universe, Who has sanctified us through His commandments and commanded us concerning the eating of matzah.

A *k'zayis* of matzah is eaten while reclining on the left side.

We don't dip the matzah in salt at the Seder because it is supposed to be לחם עוני, poor man's bread, without any extra ingredients added for taste.

MEASURING AND DISTRIBUTING THE MATZAH

The quantity of matzah that needs to be eaten is one *kezayis*. There is a great debate among the *Poskim* regarding how to measure this. For the sake of brevity and clarity, we will avoid this discussion and focus on the practical amount that should be eaten. The strictest opinion is that one should eat slightly more than one-third of a hand-baked matzah for this part of the Seder. This can also be measured based on an average-sized adult hand with the fingers spread out. The area of the hand will be around the amount needed to fulfill the mitzvah according to the strictest opinion.

If someone prefers to eat a smaller quantity of matzah (for digestive or other reasons), they need not follow the strictest opinion. They can measure the matzah based on the entire area of the hand with the fingers closed. For those who find even this quantity too much, the amount of matzah that fits the area of the palm or even a credit card would be sufficient.[45]

Some people find themselves feeling stressed at the Seder about consuming the correct quantity of matzah—often due to the mistaken understanding that it is necessary to eat a large amount to fulfill the mitzvah. The above guidelines can help alleviate this stress.

When eating the matzah, the person leading the Seder should demonstrate a sense of joy and excitement. If the leader of the Seder complains about the taste, cost, or amount of matzah, verbally or with facial expressions, it will sour the experience for the children. This is a beautiful opportunity to show and teach our children about *simchah shel mitzvah*.

45 Based on *Hidurei Hamiddos* by Rav Hadar Margolin.

MAROR

One should try and eat the maror before *chatzos*. Hopefully, you have been maintaining a good speed so as to keep up the attention and interest of all the participants, and this should not be an issue.

The Torah tells us (*Shemos* 1:14), "וַיְמָרְרוּ אֶת חַיֵּיהֶם בַּעֲבֹדָה קָשָׁה," the Egyptians embittered the lives of the Jews with difficult labor. From here the Torah tells us to eat a bitter vegetable. This is the maror.

The Gemara (*Pesachim* 115a) says there are five vegetables that can be used for maror. The *Shulchan Aruch* (473:5) quotes both the *Talmud Bavli* and *Yerushalmi*, which say that these five vegetables are listed in descending order of importance. First on the list is *chazeres*, which is therefore considered the best option. The Gemara identifies *chazeres* as *chasa* (חסא), which *Rashi* explains is called "ליטוגנא." This is generally understood to be romaine lettuce. The *Talmud Yerushalmi* says that *chazeres* becomes bitter when left in the ground for a long time. This corresponds to our slavery in Egypt, which began sweet and then turned bitter, which explains why *chazeres* is the preferable form of maror.

> For those who always use romaine lettuce for maror, this is a great explanation. However, those who use horseradish—which is the third-ranked type of maror, after endives—may want to consider switching to romaine lettuce, though one is not obligated to change from their family custom. If your custom is to use horseradish, but your children or other Seder participants find this too harsh, it would be good to also provide some romaine lettuce so that everyone can participate in this part of the Seder.

The amount of maror that should be eaten is a *k'zayis*. This is about the size of a whole romaine leaf.

Remind those present that the *charoses* is not meant to be eaten as a spread or a dip. It is there to take away the bitterness of the maror or to counteract any bugs that may be in the maror (see Rabbeinu Chananel, *Pesachim* 115b). If they are interested in eating *charoses* then they can eat some during Shulchan Orech. Eating a *k'zayis* of *charoses* is a mitzvah according to the *Rambam*. The maror should be dipped in the *charoses*, and then the *charoses* should be shaken off.

Once the maror is ready, make the following berachah:

בָּרוּךְ אַתָּה יהוה אֱלֹהֵינוּ מֶלֶךְ הָעוֹלָם, אֲשֶׁר קִדְּשָׁנוּ בְּמִצְוֹתָיו וְצִוָּנוּ עַל אֲכִילַת מָרוֹר.

Blessed are You, Hashem, our God, King of the universe, Who has sanctified us through His commandments and commanded us concerning the eating of maror.

Because the maror represents slavery and bitterness, we do not lean while eating it.

KORECH

There is a general lack of understanding as to what the point of Korech is and the reasoning behind it. The Gemara (*Pesachim* 115a) notes that there are two opinions among the Tanna'im regarding how one must eat the *Korban Pesach*. It states in *Shemos* (12:8) that the *Korban Pesach* should be eaten with matzah and maror. According to Hillel, this means that one should eat all three items together. The Chachamim disagree and maintain that it is not necessary to eat all three together. Within the opinion of Chachamim, the Gemara quotes a dispute over whether it is permissible to eat all three together but not necessary, or whether one may not eat all three together. The Gemara concludes that since there is no definitive ruling on whether one should follow the opinion of Hillel or the Chachamim, the preferred practice nowadays—when we don't eat a *Korban Pesach*—is to recite a berachah on matzah, eat the matzah, recite a berachah on maror, eat the maror, and then eat both together without reciting a berachah, as a *zecher l'Mikdash*, remembrance for the Temple.

> Take another *k'zayis* of matzah and another *k'zayis* of maror and dip them in the *charoses.*

A bit of practical advice: If the lettuce inside the pieces of matzah is too unwieldy, and you find the matzah is crumbling, it is a good idea to take the lettuce leaf and wrap the matzah inside (see *Rav Schachter on the Haggadah*, pp. 194–95). This will prevent too many crumbs and broken pieces from getting all over the place.

Some have the custom to recite the paragraph describing the Korech before eating it. Others have the custom to say it after eating it, because of the opinion that reciting it before eating is a *hefsek* between the original berachah on the matzah and eating the Korech. Each family should follow their custom.

זֵכֶר לְמִקְדָּשׁ כְּהִלֵּל. כֵּן עָשָׂה הִלֵּל, בִּזְמַן שֶׁבֵּית הַמִּקְדָּשׁ הָיָה קַיָּם: הָיָה כּוֹרֵךְ מַצָּה וּמָרוֹר וְאוֹכֵל בְּיַחַד, לְקַיֵּם מַה שֶּׁנֶּאֱמַר, עַל מַצּוֹת וּמְרֹרִים יֹאכְלֻהוּ.

In remembrance of the Temple, like Hillel. This is what Hillel did, when the Temple was still standing. He would combine matzah and maror and eat them together, in fulfillment of what it says: "They shall eat it together with matzos and maror" (*Bamidbar* 9:11).

SHULCHAN ORECH

It is now time to enjoy the Yom Tov *seudah*. One should be careful not to eat so much so that it is uncomfortable to eat the afikoman later in the meal. If one is able to eat this meal comfortably while leaning, this is praiseworthy, though not required. Many of those who have the *minhag* of eating the egg do so at this point. The *minhag* is not dip our foods in liquids and sauces, in order to highlight the two special acts of dipping that we did earlier in the Seder.

Most likely there was not enough time during Maggid for the children to share their *divrei Torah* on the Haggadah, show off the beautiful Haggadahs they made in school, and sing the Pesach songs they learned. Shulchan Orech is a wonderful time for this. Go around the table and have the young people share what they've learned about Pesach. Pass around the adorable Haggadahs that the students and teachers put many hours into creating.

The conversation during the meal should ideally be focused on the mitzvos of the night—*emunah* and *yetzias Mitzrayim*. If this is not possible, light conversation about other topics is okay, but one should be vigilant to stay away from things that are way off topic, like politics and sports. One should be extra careful to avoid *lashon hara* in this very holy setting. In addition, we should not forget to thank those who were involved in the preparation of the *seudah* both physically and monetarily.

TZAFUN

After the meal, we eat the afikoman, the matzah that was hidden away. The word *tzafun* means "hidden," referring to the piece of matzah that was hidden away for later. It is ideal to take two *k'zeisim* for the afikoman: one to represent the *Korban Pesach* and another to represent either (1) the matzah that was eaten with the *Korban Pesach*, or (2) the *Korban Chagigah* that was eaten with the *Korban Pesach*. Both men and women must eat the afikoman, and it should be eaten while leaning. If you ate the afikoman without leaning, it would be preferable to eat another *kezyis* while leaning if it's not too difficult. The afikoman should be eaten by *chatzos*. If your Seder is moving at the appropriate pace, especially for children, this shouldn't be a concern.

The *poskim* note that we shouldn't feel burdened over having to eat the afikoman, because eating it in this way would detract from fulfilling the mitzvah properly. It is so important for the adults at the Seder not to complain or groan about having to eat another piece of matzah. Aside from demonstrating a lack of respect for the mitzvah, it sets a terrible example for the children. The children should see an excitement and passion for this mitzvah, regardless of how full you are or late it may be. There should be a sense of joy and excitement leading up to and during the eating of the afikoman.

If the afikoman was lost, then eat a *k'zayis* from any *shemurah matzah* instead. After eating the afikoman, nothing else should be eaten for the rest of the evening (this excludes the last two cups of wine at the Seder). Just like the *Korban Pesach* was the last thing that was eaten so that "טעם פסח בפיו," the taste of the *Korban Pesach* stayed in the mouth the rest of the evening, so too with the afikoman. The *Rashbam* explains that ensuring this taste is the last thing we have in our mouths for the rest of the night shows a love for the mitzvah. If a person does eat something else besides matzah after the afikoman, they should eat another *k'zayis* of matzah, having in mind that it is the afikoman. One may drink only water or tea after the afikoman.

BARECH

We pour the third cup as we prepare to recite *Birkas Hamazon*. It is proper to make sure the cup for *Birkas Hamazon* is washed out before refilling it, even if one is not usually careful about this during the rest of the year.

It is proper to remind the children and those present that we are going to thank Hashem for the beautiful meal we just enjoyed.

At this point, those who wash *mayim acharonim* should do so.

שִׁיר הַמַּעֲלוֹת, בְּשׁוּב יהוה אֶת שִׁיבַת צִיּוֹן הָיִינוּ כְּחֹלְמִים. אָז יִמָּלֵא שְׂחוֹק פִּינוּ וּלְשׁוֹנֵנוּ רִנָּה. אָז יֹאמְרוּ בַגּוֹיִם הִגְדִּיל יהוה לַעֲשׂוֹת עִם אֵלֶּה: הִגְדִּיל יהוה לַעֲשׂוֹת עִמָּנוּ, הָיִינוּ שְׂמֵחִים: שׁוּבָה יהוה אֶת שְׁבִיתֵנוּ כַּאֲפִיקִים בַּנֶּגֶב: הַזֹּרְעִים בְּדִמְעָה, בְּרִנָּה יִקְצֹרוּ: הָלוֹךְ יֵלֵךְ וּבָכֹה נֹשֵׂא מֶשֶׁךְ הַזָּרַע, בֹּא יָבֹא בְרִנָּה נֹשֵׂא אֲלֻמֹּתָיו.

A song of ascents. When Hashem will return the exiles of Zion, we will be like dreamers. Then our mouth will be filled with laughter, and our tongue with shouts of joy. Then will they say among the nations, "Hashem has done great things for these people." Hashem has done great things for us. Then we will be joyful. Hashem, return our exiles, like streams in parched land. Those who sow in tears will reap with shouts of joy. He keeps going along weeping, carrying the load of seed; but he will surely come back with shouts of joy, carrying his sheaves. (*Tehillim* 126)

It is proper for the leader of the Seder or the head of the household to lead the *zimun* for *Birkas Hamazon*. However, if there is any reason for someone else to lead the *zimun*, it is fine.

If at least three males above the age of bar mitzvah ate together, *Birkas Hamazon* begins here. If there are ten males above the age of bar mitzvah, everyone present should include the words in the brackets.

One should make sure to not speak from this point until the conclusion of *Birkas Hamazon*. If someone does speak, they do not have to repeat *Birkas Hamazon*.

רַבּוֹתַי נְבָרֵךְ:

יְהִי שֵׁם יהוה מְבֹרָךְ מֵעַתָּה וְעַד עוֹלָם.

בִּרְשׁוּת מָרָנָן וְרַבָּנָן וְרַבּוֹתַי, נְבָרֵךְ (אֱלֹהֵינוּ) שֶׁאָכַלְנוּ מִשֶּׁלּוֹ.

בָּרוּךְ (אֱלֹהֵינוּ) שֶׁאָכַלְנוּ מִשֶּׁלּוֹ וּבְטוּבוֹ חָיִינוּ.

בָּרוּךְ (אֱלֹהֵינוּ) שֶׁאָכַלְנוּ מִשֶּׁלּוֹ וּבְטוּבוֹ חָיִינוּ.

Leader: Gentlemen, let us bless!
Others: May the Name of Hashem be blessed from now to eternity.
Leader: May the Name of Hashem be blessed from now to eternity. With the permission of my masters, teachers and gentlemen, let us bless Him (our God), of Whose [bounty] we have eaten.
Others: Blessed be He (our God) of Whose bounty we have eaten, and by Whose grace we live.
Leader: Blessed be He (our God) of Whose bounty we have eaten, and by Whose grace we live.

בָּרוּךְ אַתָּה יהוה אֱלֹהֵינוּ מֶלֶךְ הָעוֹלָם, הַזָּן אֶת הָעוֹלָם כֻּלּוֹ בְּטוּבוֹ בְּחֵן בְּחֶסֶד וּבְרַחֲמִים, הוּא נוֹתֵן לֶחֶם לְכָל בָּשָׂר כִּי לְעוֹלָם חַסְדּוֹ, וּבְטוּבוֹ הַגָּדוֹל תָּמִיד לֹא חָסַר לָנוּ וְאַל יֶחְסַר לָנוּ מָזוֹן לְעוֹלָם וָעֶד, בַּעֲבוּר שְׁמוֹ הַגָּדוֹל, כִּי הוּא אֵל זָן וּמְפַרְנֵס לַכֹּל וּמֵטִיב לַכֹּל, וּמֵכִין מָזוֹן לְכָל בְּרִיּוֹתָיו אֲשֶׁר בָּרָא. בָּרוּךְ אַתָּה יהוה, הַזָּן אֶת הַכֹּל.

Blessed are You, Hashem, our God, King of the universe, Who feeds the whole world in His benevolence, with graciousness, with kindness and with compassion. He "gives food to all flesh, for His kindness is forever" (*Tehillim* 136:25). And in His great benevolence, we have never lacked food, nor will we ever lack food, for the sake of His great Name, for He is God, Who feeds and sustains all, is benevolent to all, and prepares food for all His creatures that He created. Blessed are You, Hashem, Who provides food for all.

נוֹדֶה לְּךָ יהוה אֱלֹהֵינוּ עַל שֶׁהִנְחַלְתָּ
לַאֲבוֹתֵינוּ, אֶרֶץ חֶמְדָּה טוֹבָה וּרְחָבָה, וְעַל
שֶׁהוֹצֵאתָנוּ יהוה אֱלֹהֵינוּ מֵאֶרֶץ מִצְרַיִם,
וּפְדִיתָנוּ מִבֵּית עֲבָדִים, וְעַל בְּרִיתְךָ שֶׁחָתַמְתָּ
בִּבְשָׂרֵנוּ, וְעַל תּוֹרָתְךָ שֶׁלִּמַּדְתָּנוּ, וְעַל חֻקֶּיךָ
שֶׁהוֹדַעְתָּנוּ, וְעַל חַיִּים חֵן וָחֶסֶד שֶׁחוֹנַנְתָּנוּ,
וְעַל אֲכִילַת מָזוֹן שָׁאַתָּה זָן וּמְפַרְנֵס אוֹתָנוּ
תָּמִיד, בְּכָל יוֹם וּבְכָל עֵת וּבְכָל שָׁעָה:

We thank You, Hashem, our God, for having bestowed upon our ancestors a precious, good and spacious land; for having brought us out, Hashem our God, from the land of Egypt and redeeming us from the house of bondage; for Your covenant, which You have sealed in our flesh, and for Your Torah, which You have taught us; for Your statutes, which You have made known to us; for life, grace and kindness which You have graciously granted us; and for our eating of the food that You provide and sustain us with constantly, every day, at all times, and at every hour.

וְעַל הַכֹּל יהוה אֱלֹהֵינוּ אֲנַחְנוּ מוֹדִים לָךְ,
וּמְבָרְכִים אוֹתָךְ, יִתְבָּרַךְ שִׁמְךָ בְּפִי כָּל
חַי תָּמִיד לְעוֹלָם וָעֶד. כַּכָּתוּב, וְאָכַלְתָּ
וְשָׂבָעְתָּ, וּבֵרַכְתָּ אֶת יהוה אֱלֹהֶיךָ
עַל הָאָרֶץ הַטֹּבָה אֲשֶׁר נָתַן לָךְ.
בָּרוּךְ אַתָּה יהוה עַל הָאָרֶץ וְעַל הַמָּזוֹן:

For everything, Hashem our God, we are thankful to You and bless You. May Your Name always be blessed in the mouth of every living being, forever. Thus it is written: "And you will eat and become sated, and you shall bless Hashem your God for the fine land that He has given you" (*Devarim* 8:10). Blessed are You, Hashem, for the land and for the food.

רַחֵם נָא יהוה אֱלֹהֵינוּ, עַל יִשְׂרָאֵל עַמֶּךָ,
וְעַל יְרוּשָׁלַיִם עִירֶךָ, וְעַל צִיּוֹן מִשְׁכַּן כְּבוֹדֶךָ,
וְעַל מַלְכוּת בֵּית דָּוִד מְשִׁיחֶךָ, וְעַל הַבַּיִת
הַגָּדוֹל וְהַקָּדוֹשׁ שֶׁנִּקְרָא שִׁמְךָ עָלָיו.

Have mercy, Hashem our God, upon Israel Your people, upon Jerusalem Your city, upon Zion the abode of Your glory, upon the kingship of the House

אֱלֹהֵינוּ אָבִינוּ, רְעֵנוּ זוּנֵנוּ פַּרְנְסֵנוּ וְכַלְכְּלֵנוּ וְהַרְוִיחֵנוּ, וְהַרְוַח לָנוּ יהוה אֱלֹהֵינוּ מְהֵרָה מִכָּל צָרוֹתֵינוּ. וְנָא אַל תַּצְרִיכֵנוּ יהוה אֱלֹהֵינוּ לֹא לִידֵי מַתְּנַת בָּשָׂר וָדָם, וְלֹא לִידֵי הַלְוָאָתָם, כִּי אִם לְיָדְךָ הַמְּלֵאָה הַפְּתוּחָה הַקְּדוֹשָׁה וְהָרְחָבָה, שֶׁלֹּא נֵבוֹשׁ וְלֹא נִכָּלֵם לְעוֹלָם וָעֶד.

of David Your anointed one, and upon the great and holy Temple with which Your Name is associated. Our God, our Father! Provide for us, nourish us, sustain us, support us and relieve us; and speedily grant us relief, Hashem our God, from all our troubles. And do not make us dependent, Hashem our God, upon gifts of mortal men nor upon their loans—but only upon Your full, open, holy and bountiful hand, that we may never be ashamed or embarrassed.

On Shabbos add:

רְצֵה וְהַחֲלִיצֵנוּ יהוה אֱלֹהֵינוּ בְּמִצְוֹתֶיךָ, וּבְמִצְוַת יוֹם הַשְּׁבִיעִי הַשַּׁבָּת הַגָּדוֹל וְהַקָּדוֹשׁ הַזֶּה, כִּי יוֹם זֶה גָּדוֹל וְקָדוֹשׁ הוּא לְפָנֶיךָ, לִשְׁבָּת בּוֹ וְלָנוּחַ בּוֹ בְּאַהֲבָה כְּמִצְוַת רְצוֹנֶךָ, וּבִרְצוֹנְךָ הָנִיחַ לָנוּ יהוה אֱלֹהֵינוּ שֶׁלֹּא תְהֵא צָרָה וְיָגוֹן וַאֲנָחָה בְּיוֹם מְנוּחָתֵנוּ, וְהַרְאֵנוּ יהוה אֱלֹהֵינוּ בְּנֶחָמַת צִיּוֹן עִירֶךָ וּבְבִנְיַן יְרוּשָׁלַיִם עִיר קָדְשֶׁךָ, כִּי אַתָּה הוּא בַּעַל הַיְשׁוּעוֹת וּבַעַל הַנֶּחָמוֹת.

May it please You, Hashem our God, to grant us strength through Your commandments, and through the commandment of the seventh day—this great and holy Sabbath. For this day is a great and holy one before You, to refrain from work and to rest on it with love, in accordance with the commandment of Your will. And may it be Your will, Hashem, our God, to grant us tranquility, that there should be no misfortune, sorrow or anguish on our day of our rest. And allow us to behold, Hashem our God, the solace of Zion Your city and the rebuilding of Jerusalem Your holy city, for You are the Master of salvations and the Master of consolations.

אֱלֹהֵינוּ וֵאלֹהֵי אֲבוֹתֵינוּ, יַעֲלֶה וְיָבֹא וְיַגִּיעַ וְיֵרָאֶה וְיֵרָצֶה וְיִשָּׁמַע וְיִפָּקֵד וְיִזָּכֵר זִכְרוֹנֵנוּ וּפִקְדוֹנֵנוּ, וְזִכְרוֹן אֲבוֹתֵינוּ, וְזִכְרוֹן מָשִׁיחַ בֶּן דָּוִד עַבְדֶּךָ, וְזִכְרוֹן יְרוּשָׁלַיִם עִיר קָדְשֶׁךָ, וְזִכְרוֹן כָּל עַמְּךָ בֵּית יִשְׂרָאֵל לְפָנֶיךָ, לִפְלֵיטָה לְטוֹבָה לְחֵן וּלְחֶסֶד וּלְרַחֲמִים

Our God and God of our fathers! May they ascend, come and reach, be seen and accepted, heard, recalled, and remembered before You—the remembrance and recollection of us,

לְחַיִּים וּלְשָׁלוֹם בְּיוֹם חַג הַמַּצּוֹת הַזֶּה, זָכְרֵנוּ יהוה אֱלֹהֵינוּ בּוֹ לְטוֹבָה, וּפָקְדֵנוּ בוֹ לִבְרָכָה, וְהוֹשִׁיעֵנוּ בוֹ לְחַיִּים, וּבִדְבַר יְשׁוּעָה וְרַחֲמִים חוּס וְחָנֵּנוּ וְרַחֵם עָלֵינוּ וְהוֹשִׁיעֵנוּ, כִּי אֵלֶיךָ עֵינֵינוּ, כִּי אֵל מֶלֶךְ חַנּוּן וְרַחוּם אָתָּה.

the remembrance of our fathers, the remembrance of the Messiah, the descendant of David Your servant, the remembrance of Jerusalem Your holy city, and the remembrance of all Your people the House of Israel, for deliverance, welfare, grace, kindness, mercy, life, and peace, on this day of the Festival of Matzos. Remember us on it, Hashem, our God, for good; recall us on it for a blessing; and spare us on it for life. And with a word of salvation and compassion, pity us and be gracious to us, and have mercy upon us and save us; for our eyes are [lifted] towards You, for You are a gracious and merciful God (and King).

וּבְנֵה יְרוּשָׁלַיִם עִיר הַקֹּדֶשׁ בִּמְהֵרָה בְיָמֵינוּ. בָּרוּךְ אַתָּה יהוה בּוֹנֵה בְרַחֲמָיו יְרוּשָׁלַיִם, אָמֵן.

Rebuild Jerusalem the holy city speedily in our days. Blessed are You, Hashem, Who rebuilds Jerusalem in His mercy. Amen.

בָּרוּךְ אַתָּה יהוה אֱלֹהֵינוּ מֶלֶךְ הָעוֹלָם, הָאֵל אָבִינוּ מַלְכֵּנוּ אַדִּירֵנוּ בּוֹרְאֵנוּ גּוֹאֲלֵנוּ יוֹצְרֵנוּ קְדוֹשֵׁנוּ קְדוֹשׁ יַעֲקֹב, רוֹעֵנוּ רוֹעֵה יִשְׂרָאֵל, הַמֶּלֶךְ הַטּוֹב וְהַמֵּטִיב לַכֹּל, שֶׁבְּכָל יוֹם וָיוֹם הוּא הֵטִיב הוּא מֵטִיב הוּא יֵיטִיב לָנוּ, הוּא גְמָלָנוּ הוּא גוֹמְלֵנוּ הוּא יִגְמְלֵנוּ לָעַד, לְחֵן, לְחֶסֶד וּלְרַחֲמִים וּלְרֶוַח הַצָּלָה

Blessed are You, Hashem, our God, King of the universe, the God, our Father, our Mighty One, our Creator, our Redeemer, our Maker, our Holy One, the Holy One of Yaakov, our Shepherd, the Shepherd of Israel, the King Who is benevolent

וְהַצְלָחָה, בְּרָכָה וִישׁוּעָה נֶחָמָה פַּרְנָסָה וְכַלְכָּלָה, וְרַחֲמִים וְחַיִּים וְשָׁלוֹם וְכָל טוֹב, וּמִכָּל טוּב לְעוֹלָם אַל יְחַסְּרֵנוּ.

and bestows benevolence upon all, Who each and every day has done good for us, does good for us, and will do good for us; He has bestowed upon us, bestows upon us, and will forever bestow upon us grace, kindness and mercy, relief, salvation, success, blessing, deliverance, consolation, sustenance and nourishment, mercy, life, peace and all goodness; and may He never allow us any lack of bounty.

הָרַחֲמָן, הוּא יִמְלוֹךְ עָלֵינוּ לְעוֹלָם וָעֶד.

הָרַחֲמָן, הוּא יִתְבָּרֵךְ בַּשָּׁמַיִם וּבָאָרֶץ.

הָרַחֲמָן, הוּא יִשְׁתַּבַּח לְדוֹר דוֹרִים, וְיִתְפָּאַר בָּנוּ לָעַד וּלְנֵצַח נְצָחִים, וְיִתְהַדַּר בָּנוּ לָעַד וּלְעוֹלְמֵי עוֹלָמִים.

הָרַחֲמָן, הוּא יְפַרְנְסֵנוּ בְּכָבוֹד.

הָרַחֲמָן, הוּא יִשְׁבּוֹר עֻלֵּנוּ מֵעַל צַוָּארֵנוּ וְהוּא יוֹלִיכֵנוּ קוֹמְמִיּוּת לְאַרְצֵנוּ.

הָרַחֲמָן, הוּא יִשְׁלַח לָנוּ בְּרָכָה מְרֻבָּה בַּבַּיִת הַזֶּה, וְעַל שֻׁלְחָן זֶה שֶׁאָכַלְנוּ עָלָיו.

הָרַחֲמָן, הוּא יִשְׁלַח לָנוּ אֶת אֵלִיָּהוּ הַנָּבִיא זָכוּר לַטּוֹב וִיבַשֶּׂר לָנוּ בְּשׂוֹרוֹת טוֹבוֹת יְשׁוּעוֹת וְנֶחָמוֹת.

May the Merciful One reign over us forever and ever. May the Merciful One be blessed in heaven and on earth. May the Merciful One be praised for all generations, and may He be glorified among us forever and ever, and may He be honored among us for all eternity. May the Merciful One grant us honorable sustenance. May the Merciful One break off our yoke from our necks and lead us upright to our land. May the Merciful One send us abundant blessing into this house, and upon this table at which we have eaten. May the Merciful One send us Elijah the Prophet—may he be remembered for a blessing—to proclaim good tidings of salvation and consolation to us.

הָרַחֲמָן, הוּא יְבָרֵךְ אֶת [אָבִי מוֹרִי]
בַּעַל הַבַּיִת הַזֶּה וְאֶת [אִמִּי מוֹרָתִי]
בַּעֲלַת הַבַּיִת הַזֶּה, אוֹתָם וְאֶת בֵּיתָם וְאֶת
זַרְעָם וְאֶת כָּל אֲשֶׁר לָהֶם, אוֹתָנוּ וְאֶת כָּל
אֲשֶׁר לָנוּ, כְּמוֹ שֶׁנִּתְבָּרְכוּ אֲבוֹתֵינוּ אַבְרָהָם
יִצְחָק וְיַעֲקֹב בַּכֹּל מִכֹּל כֹּל, כֵּן יְבָרֵךְ אוֹתָנוּ
כֻּלָּנוּ יַחַד, בִּבְרָכָה שְׁלֵמָה, וְנֹאמַר אָמֵן.

May the Merciful One bless [my father, my teacher] the master of this house and [my mother, my teacher] the lady of this house—them, their household, their offspring, and all that is theirs, as well as us and all that is ours. Just as our forefathers Avraham, Yitzchak, and Yaakov, were blessed with everything, from everything, and everything, so may He bless all of us together, with a complete blessing. And let us say Amen.

בַּמָּרוֹם יְלַמְּדוּ עֲלֵיהֶם וְעָלֵינוּ זְכוּת שֶׁתְּהֵא
לְמִשְׁמֶרֶת שָׁלוֹם, וְנִשָּׂא בְרָכָה מֵאֵת יהוה
וּצְדָקָה מֵאֱלֹהֵי יִשְׁעֵנוּ, וְנִמְצָא חֵן וְשֵׂכֶל
טוֹב בְּעֵינֵי אֱלֹהִים וְאָדָם.

On High, may there be invoked merit for them and for us, which will serve them as a safeguard for peace. And may we receive blessing from Hashem and kindness from the God of our salvation, and may we find grace and good repute in the eyes of God and man.

On Shabbos, the following is added:

הָרַחֲמָן, הוּא יַנְחִילֵנוּ יוֹם שֶׁכֻּלּוֹ שַׁבָּת
וּמְנוּחָה לְחַיֵּי הָעוֹלָמִים.

May the Merciful One allow us to inherit that day that will be a complete Sabbath and rest, for eternal life.

הָרַחֲמָן הוּא יַנְחִילֵנוּ יוֹם שֶׁכֻּלּוֹ טוֹב.
(יוֹם שֶׁכֻּלּוֹ אָרוּךְ, יוֹם שֶׁצַּדִּיקִים יוֹשְׁבִים
וְעַטְרוֹתֵיהֶם בְּרָאשֵׁיהֶם וְנֶהֱנִים מִזִּיו הַשְּׁכִינָה,
וִיהִי חֶלְקֵנוּ עִמָּהֶם).

May the Merciful One allow us to inherit that day that will be total goodness, that day when the righteous sit with their crowns of glory on their heads, benefiting from the splendor of the Divine Presence; and may our portion be among them.

הָרַחֲמָן הוּא יְזַכֵּנוּ לִימוֹת הַמָּשִׁיחַ וּלְחַיֵּי הָעוֹלָם הַבָּא.

May the Merciful One grant us the privilege of experiencing the Messianic era and the life of the Next World.

מַגְדִּיל יְשׁוּעוֹת מַלְכּוֹ וְעֹשֶׂה חֶסֶד לִמְשִׁיחוֹ לְדָוִד וּלְזַרְעוֹ עַד עוֹלָם: עֹשֶׂה שָׁלוֹם בִּמְרוֹמָיו הוּא יַעֲשֶׂה שָׁלוֹם עָלֵינוּ וְעַל כָּל יִשְׂרָאֵל, וְאִמְרוּ אָמֵן.

He is a tower of His king's salvation, and does kindness for His anointed one, for David and his descendants forever. He Who makes peace in His heights—may He make peace over us and over all Israel. And say, Amen.

יְראוּ אֶת יהוה קְדֹשָׁיו, כִּי אֵין מַחְסוֹר לִירֵאָיו: כְּפִירִים רָשׁוּ וְרָעֵבוּ, וְדֹרְשֵׁי יהוה לֹא יַחְסְרוּ כָל טוֹב: הוֹדוּ לַיהוה כִּי טוֹב, כִּי לְעוֹלָם חַסְדּוֹ: פּוֹתֵחַ אֶת יָדֶךָ, וּמַשְׂבִּיעַ לְכָל חַי רָצוֹן: בָּרוּךְ הַגֶּבֶר אֲשֶׁר יִבְטַח בַּיהוה, וְהָיָה יהוה מִבְטַחוֹ: נַעַר הָיִיתִי גַּם זָקַנְתִּי, וְלֹא רָאִיתִי צַדִּיק נֶעֱזָב וְזַרְעוֹ מְבַקֶּשׁ לָחֶם: יהוה עֹז לְעַמּוֹ יִתֵּן, יהוה יְבָרֵךְ אֶת עַמּוֹ בַשָּׁלוֹם.

Fear Hashem, you, His holy ones, for those who fear Him want for nothing. Young lions may be deprived and go hungry, but those who seek out Hashem shall not lack any goodness. Give thanks to Hashem, for He is good, for His kindness is forever. You open Your hand and satisfy the desire of every living thing. Blessed be the man who trusts in Hashem and makes Hashem his security. I was once a boy, and have also grown old, and I have never seen a righteous man forsaken or his offspring begging for bread. Hashem will give strength to His people; Hashem will bless His people with peace.

If you realized at this point that you forgot to eat the afikoman, you must wash *netilas yadayim* with a berachah, make *Hamotzi* and eat the afikoman, then say *Birkas Hamazon* and drink the third cup. If you already drank the third cup, go back and follow the above procedure without drinking another cup.

בָּרוּךְ אַתָּה יהוה אֱלֹהֵינוּ מֶלֶךְ הָעוֹלָם, בּוֹרֵא פְּרִי הַגָּפֶן.

Blessed are You, Hashem, our God, King of the universe, who creates the fruit of the vine.

Drink the third cup while leaning to the left.

If you forgot to lean, don't drink another cup.

This next paragraph is a collection of verses detailing our request for Hashem to take revenge on the non-Jews who have persecuted us. The practice of reciting this paragraph is quite old, and is even found in the ninth-century siddur of Rav Amram Gaon. Many of the Rishonim cite the *Talmud Yerushalmi* (*Pesachim* 10:1), which suggests that the four cups on Seder night are meant to correspond to the four cups of retribution that Hashem will serve to the nations who persecuted the Jewish People. Now we ask Hashem to pour the cups of retribution on our enemies and redeem us. Other commentaries view this as an introduction to the second half of Hallel, which begins by mentioning the false and frivolous pursuits of our enemies, who do not follow Hashem.

The custom is to open the door of the house while saying these verses to remind us that tonight is a *leil shimurim*, an evening of special Divine protection. In the merit of our trust in God, Mashiach will come and our enemies will be punished.

Pour the fourth cup.

The *Mishnah Berurah* notes the custom of Ashkenazim to pour a fifth cup at this point and name it the "*Kos shel Eliyahu HaNavi*," the cup of Eliyahu HaNavi. Rav Yaakov Emden notes that this cup should be larger than those used for the other four cups. The idea behind this fifth cup is that just as Hashem took us out of Egypt, we sincerely believe that He will redeem us from our current exile. This process will begin with Eliyahu coming to announce the redemption. What does this have to do with pouring an additional cup of wine? We eagerly await the arrival of Eliyahu on this evening specifically, and we understand that he will also need a cup of wine so that he too can take part in the Pesach Seder (*Maharaz MiBinga*, *Pesachim* 81:11).

Another explanation of the fifth cup is based on the opinion that there should be five cups of wine at the Seder, not four. Because of this debate, we compromise by pouring a fifth cup—but not making a blessing on or drinking it. We will not truly know how to settle this debate over the number of cups of wine until Eliyahu HaNavi comes and helps us settle our halachic disputes. Therefore, it is referred to as the Cup of Eliyahu.

This moment of anticipating Eliyahu HaNavi is an important demonstration of *emunah* and our belief in and desire for the *geulah*. It shouldn't be cheapened with frivolities like people dressing up as Eliyahu or teasing young children with nonsense about Eliyahu HaNavi actually drinking from the cup. We have no source in our tradition that Eliyahu actually drinks from the cup. We believe in the coming of Mashiach, and this is a powerful moment to express our deep desire in and belief that Mashiach can come any day.

שְׁפֹךְ חֲמָתְךָ אֶל הַגּוֹיִם אֲשֶׁר לֹא יְדָעוּךָ וְעַל מַמְלָכוֹת אֲשֶׁר בְּשִׁמְךָ לֹא קָרָאוּ.

Pour Your anger that was meant to be directed at us **on the nations that don't recognize You, and on the kingdoms** that know of you **but don't call out to Your name.**

כִּי אָכַל אֶת יַעֲקֹב וְאֶת נָוֵהוּ הֵשַׁמּוּ.

Even more so **that they consume Yaakov** who do call out to You **and they destroyed the Beis Hamikdash.**

שְׁפָךְ עֲלֵיהֶם זַעֲמֶךָ וַחֲרוֹן אַפְּךָ יַשִּׂיגֵם.

Pour Your anger so that they cannot escape from You.

תִּרְדֹּף בְּאַף וְתַשְׁמִידֵם מִתַּחַת שְׁמֵי יהוה.

Pursue them with your anger and destroy them from under the Heavens of God so that there is no remembrance of them.

The door is closed and the Seder continues with *Hallel.*

HALLEL

Ideally, *Hallel* should be recited before *chatzos*. If you are unable to recite *Hallel* before *chatzos*, it is the position of most *poskim* that you can still recite it with a berachah.

We recite *Hallel* while seated on the night of the Seder, even though we usually recite it standing. This is because this is a special *Hallel* that reflects our feeling of being freed from Egypt.

> The person leading the Seder should allow the children who are present to pick the tunes for *Hallel* that they are familiar with from school or shul. Doing so will allow them to be more engaged in the singing and to feel connected to the Seder. If needed, discuss beforehand and prepare a list of tunes so that they will be engaging for everyone present. As we draw closer to the end of this exalted night, we should try to sing with inspiration and feeling. Don't succumb to the *yetzer hara* of wanting to wrap things up because people are tired. Rally the troops; make the singing (and if necessary, dancing) lively to make this *Hallel* the highlight of the year.[46]

46   The *Netziv*, in his Haggadah, introduces the *Hallel* of the Seder night by citing *Maseches Sofrim* (20:7), which says it is a preferable to recite *Hallel* on both nights with a beautiful melody. He explains that this is a fulfillment of "ורוממה שמו יחדיו," to raise up the name of God together. The melody, the *ne'imah*, while singing *Hallel* brings one to love Hashem and feel His closeness. The *Netziv* understands that "ורוממה," to raise up, refers to us—that we are raised up to levels of *ahavas Hashem* through the singing of *Hallel*.

לֹא לָנוּ יהוה לֹא לָנוּ, כִּי לְשִׁמְךָ תֵּן כָּבוֹד עַל חַסְדְּךָ עַל אֲמִתֶּךָ: לָמָּה יֹאמְרוּ הַגּוֹיִם, אַיֵּה נָא אֱלֹהֵיהֶם: וֵאלֹהֵינוּ בַשָּׁמָיִם, כֹּל אֲשֶׁר חָפֵץ עָשָׂה: עֲצַבֵּיהֶם כֶּסֶף וְזָהָב, מַעֲשֵׂה יְדֵי אָדָם: פֶּה לָהֶם וְלֹא יְדַבֵּרוּ, עֵינַיִם לָהֶם וְלֹא יִרְאוּ: אָזְנַיִם לָהֶם וְלֹא יִשְׁמָעוּ, אַף לָהֶם וְלֹא יְרִיחוּן: יְדֵיהֶם וְלֹא יְמִישׁוּן רַגְלֵיהֶם וְלֹא יְהַלֵּכוּ, לֹא יֶהְגּוּ בִּגְרוֹנָם: כְּמוֹהֶם יִהְיוּ עֹשֵׂיהֶם, כֹּל אֲשֶׁר בֹּטֵחַ בָּהֶם: יִשְׂרָאֵל בְּטַח בַּיהוה, עֶזְרָם וּמָגִנָּם הוּא: בֵּית אַהֲרֹן בִּטְחוּ בַיהוה, עֶזְרָם וּמָגִנָּם הוּא: יִרְאֵי יהוה בִּטְחוּ בַיהוה, עֶזְרָם וּמָגִנָּם הוּא.

Not for us, Hashem, not for us, but for Your Name give glory, for the sake of Your kindness and Your truth. Why should the nations say, "Where, now, is their God?" But our God is in heaven; He does whatever He desires. Their idols are silver and gold, the product of human hands. They have a mouth but cannot speak; they have eyes but cannot see; they have ears but cannot hear; they have a nose but cannot smell; they have hands but cannot feel; they have feet but cannot walk; they can utter no sound with their throat. May those who make them be like them—all those who trust in them! Israel, trust in Hashem; He is their help and their shield. House of Aaron, trust in Hashem; He is their help and their shield. You who fear Hashem, trust in Hashem; He is their help and their shield.

יהוה זְכָרָנוּ יְבָרֵךְ. יְבָרֵךְ אֶת בֵּית יִשְׂרָאֵל, יְבָרֵךְ אֶת בֵּית אַהֲרֹן: יְבָרֵךְ יִרְאֵי יהוה, הַקְּטַנִּים עִם הַגְּדֹלִים: יֹסֵף יהוה עֲלֵיכֶם, עֲלֵיכֶם וְעַל בְּנֵיכֶם: בְּרוּכִים אַתֶּם לַיהוה, עֹשֵׂה שָׁמַיִם וָאָרֶץ: הַשָּׁמַיִם שָׁמַיִם לַיהוה, וְהָאָרֶץ נָתַן לִבְנֵי אָדָם: לֹא הַמֵּתִים יְהַלְלוּ יָהּ, וְלֹא כָּל יֹרְדֵי דוּמָה: וַאֲנַחְנוּ נְבָרֵךְ יָהּ, מֵעַתָּה וְעַד עוֹלָם, הַלְלוּיָהּ.

Hashem, Who has always remembered us, will bless—He will bless the House of Israel, He will bless the House of Aaron, He will bless those who fear Hashem, the smaller ones along with the greater ones. Hashem will increase you—you and your children. Blessed are you for Hashem, the Maker of heaven and earth. The heavens are the heavens of Hashem, but the earth He gave to mankind. The dead do not praise God, nor do those who go down to the grave. But we will bless God, from now to eternity. Halleluyah! (*Tehillim* 115)

אָהַבְתִּי כִּי יִשְׁמַע יהוה, אֶת קוֹלִי תַּחֲנוּנָי: כִּי הִטָּה אָזְנוֹ לִי, וּבְיָמַי אֶקְרָא: אֲפָפוּנִי חֶבְלֵי מָוֶת, וּמְצָרֵי שְׁאוֹל מְצָאוּנִי, צָרָה וְיָגוֹן אֶמְצָא: וּבְשֵׁם יהוה אֶקְרָא, אָנָּה יהוה מַלְּטָה נַפְשִׁי: חַנּוּן יהוה וְצַדִּיק, וֵאלֹהֵינוּ מְרַחֵם: שֹׁמֵר פְּתָאיִם יהוה, דַּלּוֹתִי וְלִי יְהוֹשִׁיעַ: שׁוּבִי נַפְשִׁי לִמְנוּחָיְכִי, כִּי יהוה גָּמַל עָלָיְכִי: כִּי חִלַּצְתָּ נַפְשִׁי מִמָּוֶת, אֶת עֵינִי מִן דִּמְעָה אֶת רַגְלִי מִדֶּחִי: אֶתְהַלֵּךְ לִפְנֵי יהוה, בְּאַרְצוֹת הַחַיִּים: הֶאֱמַנְתִּי כִּי אֲדַבֵּר, אֲנִי עָנִיתִי מְאֹד: אֲנִי אָמַרְתִּי בְחָפְזִי, כָּל הָאָדָם כֹּזֵב.

I loved that Hashem hears my voice, my prayers. For He inclined His ear to me, so all my days I will call [Him]. The pains of death encompassed me, and the anguish of dying came upon me, I encounter misfortune and sorrow—and I call out in the Name of Hashem, "Please, Hashem, rescue my life!" Hashem is gracious and righteous, and our God shows compassion. Hashem watches over simple people; when I sink low, He will save me. Return, my soul, to your rest, for Hashem has dealt kindly with you. For You have released my soul from death, my eyes from tears, my foot from stumbling. I will walk before Hashem in the lands of the living. I had faith when I said, "I am greatly distressed"; I said in my haste, "All men are deceitful."

מָה אָשִׁיב לַיהוה, כָּל תַּגְמוּלוֹהִי עָלָי: כּוֹס יְשׁוּעוֹת אֶשָּׂא, וּבְשֵׁם יהוה אֶקְרָא: נְדָרַי לַיהוה אֲשַׁלֵּם, נֶגְדָה נָּא לְכָל עַמּוֹ: יָקָר בְּעֵינֵי יהוה, הַמָּוְתָה לַחֲסִידָיו: אָנָּה יהוה כִּי אֲנִי עַבְדֶּךָ, אֲנִי עַבְדְּךָ בֶּן אֲמָתֶךָ, פִּתַּחְתָּ לְמוֹסֵרָי: לְךָ אֶזְבַּח זֶבַח תּוֹדָה וּבְשֵׁם יהוה אֶקְרָא: נְדָרַי לַיהוה אֲשַׁלֵּם, נֶגְדָה נָּא לְכָל עַמּוֹ: בְּחַצְרוֹת בֵּית יהוה, בְּתוֹכֵכִי יְרוּשָׁלָיִם, הַלְלוּיָהּ.

With what can I repay Hashem for all His kindness to me? I will raise a cup of salvation and call the Name of Hashem. I will fulfill my vows to Hashem now, in the presence of all His people. The death of His pious ones is difficult in the eyes of Hashem. I thank you, Hashem, for I am Your servant; I am Your servant, the son of Your maidservant, and You have broken open my bonds. I will sacrifice a thanksgiving-offering to You, and I will call the

Name of Hashem. I will fulfill my vows to Hashem now, in the presence of all His people, in the courtyards of the Temple of Hashem, in the midst of Jerusalem. Halleluyah! (*Tehillim* 116)

הַלְלוּ אֶת יהוה כָּל גּוֹיִם, שַׁבְּחוּהוּ כָּל הָאֻמִּים: כִּי גָבַר עָלֵינוּ חַסְדּוֹ, וֶאֱמֶת יהוה לְעוֹלָם, הַלְלוּיָהּ.

Praise Hashem, all nations! Laud Him, all peoples! For His kindness has overwhelmed us, and the truth of Hashem is forever. Halleluyah! (*Tehillim* 117)

The following should be recited responsively, as in shul:

Seder Leader

הוֹדוּ לַיהוה כִּי טוֹב כִּי לְעוֹלָם חַסְדּוֹ:

Give thanks to Hashem, for He is good, for His kindness is forever.

Those present

הוֹדוּ לַיהוה כִּי טוֹב כִּי לְעוֹלָם חַסְדּוֹ:
יֹאמַר נָא יִשְׂרָאֵל כִּי לְעוֹלָם חַסְדּוֹ:

Seder Leader

יֹאמַר נָא יִשְׂרָאֵל כִּי לְעוֹלָם חַסְדּוֹ:

Let Israel say: For His kindness is forever.

Those present

הוֹדוּ לַיהוה כִּי טוֹב כִּי לְעוֹלָם חַסְדּוֹ:
יֹאמְרוּ נָא בֵית אַהֲרֹן כִּי לְעוֹלָם חַסְדּוֹ:

יֹאמְרוּ נָא בֵית אַהֲרֹן
כִּי לְעוֹלָם חַסְדּוֹ:

Let the House of Aaron
say: For His kindness
is forever.

הוֹדוּ לַיהוה כִּי טוֹב כִּי לְעוֹלָם חַסְדּוֹ:
יֹאמְרוּ נָא יִרְאֵי יהוה כִּי לְעוֹלָם חַסְדּוֹ:

יֹאמְרוּ נָא יִרְאֵי יהוה
כִּי לְעוֹלָם חַסְדּוֹ:

Let those who fear
Hashem say: For His
kindness is forever.

הוֹדוּ לַיהוה כִּי טוֹב כִּי לְעוֹלָם חַסְדּוֹ.

מִן הַמֵּצַר קָרָאתִי יָּהּ, עָנָנִי בַמֶּרְחָב יָהּ: יהוה
לִי לֹא אִירָא, מַה יַּעֲשֶׂה לִי אָדָם: יהוה לִי
בְּעֹזְרָי, וַאֲנִי אֶרְאֶה בְשֹׂנְאָי: טוֹב לַחֲסוֹת
בַּיהוה, מִבְּטֹחַ בָּאָדָם: טוֹב לַחֲסוֹת בַּיהוה,
מִבְּטֹחַ בִּנְדִיבִים: כָּל גּוֹיִם סְבָבוּנִי, בְּשֵׁם
יהוה כִּי אֲמִילַם: סַבּוּנִי גַם סְבָבוּנִי, בְּשֵׁם
יהוה כִּי אֲמִילַם: סַבּוּנִי כִדְבוֹרִים דֹּעֲכוּ כְּאֵשׁ
קוֹצִים, בְּשֵׁם יהוה כִּי אֲמִילַם:

Out of the narrow straits
I called to God; God
answered me by [granting
me] spaciousness.
Hashem is with me, I shall
not fear; what can man do
to me? Hashem is with me
among those who help me,
and I will see my enemies'
[downfall]. It is better to
seek shelter

דָּחֹה דְחִיתַנִי לִנְפֹּל, וַיהוה עֲזָרָנִי: עָזִּי וְזִמְרָת
יָהּ, וַיְהִי לִי לִישׁוּעָה: קוֹל רִנָּה וִישׁוּעָה
בְּאָהֳלֵי צַדִּיקִים, יְמִין יהוה עֹשָׂה חָיִל: יְמִין
יהוה רוֹמֵמָה, יְמִין יהוה עֹשָׂה חָיִל: לֹא
אָמוּת כִּי אֶחְיֶה, וַאֲסַפֵּר מַעֲשֵׂי יָהּ: יַסֹּר
יִסְּרַנִּי יָּהּ, וְלַמָּוֶת לֹא נְתָנָנִי: פִּתְחוּ לִי שַׁעֲרֵי
צֶדֶק, אָבֹא בָם אוֹדֶה יָהּ: זֶה הַשַּׁעַר לַיהוה,
צַדִּיקִים יָבֹאוּ בוֹ: אוֹדְךָ כִּי עֲנִיתָנִי, וַתְּהִי לִי
לִישׁוּעָה: אוֹדְךָ כִּי עֲנִיתָנִי, וַתְּהִי לִי לִישׁוּעָה:
אֶבֶן מָאֲסוּ הַבּוֹנִים, הָיְתָה לְרֹאשׁ פִּנָּה: אֶבֶן
מָאֲסוּ הַבּוֹנִים, הָיְתָה לְרֹאשׁ פִּנָּה: מֵאֵת
יהוה הָיְתָה זֹּאת, הִיא נִפְלָאת בְּעֵינֵינוּ: מֵאֵת
יהוה הָיְתָה זֹּאת, הִיא נִפְלָאת בְּעֵינֵינוּ: זֶה
הַיּוֹם עָשָׂה יהוה, נָגִילָה וְנִשְׂמְחָה בוֹ: זֶה
הַיּוֹם עָשָׂה יהוה, נָגִילָה וְנִשְׂמְחָה בוֹ.

with Hashem than to trust in man; it is better to seek shelter in Hashem than to trust in nobles. If all the nations surround me, I will cut them down in the Name of Hashem. If they surround me and they encompass me, I will cut them down in the Name of Hashem. If they surround me like bees, they are extinguished like a fire of thorns; I will cut them down in the Name of Hashem. You may push me repeatedly to make me fall, but Hashem helps me. God is my strength and my song, and He has always been my salvation. The sound of shouts of joy and salvation is in the tents of the righteous: "The right hand of Hashem acts valiantly. The right hand of Hashem is exalted; the right hand of Hashem acts valiantly!" I shall not die, but I shall live, and I shall relate the deeds of God. God may chastise me, but He has not given me over to death. Open for me the gates of righteousness; I will enter them and give thanks to God. This is the gate of Hashem; the righteous will enter it. I give thanks to You for You have answered me, and You have been my salvation. I give thanks to You for You have answered me, and You have been my salvation. The stone rejected by the builders has become the main cornerstone. The stone rejected by the builders has become the main cornerstone. This took place because of Hashem; it is wondrous in our eyes. This took place because of Hashem; it is wondrous in our eyes. This is the day that Hashem has made, let us be glad and rejoice on it. This is the day that Hashem has made, let us be glad and rejoice on it.

The leader of the Seder should call out the following
and those present should repeat after him:

אָנָּא יהוה הוֹשִׁיעָה נָּא:

אָנָּא יהוה הוֹשִׁיעָה נָּא:

אָנָּא יהוה הַצְלִיחָה נָּא:

אָנָּא יהוה הַצְלִיחָה נָּא.

Please, Hashem,
save us now!
Please, Hashem,
save us now!
Please, Hashem,
grant us success now!
Please, Hashem,
grant us success now!

בָּרוּךְ הַבָּא בְּשֵׁם יהוה,
בֵּרַכְנוּכֶם מִבֵּית יהוה:

בָּרוּךְ הַבָּא בְּשֵׁם יהוה,
בֵּרַכְנוּכֶם מִבֵּית יהוה:

אֵל יהוה וַיָּאֶר לָנוּ, אִסְרוּ חַג
בַּעֲבֹתִים עַד קַרְנוֹת הַמִּזְבֵּחַ:

אֵל יהוה וַיָּאֶר לָנוּ, אִסְרוּ חַג
בַּעֲבֹתִים עַד קַרְנוֹת הַמִּזְבֵּחַ:

אֵלִי אַתָּה וְאוֹדֶךָּ, אֱלֹהַי אֲרוֹמְמֶךָּ:

אֵלִי אַתָּה וְאוֹדֶךָּ, אֱלֹהַי אֲרוֹמְמֶךָּ:

הוֹדוּ לַיהוה כִּי טוֹב, כִּי לְעוֹלָם חַסְדּוֹ:

הוֹדוּ לַיהוה כִּי טוֹב, כִּי לְעוֹלָם חַסְדּוֹ.

Blessed is he who comes
in the Name of Hashem;
we bless you from the
House of Hashem. Blessed
is he who comes in the
Name of Hashem; we bless
you from the House of
Hashem. Hashem is God,
and He made light shine
for us; bind the festival-
offering up to the corners
of the altar. Hashem is
God, and He made light
shine for us; bind the
festival-offering up to the
corners of the altar. You
are my God and I will give
thanks to You; my God,
I will exalt You. You are my
God and I will give thanks
to You; my God, I will exalt You. Give thanks to Hashem, for He is good, for His
kindness is forever. Give thanks to Hashem, for He is good, for His kindness is
forever. (*Tehillim* 118)

יְהַלְלוּךָ יהוה אֱלֹהֵינוּ כָּל מַעֲשֶׂיךָ, וַחֲסִידֶיךָ צַדִּיקִים עוֹשֵׂי רְצוֹנֶךָ, וְכָל עַמְּךָ בֵּית יִשְׂרָאֵל, בְּרִנָּה יוֹדוּ וִיבָרְכוּ וִישַׁבְּחוּ וִיפָאֲרוּ וִירוֹמְמוּ וְיַעֲרִיצוּ וְיַקְדִּישׁוּ וְיַמְלִיכוּ אֶת שִׁמְךָ מַלְכֵּנוּ, כִּי לְךָ טוֹב לְהוֹדוֹת וּלְשִׁמְךָ נָאֶה לְזַמֵּר, כִּי מֵעוֹלָם וְעַד עוֹלָם אַתָּה אֵל.

All Your works shall praise You, Hashem, our God, along with Your pious ones, the righteous who do Your will. And all Your people, the House of Israel, with shouts of joy, will give thanks, bless, laud, glorify, exalt, acclaim, sanctify, and proclaim the sovereignty of Your Name, our King. For it is good to give thanks to You, and it is befitting to sing to Your Name, for You are God for all eternity.

הוֹדוּ לַיהוה כִּי טוֹב
כִּי לְעוֹלָם חַסְדּוֹ:

Give thanks to Hashem, for He is good for His kindness is forever.

הוֹדוּ לֵאלֹהֵי הָאֱלֹהִים
כִּי לְעוֹלָם חַסְדּוֹ:

Give thanks to the God of gods for His kindness is forever.

הוֹדוּ לַאֲדֹנֵי הָאֲדֹנִים
כִּי לְעוֹלָם חַסְדּוֹ:

Give thanks to the Lord of lords for His kindness is forever.

לְעֹשֵׂה נִפְלָאוֹת גְּדֹלוֹת לְבַדּוֹ
כִּי לְעוֹלָם חַסְדּוֹ:

To the One Who alone does great wonders for His kindness is forever.

לְעֹשֵׂה הַשָּׁמַיִם בִּתְבוּנָה
כִּי לְעוֹלָם חַסְדּוֹ:

To the One Who made the heavens with understanding for His kindness is forever.

לְרֹקַע הָאָרֶץ עַל הַמָּיִם
כִּי לְעוֹלָם חַסְדּוֹ:

To the One Who stretched out the earth over the waters for His kindness is forever.

לְעֹשֵׂה אוֹרִים גְּדֹלִים
כִּי לְעוֹלָם חַסְדּוֹ:

To the One Who made the great lights for His kindness is forever.

אֶת הַשֶּׁמֶשׁ לְמֶמְשֶׁלֶת בַּיּוֹם
כִּי לְעוֹלָם חַסְדּוֹ:

The sun to rule by day for His kindness is forever.

אֶת הַיָּרֵחַ וְכוֹכָבִים לְמֶמְשְׁלוֹת בַּלָּיְלָה
כִּי לְעוֹלָם חַסְדּוֹ:

The moon and stars to rule by night for His kindness is forever.

לְמַכֵּה מִצְרַיִם בִּבְכוֹרֵיהֶם
כִּי לְעוֹלָם חַסְדּוֹ:

To the One Who struck Egypt in their firstborn for His kindness is forever.

וַיּוֹצֵא יִשְׂרָאֵל מִתּוֹכָם
כִּי לְעוֹלָם חַסְדּוֹ:

And took Israel out of their midst for His kindness is forever.

בְּיָד חֲזָקָה וּבִזְרוֹעַ נְטוּיָה
כִּי לְעוֹלָם חַסְדּוֹ:

With a strong hand and with an outstretched arm for His kindness is forever.

לְגֹזֵר יַם סוּף לִגְזָרִים
כִּי לְעוֹלָם חַסְדּוֹ:

To the One Who carved the Red Sea into sections for His kindness is forever.

וְהֶעֱבִיר יִשְׂרָאֵל בְּתוֹכוֹ
כִּי לְעוֹלָם חַסְדּוֹ:

And had Israel pass through it for His kindness is forever.

וְנִעֵר פַּרְעֹה וְחֵילוֹ בְיַם סוּף
כִּי לְעוֹלָם חַסְדּוֹ:

And stirred up Pharaoh and his army in the Red Sea for His kindness is forever.

לְמוֹלִיךְ עַמּוֹ בַּמִּדְבָּר
כִּי לְעוֹלָם חַסְדּוֹ:

To the One Who led His people through the desert for His kindness is forever.

לְמַכֵּה מְלָכִים גְּדֹלִים
כִּי לְעוֹלָם חַסְדּוֹ:

To the One Who struck
great kings for His
kindness is forever.

וַיַּהֲרֹג מְלָכִים אַדִּירִים
כִּי לְעוֹלָם חַסְדּוֹ:

And killed mighty kings for
His kindness is forever.

לְסִיחוֹן מֶלֶךְ הָאֱמֹרִי
כִּי לְעוֹלָם חַסְדּוֹ:

Sichon king of the
Amorites for His kindness
is forever.

וּלְעוֹג מֶלֶךְ הַבָּשָׁן
כִּי לְעוֹלָם חַסְדּוֹ:

And Og, king of Bashan for
His kindness is forever.

וְנָתַן אַרְצָם לְנַחֲלָה
כִּי לְעוֹלָם חַסְדּוֹ:

And gave their land as
an inheritance for His
kindness is forever.

נַחֲלָה לְיִשְׂרָאֵל עַבְדּוֹ
כִּי לְעוֹלָם חַסְדּוֹ:

An inheritance to His
servant Israel for His
kindness is forever.

שֶׁבְּשִׁפְלֵנוּ זָכַר לָנוּ
כִּי לְעוֹלָם חַסְדּוֹ:

[To the One] Who
remembered us when
we were lowly for His
kindness is forever.

וַיִּפְרְקֵנוּ מִצָּרֵינוּ
כִּי לְעוֹלָם חַסְדּוֹ:

And delivered us from our
enemies for His kindness
is forever.

נֹתֵן לֶחֶם לְכָל בָּשָׂר
כִּי לְעוֹלָם חַסְדּוֹ:

He gives food to all flesh
for His kindness is forever.

הוֹדוּ לְאֵל הַשָּׁמָיִם
כִּי לְעוֹלָם חַסְדּוֹ:

Give thanks to the God of
heaven for His kindness
is forever.

(Tehillim 136,
the "Great Hallel")

נִשְׁמַת כָּל חַי תְּבָרֵךְ אֶת שִׁמְךָ יהוה אֱלֹהֵינוּ, וְרוּחַ כָּל בָּשָׂר תְּפָאֵר וּתְרוֹמֵם זִכְרְךָ מַלְכֵּנוּ תָּמִיד, מִן הָעוֹלָם וְעַד הָעוֹלָם אַתָּה אֵל, וּמִבַּלְעָדֶיךָ אֵין לָנוּ מֶלֶךְ גּוֹאֵל וּמוֹשִׁיעַ, פּוֹדֶה וּמַצִּיל וּמְפַרְנֵס וּמְרַחֵם בְּכָל עֵת צָרָה וְצוּקָה, אֵין לָנוּ מֶלֶךְ אֶלָּא אָתָּה. אֱלֹהֵי הָרִאשׁוֹנִים וְהָאַחֲרוֹנִים, אֱלוֹהַּ כָּל בְּרִיּוֹת, אֲדוֹן כָּל תּוֹלָדוֹת, הַמְהֻלָּל בְּרֹב הַתִּשְׁבָּחוֹת, הַמְנַהֵג עוֹלָמוֹ בְּחֶסֶד וּבְרִיּוֹתָיו בְּרַחֲמִים. וַיהוה לֹא יָנוּם וְלֹא יִישָׁן, הַמְעוֹרֵר יְשֵׁנִים, וְהַמֵּקִיץ נִרְדָּמִים, וְהַמֵּשִׂיחַ אִלְּמִים, וְהַמַּתִּיר אֲסוּרִים, וְהַסּוֹמֵךְ נוֹפְלִים, וְהַזּוֹקֵף כְּפוּפִים, לְךָ לְבַדְּךָ אֲנַחְנוּ מוֹדִים. אִלּוּ פִינוּ מָלֵא שִׁירָה כַּיָּם, וּלְשׁוֹנֵנוּ רִנָּה כַּהֲמוֹן גַּלָּיו, וְשִׂפְתוֹתֵינוּ שֶׁבַח כְּמֶרְחֲבֵי רָקִיעַ, וְעֵינֵינוּ מְאִירוֹת כַּשֶּׁמֶשׁ וְכַיָּרֵחַ, וְיָדֵינוּ פְרוּשׂוֹת כְּנִשְׁרֵי שָׁמָיִם, וְרַגְלֵינוּ קַלּוֹת כָּאַיָּלוֹת—אֵין אֲנַחְנוּ מַסְפִּיקִים לְהוֹדוֹת לְךָ יהוה אֱלֹהֵינוּ וֵאלֹהֵי אֲבוֹתֵינוּ, וּלְבָרֵךְ אֶת שְׁמֶךָ עַל אַחַת מֵאֶלֶף אֶלֶף אַלְפֵי אֲלָפִים וְרִבֵּי רְבָבוֹת פְּעָמִים, הַטּוֹבוֹת שֶׁעָשִׂיתָ עִם אֲבוֹתֵינוּ וְעִמָּנוּ. מִמִּצְרַיִם גְּאַלְתָּנוּ יהוה אֱלֹהֵינוּ, וּמִבֵּית עֲבָדִים פְּדִיתָנוּ, בְּרָעָב זַנְתָּנוּ וּבְשָׂבָע כִּלְכַּלְתָּנוּ, מֵחֶרֶב הִצַּלְתָּנוּ וּמִדֶּבֶר מִלַּטְתָּנוּ, וּמֵחֳלָיִם רָעִים וְנֶאֱמָנִים דִּלִּיתָנוּ. עַד הֵנָּה עֲזָרוּנוּ רַחֲמֶיךָ

The soul of every living being shall bless Your Name, Hashem, our God; and the spirit of all flesh shall always glorify and exalt Your remembrance, our King. For all eternity You are God, and other than You we have no king who redeems and saves us. You deliver, rescue, sustain, and show mercy in all times of trouble and distress; we have no king but You—the God of the first and of the last, God of all creatures, Lord of all generations, Who is lauded with a multitude of praises, Who guides His world with kindness and His creatures with compassion. Hashem neither slumbers nor sleeps; He awakens sleepers and rouses those who slumber; He makes the mute speak, releases the bound, supports those who are falling and straightens those who are bent over. To You alone do we give thanks. Even if our mouths were as full with song as the sea, and our tongues [as full] with

וְלֹא עֲזָבוּנוּ חֲסָדֶיךָ, וְאַל תִּטְּשֵׁנוּ יהוה אֱלֹהֵינוּ לָנֶצַח. עַל כֵּן אֵבָרִים שֶׁפִּלַּגְתָּ בָּנוּ, וְרוּחַ וּנְשָׁמָה שֶׁנָּפַחְתָּ בְּאַפֵּינוּ, וְלָשׁוֹן אֲשֶׁר שַׂמְתָּ בְּפִינוּ, הֵן הֵם יוֹדוּ וִיבָרְכוּ וִישַׁבְּחוּ וִיפָאֲרוּ וִירוֹמְמוּ וְיַעֲרִיצוּ וְיַקְדִּישׁוּ וְיַמְלִיכוּ אֶת שִׁמְךָ מַלְכֵּנוּ. כִּי כָל פֶּה לְךָ יוֹדֶה, וְכָל לָשׁוֹן לְךָ תִּשָּׁבַע, וְכָל בֶּרֶךְ לְךָ תִכְרַע, וְכָל קוֹמָה לְפָנֶיךָ תִשְׁתַּחֲוֶה וְכָל לְבָבוֹת יִירָאוּךָ, וְכָל קֶרֶב וּכְלָיוֹת יְזַמְּרוּ לִשְׁמֶךָ. כַּדָּבָר שֶׁכָּתוּב, כָּל עַצְמוֹתַי תֹּאמַרְנָה יהוה מִי כָמוֹךָ. מַצִּיל עָנִי מֵחָזָק מִמֶּנּוּ, וְעָנִי וְאֶבְיוֹן מִגֹּזְלוֹ. מִי יִדְמֶה לָּךְ וּמִי יִשְׁוֶה לָּךְ וּמִי יַעֲרָךְ לָךְ, הָאֵל הַגָּדוֹל הַגִּבּוֹר וְהַנּוֹרָא אֵל עֶלְיוֹן, קֹנֵה שָׁמַיִם וָאָרֶץ. נְהַלֶּלְךָ וּנְשַׁבֵּחֲךָ וּנְפָאֶרְךָ וּנְבָרֵךְ אֶת שֵׁם קָדְשֶׁךָ, כָּאָמוּר, לְדָוִד, בָּרְכִי נַפְשִׁי אֶת יהוה, וְכָל קְרָבַי אֶת שֵׁם קָדְשׁוֹ.

shouts of joy as the multitudes of its waves, and our lips [as full] with praise as the expanse of the sky, and our eyes as gleaming as the sun and the moon, and our hands as spread out as the eagles of heaven, and our feet as swift as hinds—we would still be insufficient to thank You, Hashem, our God and God of our fathers, and to bless Your Name for even one of the millions and billions of benevolent acts that You have done for our fathers and for us. You redeemed us from Egypt, Hashem, our God, and You delivered us from the house of bondage. You have fed us during famine and nourished us in times of plenty; You have saved us from the sword and rescued us from pestilence, and extricated us from dire and serious diseases. Up to now Your compassion has always helped us, and Your kindnesses have not left us; so too, do not abandon us, Hashem our God, forever more! Therefore, the limbs that You have supplied us with, and the spirit and soul that You have breathed into our nostrils, and the tongue that You have placed in our mouth—they shall all thank, bless, praise, glorify, exalt, acclaim, sanctify and proclaim the sovereignty of Your Name, our King. For every mouth shall give thanks to You, every tongue shall swear allegiance to You, every knee shall kneel to You, every spine shall bow down before You, every heart shall fear You, and every organ and mind shall sing praises to Your Name, as it is written, "All my bones say: Hashem, who is like You? You save the poor man from those stronger than he, and the poor and needy man from one who tries to rob him" (*Tehillim* 35:10). Who can be likened to You, who is equal to You, who can be compared to You, the great, mighty, awesome God, supreme God, Possessor of Heaven and earth! We shall praise You, laud You and glorify You, and we will bless Your holy Name, as it says, "By David. Bless Hashem, O my soul, and all that is within me [bless] His holy Name" (*Tehillim* 103:1).

הָאֵל בְּתַעֲצֻמוֹת עֻזֶּךָ, הַגָּדוֹל בִּכְבוֹד שְׁמֶךָ, הַגִּבּוֹר לָנֶצַח וְהַנּוֹרָא בְּנוֹרְאוֹתֶיךָ, הַמֶּלֶךְ הַיּוֹשֵׁב עַל כִּסֵּא רָם וְנִשָּׂא שׁוֹכֵן עַד מָרוֹם וְקָדוֹשׁ שְׁמוֹ, וְכָתוּב, רַנְּנוּ צַדִּיקִים בַּיהוה, לַיְשָׁרִים נָאוָה תְהִלָּה. בְּפִי יְשָׁרִים תִּתְהַלָּל, וּבְדִבְרֵי צַדִּיקִים תִּתְבָּרַךְ, וּבִלְשׁוֹן חֲסִידִים תִּתְרוֹמָם, וּבְקֶרֶב קְדוֹשִׁים תִּתְקַדָּשׁ.

You are the God—in the might of Your strength; great in the glory of Your Name; mighty forever; and awesome in Your awesome deeds; the King Who sits upon an exalted and lofty throne. He abides forever, exalted and holy is His Name. And it is written, "Shout out with joy to Hashem, you righteous ones; it is befitting for the upright to offer praise" (*Tehillim* 33:1). By the mouth of the upright You shall be praised; by the words of the righteous You shall be blessed; by the tongue of the pious You shall be exalted; and among the holy ones You shall be sanctified.

וּבְמַקְהֲלוֹת רִבְבוֹת עַמְּךָ בֵּית יִשְׂרָאֵל, בְּרִנָּה יִתְפָּאֵר שִׁמְךָ מַלְכֵּנוּ בְּכָל דּוֹר וָדוֹר, שֶׁכֵּן חוֹבַת כָּל הַיְצוּרִים לְפָנֶיךָ יהוה אֱלֹהֵינוּ וֵאלֹהֵי אֲבוֹתֵינוּ, לְהוֹדוֹת לְהַלֵּל לְשַׁבֵּחַ לְפָאֵר לְרוֹמֵם לְהַדֵּר לְבָרֵךְ לְעַלֵּה וּלְקַלֵּס, עַל כָּל דִּבְרֵי שִׁירוֹת וְתִשְׁבָּחוֹת דָּוִד בֶּן יִשַׁי עַבְדְּךָ מְשִׁיחֶךָ.

And in the assemblies of the myriads of Your people, the House of Israel, Your Name shall be glorified with joyful shouts, our King, in every generation. For this is the duty of all creatures before You, Hashem, our God and God of our fathers—to thank, to praise, to laud, to glorify, to exalt, to honor, to bless, to elevate and to extol [You], even beyond all the words of song and praise of David son of Jesse, Your anointed servant.

יִשְׁתַּבַּח שִׁמְךָ לָעַד מַלְכֵּנוּ, הָאֵל הַמֶּלֶךְ הַגָּדוֹל וְהַקָּדוֹשׁ בַּשָּׁמַיִם וּבָאָרֶץ, כִּי לְךָ נָאֶה יהוה אֱלֹהֵינוּ וֵאלֹהֵי אֲבוֹתֵינוּ, שִׁיר וּשְׁבָחָה הַלֵּל וְזִמְרָה עֹז וּמֶמְשָׁלָה נֶצַח גְּדֻלָּה וּגְבוּרָה תְּהִלָּה וְתִפְאֶרֶת קְדֻשָּׁה וּמַלְכוּת בְּרָכוֹת וְהוֹדָאוֹת מֵעַתָּה וְעַד עוֹלָם. בָּרוּךְ אַתָּה יהוה אֵל מֶלֶךְ גָּדוֹל בַּתִּשְׁבָּחוֹת, אֵל הַהוֹדָאוֹת, אֲדוֹן הַנִּפְלָאוֹת, הַבּוֹחֵר בְּשִׁירֵי זִמְרָה, מֶלֶךְ אֵל חֵי הָעוֹלָמִים.

May Your Name be praised forever, our King, the God and King Who is great and holy in heaven and on earth. For to You, Hashem, our God and God of our fathers, are befitting song and praise, laud and hymn, strength and dominion, eternity, greatness and might, glorification and splendor, holiness and sovereignty, blessings and thanksgiving—for all eternity. Blessed are You, Hashem, God, King, great in praises, God of thanksgiving, Lord of wonders, Who favors melodious songs of praise, the King, the Life of the universe.

בָּרוּךְ אַתָּה יהוה אֱלֹהֵינוּ מֶלֶךְ הָעוֹלָם, בּוֹרֵא פְּרִי הַגָּפֶן.

Blessed are You, Hashem, our God, King of the universe, Who creates the fruit of the vine.

Drink the fourth cup while leaning to the left.

If you did not lean, do not go back and drink again.

הגדה של פסח   122

After drinking the fourth cup, the following blessing is recited.
On Shabbos, the words in parentheses are added.

בָּרוּךְ אַתָּה יהוה אֱלֹהֵינוּ מֶלֶךְ הָעוֹלָם,
עַל הַגֶּפֶן וְעַל פְּרִי הַגֶּפֶן וְעַל תְּנוּבַת הַשָּׂדֶה
וְעַל אֶרֶץ חֶמְדָּה טוֹבָה וּרְחָבָה, שֶׁרָצִיתָ
וְהִנְחַלְתָּ לַאֲבוֹתֵינוּ, לֶאֱכֹל מִפִּרְיָהּ וְלִשְׂבֹּעַ
מִטּוּבָהּ. רַחֵם נָא יהוה אֱלֹהֵינוּ עַל יִשְׂרָאֵל
עַמֶּךָ, וְעַל יְרוּשָׁלַיִם עִירֶךָ, וְעַל צִיּוֹן מִשְׁכַּן
כְּבוֹדֶךָ וְעַל מִזְבְּחֶךָ וְעַל הֵיכָלֶךָ. וּבְנֵה יְרוּשָׁלַיִם
עִיר הַקֹּדֶשׁ בִּמְהֵרָה בְיָמֵינוּ, וְהַעֲלֵנוּ לְתוֹכָהּ
וְשַׂמְּחֵנוּ בְּבִנְיָנָהּ וְנֹאכַל מִפִּרְיָהּ וְנִשְׂבַּע
מִטּוּבָהּ, וּנְבָרֶכְךָ עָלֶיהָ בִּקְדֻשָּׁה וּבְטָהֳרָה,
(וּרְצֵה וְהַחֲלִיצֵנוּ בְּיוֹם הַשַּׁבָּת הַזֶּה) וְשַׂמְּחֵנוּ בְּיוֹם חַג
הַמַּצּוֹת הַזֶּה כִּי אַתָּה יהוה טוֹב וּמֵטִיב לַכֹּל,
וְנוֹדֶה לְּךָ עַל הָאָרֶץ וְעַל פְּרִי הַגֶּפֶן.
בָּרוּךְ אַתָּה יהוה, עַל הָאָרֶץ וְעַל פְּרִי הַגֶּפֶן.

When drinking wine from Eretz Yisrael
conclude with the following instead:

בָּרוּךְ אַתָּה יהוה, עַל הָאָרֶץ וְעַל פְּרִי גַפְנָהּ.

Blessed are You, Hashem our God, King of the universe, for the vine and the fruit of the vine, for the produce of the field, and for the precious, good and spacious land that You saw fit to grant as a possession to our fathers, to eat of its fruit and be sated by its goodness. Have mercy, Hashem our God, on Israel Your people, on Jerusalem Your city, on Zion the abode of Your glory, on Your altar and on Your Temple. Rebuild Jerusalem, the holy city, speedily in our days, and bring us up into it and let us rejoice in its rebuilding; let us partake of its fruits and be sated by its goodness, and bless You upon it in holiness and purity. (May it please You to grant us strength on this Sabbath day) and remember us for good on this day of the Festival of Matzos. For You, Hashem, are benevolent and bestow benevolence upon all, and we give thanks to You for the land and for the fruit of the vine. Blessed are You, Hashem, for the land and for the fruit of the vine.

NIRTZAH

The meaning of *Nirtzah* is that we are wanted and desired by Hashem. If the Seder has gone according to plan and we have taught those present about the Jewish People leaving Egypt, discussed Hashem's interest in us as a people, spoken about and reflected on *emunah*, and turned the night of the Seder into a spiritual journey, then we have done our job and we are now ready to celebrate.

The final poems and songs of the evening are expressions of our love for and relationship with Hashem. The ideas ensconced in these profound and moving pieces contain the past, present, and future of the Jewish People. We will sing about the triumphs and struggles of those who came before us and will soar as we imagine what the future holds for entirety of the Jewish People. After an evening of Torah and mitzvos, our hearts overflow with a deep love and passion that can only be expressed through song.

> On a much simpler level, these songs are where important connections are made between meaningful concepts at the Pesach Seder. If the Seder has followed an appropriate tempo for those present, there should be no one sleeping on the couch and everyone should be at the table. The family tunes sung during Nirtzah are an expression of tradition going back generations. Here is where the leader of the Seder passes down the tunes that were heard at his childhood Sedarim, thereby connecting the younger generation with the past. Take those songs you remember from childhood and share them with the children present so they will remember them when they lead their Sedarim.

חֲסַל סִדּוּר פֶּסַח כְּהִלְכָתוֹ, כְּכָל מִשְׁפָּטוֹ וְחֻקָּתוֹ, כַּאֲשֶׁר זָכִינוּ לְסַדֵּר אוֹתוֹ, כֵּן נִזְכֶּה לַעֲשׂוֹתוֹ, זָךְ שׁוֹכֵן מְעוֹנָה, קוֹמֵם קְהַל עֲדַת מִי מָנָה, בְּקָרוֹב נַהֵל נִטְעֵי כַנָּה, פְּדוּיִם לְצִיּוֹן בְּרִנָּה.

This is the completion of the Pesach ceremony according to its rules, in accordance with all its laws and statutes. Just as we merited to present it, so may we merit to perform it. Pure One, Who dwells on high, raise up the congregation of whom it was said, "Who can count them?" (*Bamidbar* 23:10). Soon lead the plants of your vineyard [Israel], redeemed, to Zion, with shouts of joy.

לְשָׁנָה הַבָּאָה בִּירוּשָׁלַיִם הַבְּנוּיָה.

Next year in the rebuilt Jerusalem!

On the first night, outside of Eretz Yisrael, recite the following:

וּבְכֵן וַיְהִי בַּחֲצִי הַלַּיְלָה:

"It happened at midnight" (*Shemos* 12:29).

אָז רוֹב נִסִּים הִפְלֵאתָ בַּלַּיְלָה.
בְּרֹאשׁ אַשְׁמוֹרֶת זֶה הַלַּיְלָה.
גֵּר צֶדֶק נִצַּחְתּוֹ כְּנֶחֱלַק לוֹ לַיְלָה.
וַיְהִי בַּחֲצִי הַלַּיְלָה:

Always, You have performed wondrous miracles on this night. At the beginning of the watches on this night, You granted victory to the righteous convert

[Avraham] when the night was divided in two (*Bereishis* 14:15).
It happened at midnight.

דַּנְתָּ מֶלֶךְ גְּרָר בַּחֲלוֹם הַלַּיְלָה.
הִפְחַדְתָּ אֲרַמִּי בְּאֶמֶשׁ לַיְלָה.
וַיָּשַׂר יִשְׂרָאֵל לְמַלְאָךְ וַיּוּכַל לוֹ לַיְלָה.
וַיְהִי בַּחֲצִי הַלַּיְלָה:

You judged the king of Gerar [Avimelech] in a dream at night (ibid. 20:3). You frightened the Aramean [Lavan] in the dark of the night (ibid. 31:24).

Israel struggled with an angel and overcame him at night (ibid. 32:25).
It happened at midnight.

זֶרַע בְּכוֹרֵי פַתְרוֹס מָחַצְתָּ בַּחֲצִי הַלַּיְלָה.
חֵילָם לֹא מָצְאוּ בְּקוּמָם בַּלַּיְלָה.
טִיסַת נְגִיד חֲרוֹשֶׁת סִלִּיתָ בְּכוֹכְבֵי לַיְלָה.
וַיְהִי בַּחֲצִי הַלַּיְלָה:

You crushed the firstborn offspring of Pathros [Egypt] at midnight. They did not find their vigor [firstborn sons] when they awoke in the middle of the night.

You trampled the swift army of the Prince of Harosheth [Sisera] by the stars of the night (*Shoftim* 5:20). It happened at midnight.

יָעַץ מְחָרֵף לְנוֹפֵף אִוּוּי הוֹבַשְׁתָּ פְגָרָיו בַּלַּיְלָה.
כָּרַע בֵּל וּמַצָּבוֹ בְּאִישׁוֹן לַיְלָה.
לְאִישׁ חֲמוּדוֹת נִגְלָה רָז חֲזוֹת לַיְלָה.
וַיְהִי בַּחֲצִי הַלַּיְלָה:

The blasphemer [Sancheriv] planned to wave his hand against the cherished Temple; You dried out his corpses overnight (*Melachim II* 19:35).

Bel [Babylonia] and its watchmen collapsed in the dark of night.
To the beloved man [Daniel] was revealed the secret of the vision at night (*Daniel* 5). It happened at midnight.

מִשְׁתַּכֵּר בִּכְלֵי קֹדֶשׁ נֶהֱרַג בּוֹ בַּלַּיְלָה.
נוֹשַׁע מִבּוֹר אֲרָיוֹת פּוֹתֵר בְּעִתּוּתֵי לַיְלָה.
שִׂנְאָה נָטַר אֲגָגִי וְכָתַב סְפָרִים בַּלַּיְלָה.
וַיְהִי בַּחֲצִי הַלַּיְלָה.[47]

The one who became drunk drinking from the sacred vessels [Belshazzar] was killed that very night (ibid.). The one saved from the lion's den [Daniel]

interpreted the frightening sight at night (ibid.).
The Agagite [Haman] retained his hatred and wrote writs at night (*Esther* 5:14–6:4). It happened at midnight.

---

47   The author of this song states that the downfall of Haman was on Pesach. This is based on the Gemara (*Megillah* 15a), which says that on the thirteenth of

עוֹרַרְתָּ נִצְחֲךָ עָלָיו בְּנֶדֶד שְׁנַת לַיְלָה.

פּוּרָה תִדְרוֹךְ לְשׁוֹמֵר מַה מִלַּיְלָה.

צָרַח כַּשּׁוֹמֵר וְשָׂח אָתָא בֹקֶר וְגַם לַיְלָה.

וַיְהִי בַּחֲצִי הַלַּיְלָה:

You launched Your triumph against him [Haman] when [Achashverosh's] sleep was disturbed at night (ibid). You will trample the vintage of the one [Edom] of whom it was said, "Watchman, what of the night?" (*Yeshayahu* 21:11). God shouted back like a watchman and said, "Morning is coming, but also night" (ibid. 21:12). It happened at midnight.

קָרֵב יוֹם אֲשֶׁר הוּא לֹא יוֹם וְלֹא לַיְלָה.

רָם הוֹדַע כִּי לְךָ הַיּוֹם אַף לְךָ הַלַּיְלָה.

שׁוֹמְרִים הַפְקֵד לְעִירְךָ כָּל הַיּוֹם וְכָל הַלַּיְלָה.

תָּאִיר כְּאוֹר יוֹם חֶשְׁכַּת לַיְלָה.

וַיְהִי בַּחֲצִי הַלַּיְלָה

Bring near the day [of the Messiah] which is "neither day nor night" (*Zechariah* 14:7). Exalted One, make it known that "Yours is the day and Yours is the night" (*Tehillim* 74:16). Post guardians over Your city all day and all night (*Yeshayahu* 61:6). Light up the dark of night as brightly as the light of day. It happened at midnight.

Nissan, the letters regarding the destruction of the Jews were sent out. The Jews fasted on the fourteenth, fifteenth, and sixteenth, and on the afternoon of the sixteenth, Haman was hanged. In the *Haggadah Tzuf Amarim*, there is a footnote that says it is proper to commemorate the party of Esther, which occurred on the second night of Pesach. This is first noted in the *Shelah* and then cited by the *Magen Avraham* (495) and the *Mishnah Berurah* (ibid. 2).

On the second night, outside of Eretz Yisrael, recite the following poem.
In Eretz Yisrael this poem is recited on the first night as well.

וּבְכֵן וַאֲמַרְתֶּם זֶבַח פֶּסַח:

**And you shall say,
"It is a sacrifice of Pesach"**
(*Shemos* 12:27).

אֹמֶץ גְּבוּרוֹתֶיךָ הִפְלֵאתָ בַּפֶּסַח.

בְּרֹאשׁ כָּל מוֹעֲדוֹת נִשֵּׂאתָ פֶּסַח.

גִּלִּיתָ לְאֶזְרָחִי חֲצוֹת לֵיל פֶּסַח.

וַאֲמַרְתֶּם זֶבַח פֶּסַח:

You demonstrated the
power of Your might on
Pesach. You elevated as the
first of the holidays Pesach
(*Vayikra* 23:4–5). You
revealed to the Easterner
[Avraham] the events of
the midnight of Pesach. And you shall say, "It is a sacrifice of Pesach."

דְּלָתָיו דָּפַקְתָּ כְּחוֹם הַיּוֹם בַּפֶּסַח.

הִסְעִיד נוֹצְצִים עֻגוֹת מַצּוֹת בַּפֶּסַח.

וְאֶל הַבָּקָר רָץ זֵכֶר לְשׁוֹר עֵרֶךְ פֶּסַח.

וַאֲמַרְתֶּם זֶבַח פֶּסַח:

You knocked on his
[Avraham's] door in the
heat of the day on Pesach
(*Bereishis* 18:1). He fed
angels unleavened cakes
on Pesach (ibid. 18:6).
He ran to take from the
cattle (ibid. 18:7), symbolizing the ox brought in conjunction with the sacrifice of
Pesach. And you shall say, "It is a sacrifice of Pesach."

זֹעֲמוּ סְדוֹמִים וְלֹהֲטוּ בָּאֵשׁ בַּפֶּסַח.

חֻלַּץ לוֹט מֵהֶם וּמַצּוֹת אָפָה בְּקֵץ פֶּסַח.

טִאטֵאתָ אַדְמַת מוֹף וְנוֹף בְּעָבְרְךָ בַּפֶּסַח.

וַאֲמַרְתֶּם זֶבַח פֶּסַח:

The Sodomites were
damned and burnt in
fire on Pesach. Lot was
rescued from among them;
he baked unleavened
bread (ibid. 19:3) at the
end of the eve of Pesach.
You wiped out the land of Moph and Noph [Egypt] when You passed through on
Pesach. And you shall say, "It is a sacrifice of Pesach."

יָהּ רֹאשׁ כָּל אוֹן מָחַצְתָּ בְּלֵיל שִׁמּוּר פֶּסַח. God, You crushed the first
one of all their child-
bearing, on the "night
of watching" (Shemos
12:42) of Pesach. Mighty
One, You passed over
[Your own] firstborn son

כַּבִּיר עַל בֵּן בְּכוֹר פָּסַחְתָּ בְּדַם פֶּסַח.

לְבִלְתִּי תֵּת מַשְׁחִית לָבֹא בִּפְתָחַי בַּפֶּסַח.

וַאֲמַרְתֶּם זֶבַח פֶּסַח:

because of the blood of the Pesach, Not allowing the Destroyer to enter my doors
on Pesach. And you shall say, "It is a sacrifice of Pesach."

מְסֻגֶּרֶת סֻגָּרָה בְּעִתּוֹתֵי פֶּסַח. The sealed city [Jericho]
was handed over during
the time of Pesach. Midian
was destroyed through
a loaf representing the
barley of the Omer-
sacrifice of Pesach (Shoftim

נִשְׁמְדָה מִדְיָן בִּצְלִיל שְׂעוֹרֵי עוֹמֶר פֶּסַח.

שׂוֹרְפוּ מִשְׁמַנֵּי פּוּל וְלוּד בִּיקַד יְקוֹד פֶּסַח.

וַאֲמַרְתֶּם זֶבַח פֶּסַח:

7:13). The burly warriors of Pul and Lud [Assyria] were burnt in a conflagration
on Pesach (Yeshayahu 10:16). And you shall say, "It is a sacrifice of Pesach."

עוֹד הַיּוֹם בְּנֹב לַעֲמוֹד עַד גָּעָה עוֹנַת פֶּסַח. He [Sancheriv] wanted
"to reach Nob that very
day" (ibid. 10:32)—until
it became the season
of Pesach. The palm
of a hand wrote an
inscription about the

פַּס יָד כָּתְבָה לְקַעֲקֵעַ צוּל בַּפֶּסַח.

צָפֹה הַצָּפִית עָרוֹךְ הַשֻּׁלְחָן בַּפֶּסַח.

וַאֲמַרְתֶּם זֶבַח פֶּסַח:

crushing of the well-watered country [Babylonia] on Pesach; "The chandelier was
lit and table was set" [describing the downfall of Babylonia] (ibid. 21:5) on Pesach.
And you shall say, "It is a sacrifice of Pesach."

קָהָל כִּנְּסָה הֲדַסָּה צוֹם לְשַׁלֵּשׁ בַּפֶּסַח.
רֹאשׁ מִבֵּית רָשָׁע מָחַצְתָּ בְּעֵץ
חֲמִשִּׁים בַּפֶּסַח.
שְׁתֵּי אֵלֶּה רֶגַע תָּבִיא לְעוּצִית בַּפֶּסַח.
תָּעֹז יָדְךָ וְתָרוּם יְמִינְךָ כְּלֵיל
הִתְקַדֵּשׁ חַג פֶּסַח.
וַאֲמַרְתֶּם זֶבַח פֶּסַח:

Hadassah assembled the congregation to hold a three-day fast on Pesach (*Esther* 4:16). You vanquished the chief [Haman] from the wicked family [Amalek] on a fifty-cubit wooden pole on Pesach. May You bring "these two things" (*Yeshayahu* 47:9) in an instant upon the Utzites [Babylonians] on Pesach! Let Your hand be strong and Your right hand raised, as on the night of the sanctification of the holiday of Pesach! And you shall say, "It is a sacrifice of Pesach."

כִּי לוֹ נָאֶה, כִּי לוֹ יָאֶה.

To Him it is befitting! To Him it is becoming!

אַדִּיר בִּמְלוּכָה, בָּחוּר כַּהֲלָכָה,
גְּדוּדָיו יֹאמְרוּ לוֹ.
לְךָ וּלְךָ, לְךָ כִּי לְךָ, לְךָ אַף לְךָ, לְךָ יְיָ הַמַּמְלָכָה,
כִּי לוֹ נָאֶה, כִּי לוֹ יָאֶה.

Mighty in dominion, superior indeed, His legions [angels] say to Him: To You, to You! To You, indeed to You! To You, only to You! "To you, Hashem, belongs the dominion" (*I Divrei Hayamim* 29:11)! To Him it is befitting! To Him it is becoming!

דָּגוּל בִּמְלוּכָה, הָדוּר כַּהֲלָכָה,
וָתִיקָיו יֹאמְרוּ לוֹ.
לְךָ וּלְךָ, לְךָ כִּי לְךָ, לְךָ אַף לְךָ, לְךָ יְיָ הַמַּמְלָכָה,
כִּי לוֹ נָאֶה, כִּי לוֹ יָאֶה.

Outstanding in dominion, glorious indeed, His devoted ones [Israel] say to Him: To You, to You! To You, indeed to You! To You, only to You! To you, Hashem, belongs the dominion! To Him it is befitting! To Him it is becoming!

זַכַּאי בִּמְלוּכָה, חָסִין כַּהֲלָכָה,
טַפְסְרָיו יֹאמְרוּ לוֹ.
לְךָ וּלְךָ, לְךָ כִּי לְךָ, לְךָ אַף לְךָ, לְךָ יְיָ הַמַּמְלָכָה,
כִּי לוֹ נָאֶה, כִּי לוֹ יָאֶה.

Pure in dominion, powerful indeed, His captains [angels] say to Him: To You, to You! To You, indeed to You! To You, only to You! To you, Hashem, belongs the dominion! To Him it is befitting! To Him it is becoming!

יָחִיד בִּמְלוּכָה, כַּבִּיר כַּהֲלָכָה,
לִמּוּדָיו יֹאמְרוּ לוֹ.
לְךָ וּלְךָ, לְךָ כִּי לְךָ, לְךָ אַף לְךָ, לְךָ יְיָ הַמַּמְלָכָה,
כִּי לוֹ נָאֶה, כִּי לוֹ יָאֶה.

Unique in dominion, potent indeed, His learned ones [Israel] say to Him: To You, to You! To You, indeed to You! To You, only to You! To you, Hashem, belongs the dominion! To Him it is befitting! To Him it is becoming!

מוֹשֵׁל בִּמְלוּכָה, נוֹרָא כַּהֲלָכָה,
סְבִיבָיו יֹאמְרוּ לוֹ.
לְךָ וּלְךָ, לְךָ כִּי לְךָ, לְךָ אַף לְךָ, לְךָ יְיָ הַמַּמְלָכָה,
כִּי לוֹ נָאֶה, כִּי לוֹ יָאֶה.

Exalted in dominion, awesome indeed, those surrounding Him [angels] say to Him: To You, to You! To You, indeed to You! To You, only to You! To you, Hashem, belongs the dominion! To Him it is befitting! To Him it is becoming!

עָנָיו בִּמְלוּכָה, פּוֹדֶה כַּהֲלָכָה,
צַדִּיקָיו יֹאמְרוּ לוֹ.
לְךָ וּלְךָ, לְךָ כִּי לְךָ, לְךָ אַף לְךָ, לְךָ יְיָ הַמַּמְלָכָה,
כִּי לוֹ נָאֶה, כִּי לוֹ יָאֶה.

Deigning in dominion, redeeming indeed, His righteous ones [Israel] say to Him: To You, to You! To You, indeed to You! To You, only to You! To you, Hashem, belongs the dominion! To Him it is befitting! To Him it is becoming!

קָדוֹשׁ בִּמְלוּכָה, רַחוּם כַּהֲלָכָה,
שִׁנְאַנָּיו יֹאמְרוּ לוֹ.
לְךָ וּלְךָ, לְךָ כִּי לְךָ, לְךָ אַף לְךָ, לְךָ יְיָ הַמַּמְלָכָה,
כִּי לוֹ נָאֶה, כִּי לוֹ יָאֶה.

Holy in dominion, compassionate indeed, His *shinanim* [angels] say to Him: To You, to You! To You, indeed to You! To You, only to You! To you, To Him it is becoming!

Hashem, belongs the dominion! To Him it is befitting!

תַּקִּיף בִּמְלוּכָה, תּוֹמֵךְ כַּהֲלָכָה,
תְּמִימָיו יֹאמְרוּ לוֹ.
לְךָ וּלְךָ, לְךָ כִּי לְךָ, לְךָ אַף לְךָ, לְךָ יְיָ הַמַּמְלָכָה,
כִּי לוֹ נָאֶה, כִּי לוֹ יָאֶה.

Strong in dominion, supporter indeed, His faithful ones [Israel] say to Him: To You, to You! To You, indeed to You! To You, only to You! To you, To Him it is becoming!

Hashem, belongs the dominion! To Him it is befitting!

אַדִּיר הוּא, יִבְנֶה בֵיתוֹ בְּקָרוֹב,

בִּמְהֵרָה בִּמְהֵרָה בְּיָמֵינוּ בְּקָרוֹב,
אֵל בְּנֵה אֵל בְּנֵה, בְּנֵה בֵיתְךָ בְּקָרוֹב.
בָּחוּר הוּא, גָּדוֹל הוּא, דָּגוּל הוּא,
יִבְנֶה בֵיתוֹ בְּקָרוֹב.
בִּמְהֵרָה בִּמְהֵרָה בְּיָמֵינוּ בְּקָרוֹב,
אֵל בְּנֵה אֵל בְּנֵה, בְּנֵה בֵיתְךָ בְּקָרוֹב.
הָדוּר הוּא, וָתִיק הוּא, זַכַּאי הוּא,
יִבְנֶה בֵיתוֹ בְּקָרוֹב,
בִּמְהֵרָה בִּמְהֵרָה בְּיָמֵינוּ בְּקָרוֹב,
אֵל בְּנֵה אֵל בְּנֵה, בְּנֵה בֵיתְךָ בְּקָרוֹב.
חָסִיד הוּא, טָהוֹר הוּא, יָחִיד הוּא,
יִבְנֶה בֵיתוֹ בְּקָרוֹב,

He is mighty!
May He build His Temple soon, speedily, speedily, in our days, soon!
God, build, God, build, build Your Temple soon!
He is superior! He is great! He is outstanding!
May He build His Temple soon, speedily, speedily, in our days, soon!
God, build, God, build, build Your Temple soon!
He is glorious! He is virtuous! He is blameless!
May He build His Temple soon, speedily, speedily, in our days, soon!

בִּמְהֵרָה בִּמְהֵרָה בְּיָמֵינוּ בְּקָרוֹב,
אֵל בְּנֵה אֵל בְּנֵה, בְּנֵה בֵיתְךָ בְּקָרוֹב.
כַּבִּיר הוּא, לָמוּד הוּא, מֶלֶךְ הוּא,
יִבְנֶה בֵיתוֹ בְּקָרוֹב,
בִּמְהֵרָה בִּמְהֵרָה בְּיָמֵינוּ בְּקָרוֹב,
אֵל בְּנֵה אֵל בְּנֵה, בְּנֵה בֵיתְךָ בְּקָרוֹב.
נוֹרָא הוּא, סַגִּיב הוּא, עִזּוּז הוּא,
יִבְנֶה בֵיתוֹ בְּקָרוֹב,
בִּמְהֵרָה בִּמְהֵרָה בְּיָמֵינוּ בְּקָרוֹב,
אֵל בְּנֵה אֵל בְּנֵה, בְּנֵה בֵיתְךָ בְּקָרוֹב.
פּוֹדֶה הוּא, צַדִּיק הוּא, קָדוֹשׁ הוּא,
יִבְנֶה בֵיתוֹ בְּקָרוֹב,
בִּמְהֵרָה בִּמְהֵרָה בְּיָמֵינוּ בְּקָרוֹב,
אֵל בְּנֵה אֵל בְּנֵה, בְּנֵה בֵיתְךָ בְּקָרוֹב.
רַחוּם הוּא, שַׁדַּי הוּא, תַּקִּיף הוּא,
יִבְנֶה בֵיתוֹ בְּקָרוֹב,
בִּמְהֵרָה בִּמְהֵרָה בְּיָמֵינוּ בְּקָרוֹב,
אֵל בְּנֵה אֵל בְּנֵה, בְּנֵה בֵיתְךָ בְּקָרוֹב.

God, build, God, build, build Your Temple soon!
He is kind! He is pure! He is unique!
May He build His Temple soon, speedily, speedily, in our days, soon!
God, build, God, build, build Your Temple soon!
He is powerful! He is all-knowing! He is king!
May He build His Temple soon, speedily, speedily, in our days, soon!
God, build, God, build, build Your Temple soon!
He is awesome! He is exalted! He is all-powerful!
May He build His Temple soon, speedily, speedily, in our days, soon!
God, build, God, build, build Your Temple soon!
He is the redeemer! He is righteous! He is holy!
May He build His Temple soon, speedily, speedily, in our days, soon!

God, build, God, build, build Your Temple soon!
He is compassionate! He is the Almighty! He is strong!
May He build His Temple soon, speedily, speedily, in our days, soon!
God, build, God, build, build Your Temple soon!

אֶחָד מִי יוֹדֵעַ?

Who knows one?
I know one!
One is our God, in heaven and on earth.

אֶחָד אֲנִי יוֹדֵעַ. אֶחָד אֱלֹהֵינוּ שֶׁבַּשָּׁמַיִם וּבָאָרֶץ.

שְׁנַיִם מִי יוֹדֵעַ?

Who knows two?
I know two!
Two are the tablets of the covenant; One is our God, in heaven and on earth.

שְׁנַיִם אֲנִי יוֹדֵעַ. שְׁנֵי לוּחוֹת הַבְּרִית, אֶחָד אֱלֹהֵינוּ שֶׁבַּשָּׁמַיִם וּבָאָרֶץ.

שְׁלֹשָׁה מִי יוֹדֵעַ?

Who knows three?
I know three!
Three are the patriarchs; two are the tablets of the covenant; One is our God, in heaven and on earth.

שְׁלֹשָׁה אֲנִי יוֹדֵעַ. שְׁלֹשָׁה אָבוֹת, שְׁנֵי לוּחוֹת הַבְּרִית, אֶחָד אֱלֹהֵינוּ שֶׁבַּשָּׁמַיִם וּבָאָרֶץ.

אַרְבַּע מִי יוֹדֵעַ?

Who knows four?
I know four!
Four are the matriarchs; three are the patriarchs; two are the tablets of the covenant; One is our God, in heaven and on earth.

אַרְבַּע אֲנִי יוֹדֵעַ. אַרְבַּע אִמָּהוֹת, שְׁלֹשָׁה אָבוֹת, שְׁנֵי לוּחוֹת הַבְּרִית, אֶחָד אֱלֹהֵינוּ שֶׁבַּשָּׁמַיִם וּבָאָרֶץ.

חֲמִשָּׁה מִי יוֹדֵעַ?

Who knows five?
I know five!
Five are the books of the Torah; four are the matriarchs; three are the patriarchs; two are the tablets of the covenant; One is our God, in heaven and on earth.

חֲמִשָּׁה אֲנִי יוֹדֵעַ. חֲמִשָּׁה חוּמְשֵׁי תוֹרָה, אַרְבַּע אִמָּהוֹת, שְׁלֹשָׁה אָבוֹת, שְׁנֵי לוּחוֹת הַבְּרִית, אֶחָד אֱלֹהֵינוּ שֶׁבַּשָּׁמַיִם וּבָאָרֶץ.

שִׁשָּׁה מִי יוֹדֵעַ?

שִׁשָּׁה אֲנִי יוֹדֵעַ. שִׁשָּׁה סִדְרֵי מִשְׁנָה, חֲמִשָּׁה חוּמְשֵׁי תוֹרָה, אַרְבַּע אִמָּהוֹת, שְׁלֹשָׁה אָבוֹת, שְׁנֵי לוּחוֹת הַבְּרִית, אֶחָד אֱלֹהֵינוּ שֶׁבַּשָּׁמַיִם וּבָאָרֶץ.

Who knows six?
I know six!
Six are the volumes of the Mishnah; five are the books of the Torah; four are the matriarchs; three are the patriarchs; two are the tablets of the covenant; One is our God, in heaven and on earth.

שִׁבְעָה מִי יוֹדֵעַ?

שִׁבְעָה אֲנִי יוֹדֵעַ. שִׁבְעָה יְמֵי שַׁבְּתָּא, שִׁשָּׁה סִדְרֵי מִשְׁנָה, חֲמִשָּׁה חוּמְשֵׁי תוֹרָה, אַרְבַּע אִמָּהוֹת, שְׁלֹשָׁה אָבוֹת, שְׁנֵי לוּחוֹת הַבְּרִית, אֶחָד אֱלֹהֵינוּ שֶׁבַּשָּׁמַיִם וּבָאָרֶץ.

Who knows seven?
I know seven!
Seven are the days of the week; six are the volumes of the Mishnah; five are the books of the Torah; four are the matriarchs; three are the patriarchs; two are the tablets of the covenant; One is our God, in heaven and on earth.

שְׁמוֹנָה מִי יוֹדֵעַ?

שְׁמוֹנָה אֲנִי יוֹדֵעַ. שְׁמוֹנָה יְמֵי מִילָה, שִׁבְעָה יְמֵי שַׁבְּתָּא, שִׁשָּׁה סִדְרֵי מִשְׁנָה, חֲמִשָּׁה חוּמְשֵׁי תוֹרָה, אַרְבַּע אִמָּהוֹת, שְׁלֹשָׁה אָבוֹת, שְׁנֵי לוּחוֹת הַבְּרִית, אֶחָד אֱלֹהֵינוּ שֶׁבַּשָּׁמַיִם וּבָאָרֶץ.

Who knows eight?
I know eight!
Eight are the days until circumcision; seven are the days of the week; six are the volumes of the Mishnah; five are the books of the Torah; four are the matriarchs; three are the patriarchs; two are the tablets of the covenant; One is our God, in heaven and on earth.

תִּשְׁעָה מִי יוֹדֵעַ?

תִּשְׁעָה אֲנִי יוֹדֵעַ. תִּשְׁעָה יַרְחֵי לֵידָה, שְׁמוֹנָה יְמֵי מִילָה, שִׁבְעָה יְמֵי שַׁבַּתָּא, שִׁשָּׁה סִדְרֵי מִשְׁנָה, חֲמִשָּׁה חוּמְשֵׁי תוֹרָה, אַרְבַּע אִמָּהוֹת, שְׁלֹשָׁה אָבוֹת, שְׁנֵי לוּחוֹת הַבְּרִית, אֶחָד אֱלֹהֵינוּ שֶׁבַּשָּׁמַיִם וּבָאָרֶץ.

Who knows nine?
I know nine!
Nine are the months of pregnancy; eight are the days until circumcision; seven are the days of the week; six are the volumes of the Mishnah; five are the books of the Torah; four are the matriarchs; three are the patriarchs; two are the tablets of the covenant; One is our God, in heaven and on earth.

עֲשָׂרָה מִי יוֹדֵעַ?

עֲשָׂרָה אֲנִי יוֹדֵעַ. עֲשָׂרָה דִבְּרַיָּא, תִּשְׁעָה יַרְחֵי לֵידָה, שְׁמוֹנָה יְמֵי מִילָה, שִׁבְעָה יְמֵי שַׁבַּתָּא, שִׁשָּׁה סִדְרֵי מִשְׁנָה, חֲמִשָּׁה חוּמְשֵׁי תוֹרָה, אַרְבַּע אִמָּהוֹת, שְׁלֹשָׁה אָבוֹת, שְׁנֵי לוּחוֹת הַבְּרִית, אֶחָד אֱלֹהֵינוּ שֶׁבַּשָּׁמַיִם וּבָאָרֶץ.

Who knows ten?
I know ten!
Ten are the commandments; nine are the months of pregnancy; eight are the days until circumcision; seven are the days of the week; six are the volumes of the Mishnah; five are the books of the Torah; four are the matriarchs; three are the patriarchs; two are the tablets of the covenant; One is our God, in heaven and on earth.

אַחַד עָשָׂר מִי יוֹדֵעַ?

אַחַד עָשָׂר אֲנִי יוֹדֵעַ. אַחַד עָשָׂר כּוֹכְבַיָּא, עֲשָׂרָה דִבְּרַיָּא, תִּשְׁעָה יַרְחֵי לֵידָה, שְׁמוֹנָה יְמֵי מִילָה, שִׁבְעָה יְמֵי שַׁבַּתָּא, שִׁשָּׁה סִדְרֵי מִשְׁנָה, חֲמִשָּׁה חוּמְשֵׁי תוֹרָה, אַרְבַּע אִמָּהוֹת, שְׁלֹשָׁה אָבוֹת, שְׁנֵי לוּחוֹת הַבְּרִית, אֶחָד אֱלֹהֵינוּ שֶׁבַּשָּׁמַיִם וּבָאָרֶץ.

Who knows eleven? I know eleven! Eleven are the stars [of Joseph's dream]; ten are the commandments; nine are the months of pregnancy; eight are the days until circumcision; seven are the days of the week; six are the volumes of the Mishnah; five are the books of the Torah; four are the matriarchs; three are the patriarchs; two are the tablets of the covenant; One is our God, in heaven and on earth.

שְׁנֵים עָשָׂר מִי יוֹדֵעַ?

שְׁנֵים עָשָׂר אֲנִי יוֹדֵעַ. שְׁנֵים עָשָׂר שִׁבְטַיָּא, אַחַד עָשָׂר כּוֹכְבַיָּא, עֲשָׂרָה דִבְּרַיָּא, תִּשְׁעָה יַרְחֵי לֵידָה, שְׁמוֹנָה יְמֵי מִילָה, שִׁבְעָה יְמֵי שַׁבַּתָּא, שִׁשָּׁה סִדְרֵי מִשְׁנָה, חֲמִשָּׁה חוּמְשֵׁי תוֹרָה, אַרְבַּע אִמָּהוֹת, שְׁלֹשָׁה אָבוֹת, שְׁנֵי לוּחוֹת הַבְּרִית, אֶחָד אֱלֹהֵינוּ שֶׁבַּשָּׁמַיִם וּבָאָרֶץ.

Who knows twelve? I know twelve! Twelve are the tribes of Israel; eleven are the stars [of Joseph's dream]; ten are the commandments; nine are the months of pregnancy; eight are the days until circumcision; seven are the days of the week; six are the volumes of the Mishnah; five are the books of the Torah; four are the matriarchs; three are the patriarchs; two are the tablets of the covenant; One is our God, in heaven and on earth.

שְׁלֹשָׁה עָשָׂר מִי יוֹדֵעַ?

שְׁלֹשָׁה עָשָׂר אֲנִי יוֹדֵעַ. שְׁלֹשָׁה עָשָׂר מִדַּיָּא, שְׁנֵים עָשָׂר שִׁבְטַיָּא, אַחַד עָשָׂר כּוֹכְבַיָּא, עֲשָׂרָה דִבְּרַיָּא, תִּשְׁעָה יַרְחֵי לֵידָה, שְׁמוֹנָה יְמֵי מִילָה, שִׁבְעָה יְמֵי שַׁבַּתָּא, שִׁשָּׁה סִדְרֵי מִשְׁנָה, חֲמִשָּׁה חוּמְשֵׁי תוֹרָה, אַרְבַּע אִמָּהוֹת, שְׁלֹשָׁה אָבוֹת, שְׁנֵי לוּחוֹת הַבְּרִית, אֶחָד אֱלֹהֵינוּ שֶׁבַּשָּׁמַיִם וּבָאָרֶץ.

Who knows thirteen? I know thirteen! Thirteen are God's attributes of mercy; twelve are the tribes of Israel; eleven are the stars [of Joseph's dream]; ten are the commandments; nine are the months of pregnancy; eight are the days until circumcision; seven are the days of the week; six are the volumes of the Mishnah; five are the books of the Torah; four are the matriarchs; three are the patriarchs; two are the tablets of the covenant; One is our God, in heaven and on earth.

חַד גַּדְיָא, חַד גַּדְיָא. דְּזַבִּין אַבָּא בִּתְרֵי זוּזֵי.

One kid, one kid—that my father bought for two *zuzim*.

חַד גַּדְיָא, חַד גַּדְיָא.
וְאָתָא שׁוּנְרָא, וְאָכְלָה לְגַּדְיָא, דְּזַבִּין אַבָּא בִּתְרֵי זוּזֵי.
חַד גַּדְיָא, חַד גַּדְיָא.

One kid, one kid. Along came a cat and ate the kid—that my father bought for two *zuzim*. One kid, one kid. Along came a dog and bit the cat that ate the kid—that my father bought for two *zuzim*. One kid, one kid.

וְאָתָא כַלְבָּא, וְנָשַׁךְ לְשׁוּנְרָא, דְּאָכְלָה לְגַּדְיָא, דְּזַבִּין אַבָּא בִּתְרֵי זוּזֵי.
חַד גַּדְיָא, חַד גַּדְיָא.

וְאָתָא חוּטְרָא, וְהִכָּה לְכַלְבָּא, דְּנָשַׁךְ לְשׁוּנְרָא, דְּאָכְלָה לְגַדְיָא, דְּזַבִּין אַבָּא בִּתְרֵי זוּזֵי.
חַד גַּדְיָא, חַד גַּדְיָא.

וְאָתָא נוּרָא, וְשָׂרַף לְחוּטְרָא, דְּהִכָּה לְכַלְבָּא, דְּנָשַׁךְ לְשׁוּנְרָא, דְּאָכְלָה לְגַדְיָא, דְּזַבִּין אַבָּא בִּתְרֵי זוּזֵי.
חַד גַּדְיָא, חַד גַּדְיָא.

וְאָתָא מַיָּא, וְכָבָה לְנוּרָא, דְּשָׂרַף לְחוּטְרָא, דְּהִכָּה לְכַלְבָּא, דְּנָשַׁךְ לְשׁוּנְרָא, דְּאָכְלָה לְגַדְיָא, דְּזַבִּין אַבָּא בִּתְרֵי זוּזֵי.
חַד גַּדְיָא, חַד גַּדְיָא.

וְאָתָא תוֹרָא, וְשָׁתָה לְמַיָּא, דְּכָבָה לְנוּרָא, דְּשָׂרַף לְחוּטְרָא, דְּהִכָּה לְכַלְבָּא, דְּנָשַׁךְ לְשׁוּנְרָא, דְּאָכְלָה לְגַדְיָא, דְּזַבִּין אַבָּא בִּתְרֵי זוּזֵי.
חַד גַּדְיָא, חַד גַּדְיָא.

וְאָתָא הַשּׁוֹחֵט, וְשָׁחַט לְתוֹרָא, דְּשָׁתָה לְמַיָּא, דְּכָבָה לְנוּרָא, דְּשָׂרַף לְחוּטְרָא, דְּהִכָּה לְכַלְבָּא, דְּנָשַׁךְ לְשׁוּנְרָא, דְּאָכְלָה לְגַדְיָא, דְּזַבִּין אַבָּא בִּתְרֵי זוּזֵי.
חַד גַּדְיָא, חַד גַּדְיָא.

Along came a stick and hit the dog that bit the cat that ate the kid—that my father bought for two *zuzim*.
One kid, one kid.
Along came a fire and burnt the stick that hit the dog that bit the cat that ate the kid—that my father bought for two *zuzim*.
One kid, one kid.
Along came water and extinguished the fire that burnt the stick that hit the dog that bit the cat that ate the kid—that my father bought for two *zuzim*.
One kid, one kid.
Along came an ox and drank the water that extinguished the fire that burnt the stick that hit the dog that bit the cat that ate the kid—that my father bought for two *zuzim*.
One kid, one kid.
Along came a slaughterer and slaughtered the ox that drank the water that extinguished the fire that burnt the stick that hit the dog that bit the cat that ate the kid—that my father bought for two *zuzim*.

וְאָתָא מַלְאַךְ הַמָּוֶת, וְשָׁחַט לְשׁוֹחֵט, דְּשָׁחַט לְתוֹרָא, דְּשָׁתָה לְמַיָּא, דְּכָבָה לְנוּרָא, דְּשָׂרַף לְחוּטְרָא, דְּהִכָּה לְכַלְבָּא, דְּנָשַׁךְ לְשׁוּנְרָא, דְּאָכְלָה לְגַדְיָא, דְּזַבִּין אַבָּא בִּתְרֵי זוּזֵי. חַד גַּדְיָא, חַד גַּדְיָא.

וְאָתָא הַקָּדוֹשׁ בָּרוּךְ הוּא, וְשָׁחַט לְמַלְאַךְ הַמָּוֶת, דְּשָׁחַט לְשׁוֹחֵט, דְּשָׁחַט לְתוֹרָא, דְּשָׁתָה לְמַיָּא, דְּכָבָה לְנוּרָא, דְּשָׂרַף לְחוּטְרָא, דְּהִכָּה לְכַלְבָּא, דְּנָשַׁךְ לְשׁוּנְרָא, דְּאָכְלָה לְגַדְיָא, דְּזַבִּין אַבָּא בִּתְרֵי זוּזֵי. חַד גַּדְיָא, חַד גַּדְיָא.

One kid, one kid.
Along came the angel
of death and killed
the slaughterer who
slaughtered the ox that
drank the water that
extinguished the fire that
burnt the stick that hit
the dog that bit the cat
that ate the kid—that
my father bought for
two *zuzim*.
One kid, one kid.
Then God came and killed
the angel of death who
killed the slaughterer
who slaughtered the ox
that drank the water that
extinguished the fire that
burnt the stick that hit
the dog that bit the cat
that ate the kid—that
my father bought for
two *zuzim*.
One kid, one kid.

This is the end of the Haggadah, but each person should, to the best of his ability, follow the dictum of the Sages that "whoever expounds upon the recounting of the story of the Exodus from Egypt is praiseworthy." Some have the custom of reciting *Shir Hashirim* after the Seder.

APPENDIX

ELABORATED COMMENTARY ON HALLEL AND NIRTZAH

HALLEL

אהבתי כי ישמע ה' את קולי תחנוני.

RAV MENACHEM MENDEL OF KOSOV, in *Ahavas Shalom* (*Beshalach*), explains that knowing that Hashem listens to our davening gives us tremendous joy and comfort. And not just that He listens, but that he pays attention, "כי הטה אזנו לי." He accepts our *tefillos* and our *Hallel* even though on the surface, what we are saying may appear simple and we may not fully comprehend the depth of the words of David HaMelech. Nevertheless, Hashem is "הטה אזנו," He "bends His ear" to hear the depth and draw out the inner feelings and ideas that are hidden in our *Hallel*.

צרה ויגון אמצה ובשם ה' אקרא.

The Gemara (*Pesachim* 119b) says that in the future, Hashem will prepare a feast for the righteous. After they eat and drink, the celebrants will give Avraham Avinu the cup of wine on which to recite the *Birkas Hamazon*, as he is the first of our forefathers. Avraham will say to them, "I will not lead the *bentching*, as I am blemished since Yishmael came from me." Avraham will say to Yitzchak, "Take the cup and lead *bentching*." Yitzchak will say to them, "I will not lead the *bentching* since Eisav came from me." Yitzchak will say to Yaakov, "Take the cup and lead *bentching*." Yaakov will say to them, "I will not lead the *bentching* since I married two sisters at the same time, and in the future the Torah forbade them to me." Yaakov will say to Moshe, "Take the cup and lead the *bentching*." Moshe will say to them, "I will not lead *bentching*, as I did not merit to enter Eretz Yisrael, neither in my life nor in my death." Moshe will say to Yehoshua, "Take the cup and lead *bentching*." Yehoshua will say to them, "I will not lead the *bentching*, as I did not merit to have a son." Yehoshua will say to David HaMelech, "Take the cup and lead *bentching*." David HaMelech will say to them, "I will lead *bentching*, and it is fitting for me to do so, as it is stated, 'כוס ישועות אשא ובשם ה' אקרא—I will raise the cup of salvation, and call upon the name of the Hashem.'"

Rabbi Paysach Krohn asks why this *pasuk* gives David HaMelech the right to lead the *bentching*. About which of David's merits is this verse telling us? The answer is that a few verses beforehand, David tells us, "צרה ויגון אמצא ובשם ה' אקרא." David doesn't only call out to Hashem when his cup overflows with blessing in the days of

Mashiach. Even before this, when *tzaros* and difficulties filled his life, he still called out to Hashem and still served Him with *emunah*. He epitomizes the story of the Jewish People in exile. Even when things are dark, painful, and challenging, we still pull ourselves together to daven, learn, and do mitzvos. When a person can still call out to Hashem at that point, he will certainly merit to sit at the feast of Mashiach and raise the cup of salvation and call out to Hashem.

הללו את ה׳ כל גוים, שבחוהו כל האמים. כי גבר עלינו חסדו,
ואמת ה׳ לעולם. הללויה.

The *Be'er Yosef* asks why the nations will praise Hashem for the kindness He does for the Jewish People. Why would they care how Hashem treats us? Because when Hashem freed the Jewish slaves, it was the first time the world saw that slaves could escape from their masters. It was the first time the world saw that those being oppressed could stand up and leave their bondage. Therefore, the nations of the world should thank Hashem for freeing the Jewish People because our story became the inspiration for millions of people from then on who sought redemption and freedom. (It is well documented how black slaves in America used Biblical imagery from the story of our Exodus in order to draw inspiration and hope for their own situation.)

HALLEL HAGADOL

RAV MATTISYAHU SALOMON, in the *Haggadah Matnas Chaim*, wonders why we recite the *Hallel Hagadol* (the twenty-six lines of "כי לעולם חסדו") following the regular *Hallel* at the Seder. The Gemara (*Pesachim* 118a) is the source of this practice and says that this section is called *Hallel Hagadol* because it describes how Hashem "sits in the highest realms and distributes sustenance to all of creation." *Rashi* explains that the greatness of Hashem is that He is way above us and at the same time concerned and involved in our well-being. The *Maharal* explains that the greatest understanding one can have of the kindness of Hashem is that He gives sustenance to all creatures in the world. It is a kindness that is even greater than the future redemption. That is why we first say "נותן לחם לכל בשר" and only then say "ויפרקנו מצרינו." The purpose of this type of *Hallel* at the Seder is to remind us that Hashem sustains the entire world every single moment of the day.

Rav Mattisyahu Salomon acknowledges that this is a wonderful and important idea. But why is it at the end of the Seder and what does it have to do with Pesach and *yetzias Mitzrayim*? He then adds another question. The Gemara (*Shabbos* 118b) says that someone who recites the general *Hallel* every day (as opposed to *Hallel Hagadol*) is cursed and blasphemes Hashem. What is so problematic about saying *Hallel* every day? The *Shach al HaTorah* (*Shemos* 12:40) explains that *Hallel* speaks of the major and obvious miracles, like redemption from Egypt, the splitting of the sea, and the miraculous victories in battle. If a person says *Hallel* every day, they are implying that we can only praise and acknowledge Hashem when there are amazing and open miracles. Therefore, a person who says *Hallel* every day is really belittling Hashem and not seeing that Hashem is everywhere and in everything. He is not praising Hashem for the small things in life and the hidden miracles, "על נסיך שבכל יום עמנו ועל נפלאותיך שבכל עת"—the miracles and wonders Hashem does for us each and every day. This is similar to what the *Ramban* writes at the end of *Parashas Bo*, that a Jew should strive to see Hashem in everything and acknowledge that whatever Hashem has given in the physical realm is exactly what we need.

Perhaps now we can appreciate *Hallel Hagadol* at the end of the Seder. We began the Seder with the miracles of *yetzias Mitzrayim* and we sang "בצאת ישראל ממצרים." However, this is not sufficient; it is only the beginning. Real work on *emunah* means seeing Hashem in everyday open miracles and developing an awareness of and closeness with Hashem in everything we do. The purpose of Seder night is to come to this point where we recognize that Hashem is "נותן לחם לכל בשר," and to say a *Hallel* on this idea alone.

לעשה נפלאות גדולות לבדו, כי לעולם חסדו.

Rav Zalman Sorotzkin, in his *Haggadah Hashir V'Hashevach*, notes that this line seems to be in the wrong place. The verse dealing with *nifla'os gedolos*, great wonders, should be later in the chapter when it speaks about the splitting of sea, the *mann*, and other great miracles. Instead, it is at the beginning of the chapter when we talk about the heavens, the earth, the waters, and the cosmos. The lesson is simple and profound. Instead of viewing *nifla'os gedolos* as the major and open miracles, we need to train ourselves to see the great wonders in our everyday life. The sun, stars, and planets are inanimate objects, and they move in the most wondrous fashion. David HaMelech is asking us to wake up and see the נסיך שבכל יום עמנו, ועל נפלאותיך וטובותיך שבכל עת, ערב ובקר וצהרים, as mentioned in the *Ramban* above. The *Meshech Chochmah* (*Bereishis* 5:1) says that if there is a person who is totally connected to Hashem, he sees the glory and honor of Hashem in every aspect of the creation; he doesn't need miracles. For this person we say (in *Ashrei*), "וחסידיך יברכוכה, כבוד מלכותך יאמרו." The *chassidim*, the righteous, notice Hashem in all aspects of the world, but regular people do not. It is for the regular people that Hashem makes miracles and astounding events. This is why we continue, "להודיע לבני האדם גבורתיו; וכבוד, הדר מלכותו." For regular *b'nei adam*, there is a showing of *gevurah*, power, so we will be able to understand the *kavod* and *hadar*, honor and glory, of the *malchus*, the Kingship. The *Meshech Chochmah* (*Vayikra* 26:4) adds that noticing Hashem in the nature is the highest level one can attain. This is why a person who says *Ashrei* each day goes to *Olam Haba*—this is a person who highlights the glory of Creation and sees that Hashem "opens His hand" to every part of the world.

NIRTZAH

Chasal Siddur Pesach

The Rebbe of Lelov, in the *Haggadah Birkas Moshe*, asks why only when it comes to this mitzvah do we say "כאשר זכינו לסדר אותו כן נזכה לעשותו." He explains that on other holidays, there are mitzvos to fulfill even in the absence of the Beis Hamikdash, but the main mitzvah of Pesach is the *Korban Pesach*. Without the Beis Hamikdash, it is "עיקר חסר מן הספר"—we are missing the essence of the holiday. We therefore daven, "כאשר זכינו לסדר אותו כן נזכה לעשותו." It is a prayer for the rebuilding of the Beis Hamikdash.

RAV YAAKOV UNSDORFER, a *rebbi* in Yeshivas Reishis Chochmah in Montreal, explains in the *Simanei Haseder* as follows. The Belzer Rebbe noted that *Tehillim* 63:2–3 says, "צמאה לך נפשי כמה לך בשרי...כן בקדש חזיתך—My soul thirsts for You and my flesh longs for You...so I will look for You in a holy place." Sometimes, a person prepares for something with great effort and excitement. This is certainly the case when it comes to performing mitzvos. But when it comes time for the mitzvah itself, the fire and excitement fall away, and the person is unable to serve Hashem with all of their heart. This is what David HaMelech is saying. He proclaims that his soul is thirsty with anticipation for Hashem and asks that when it is time to do the mitzvah itself, the excitement leading up to it should last. Based on this idea, we can explain "כאשר זכינו לסדר אותו." We learned the laws of Pesach, we went to the classes on the Haggadah, we cleaned and polished and prepared. Hashem, please, "כן נזכה לעשותו"—when the time comes on this holy evening, please let me maintain and end the evening on the spiritual high I so desire.

L'Shanah Ha'baah

The *Haggadah Shai LaTorah* (p. 413) writes in the name of Rav Meshulam Dovid Soloveitchik that the Haggadah begins with a prayer for the following year, "השתא הכא לשנה הבאה בארעה דישראל," and also ends with one, "לשנה הבאה בירושלים." This is by no means a coincidence. The Gemara (*Berachos* 10a) says, "כל פרשה שהיתה חביבה על דוד פתח בה באשרי וסיים באשרי—Every chapter [in *Tehillim*] that was dear to David, he began with *ashrei* and concluded with *ashrei*." Because the Haggadah begins with the idea of being in Eretz Yisrael, we conclude with the idea of being in Eretz Yisrael. This reminds us that our focus is always on the Land of Israel.

THE MOSHIAN SHEL YISRAEL (vol. 1, p. 176) brings the following idea in the name of the *Kedushas Yom Tov*. In *Tehillim* (33:22), it says, "יהי חסדך ה׳ עלינו כאשר יחלנו לך." What does this mean? Every year we come to the *Yamim Noraim* hoping Hashem will write us in the Book of Life. The prosecuting angels come before Hashem and tell Him that the Jewish People shouldn't be granted forgiveness and repentance because every year, the Jews go back to their old ways and many people don't change after Yom Kippur. In response, the defending angels appear before Hashem and point out that every year the Jewish People sit at the Seder—and also stand on the Day of Judgment—and proclaim, "לשנה הבאה בירושלים הבנויה." We wait and daven and beg for an end to the exile and for relief from our pain and uncertainty. We don't give up on Hashem and we hope that next year will be different. Therefore, isn't it fair that Hashem should believe in us for one more year just like we believe in Him for one more year? This is what it means when we say, "יהי חסדך ה׳ עלינו כאשר יחלנו לך." Just like we believe in Hashem that next year we will sit in a rebuilt Yerushalayim with a rebuilt Beis Hamikdash—even though it hasn't happened yet—so too, Hashem should believe in us that we will grow and improve in the coming year.

RAV CHAIM YOSEF BIDERMAN, in his *Haggadah Chibas Ha'avodah*, reminds us that לשנה הבאה בירושלים בנויה is not just an expression; it is meant to awaken in our hearts a desire and hunger for the coming of Mashiach so that we will soon be able to offer the *Korban Pesach* and fulfill the Biblical commandments related to Pesach. One of the questions raised about the language of the thirteen declarations of "*Ani Maamin*" (a reformulation of the *Rambam*'s Thirteen Principles of Faith), is regarding the phrase "ואף על פי שיתמהמה אחכה לו"—Even though he is delayed, I still wait for him," which seems like a strange expression. The explanation is that sometimes, we secretly desire for Mashiach to be delayed. For example, a bride and groom on the day of their wedding may think to themselves that it is certainly good if Mashiach comes today—however, it would be nice if he'd wait a few minutes until after the wedding ceremony, so as not to get in the way. Therefore, we must train ourselves to want and desire Mashiach at all times, even when it may be inconvenient for our current plans.

The story is told of a Jew who would cry each year when saying "לשנה הבאה בירושלים." When asked why he was moved to tears, he explained that he was embarrassed to face the local Polish landowner. The previous year, the landowner had heard the Jew singing "לשנה הבאה בירושלים הבנויה" and had asked him repeatedly throughout the year when he was going to Jerusalem. The Jew had no answer, so he avoided the landowner whenever he could. But now it was the next year, and he was saying "לשנה הבאה" again, and he could no longer hide from the landowner. He was crying to Hashem for Mashiach to come so he wouldn't be embarrassed in front of this gentile. If only we would be like this Jew and believe with full faith that in this coming year, we will merit the full redemption.

Adir Hu

The *Otzar Kol Minhagei Yeshurun* (16:3) says that the author of *Adir Hu* is the same author as *Mi Adir Al Ha'kol* that is sung under the chuppah at all Jewish weddings. Interestingly, there are a number of other comparisons between the Seder and a wedding:

- The *Talmud Yerushalmi* (*Pesachim*, chap. 10) says that a person who has matzah on Erev Pesach is like one who has relations with the person they are engaged to, before the actual marriage. The *Shibbolei Haleket* (209) explains that a person who has relations with his betrothed before the *chuppah* is also preempting the *sheva berachos*, which are a form of completing the marriage. So too, on the night of the Seder, there are seven berachos, and if you eat matzah beforehand, you are preempting those *sheva berachos*. He notes that the seven berachos on the Seder night are *Hagafen*, *Kedushas Ha'yom*, *Shehecheyanu*, *Ha'adamah* (on the *karpas*), the second cup, and then *Hamotzi* (*Netilas Yadayim* doesn't count because that just brings us to *Hamotzi*). The *Mahari Veil* (193) counts *Hagafen*, *Kedushas Ha'yom*, *Asher Ge'alanu*, *Achilas Maror*, *Netilas Yadayim*, *Hamotzi*, and *Achilas Matzah*.
- The *Avodas Yisrael* on the Haggadah explains that the phrase "כל דכפין ייתי וייכול" is referring to an intimate union between us and Hashem during the Seder.
- We cover the matzah like the groom covers the face of the bride.

THE LIKUTEI CHAVER BEN CHAIM (vol. 2, p. 17b) cites the *Chasam Sofer*, who brings the following explanation of the line of "יבנה ביתו בקרוב במהרה במהרה בימינו בקרוב" in the name of the *Machatzis Hashekel*, Rav Shmuel Kellin of Boskowitz. In the eyes of Hashem, "מהרה," the quick passage of time is like one thousand years for one of our days. We ask Hashem to build the Beis Hamikdash "במהרה במהרה," according to the way we experience the world, not in the very long-ranging view of Hashem.

Ki Lo Na'eh

Rav Yosef Chaver (the son of Rav Yitzchak Isaac Chaver), in the *Haggadah Zeroa Netuyah*, based on *Bereishis Rabbah* (6:2), explains the expression "לך ולך לך כי לך" as follows. In general, we associate evil with the night and good with the day. But in reality, everything comes from Hashem and is good. We say to Hashem that just like the apparently positive things in the world show Your (לך) praise and glory, so too, the seemingly negative things also show Your (לך) praise, because everything is from You. Therefore, we sing "לך ולך." When there are good things in the world, this openly demonstrates that You are there. But even at night, when things are not clear and when it appears as if Hashem is not there, we say "לך אף לך," that the good cloaked in bad is also Hashem. Why? Because "לך ה' הממלכה," all of nature and all of the world is under the direction of Hashem.

WE DESCRIBE HASHEM as "יחיד במלוכה כביר כהלכה." The *Yismach Moshe* explains in his introduction to *Navi* that once, at *seudah shelishis*, he explained "יחיד ורבים הלכה כרבים" as follows. We know that Hashem is the One and Only, like no other. He is the very definition of a *yachid*. We—the many different people who make up the Jewish People—are the *rabim*. Because we are the majority, the halachah follows whatever we decide, and we decide that there should be good for the Jewish People. Rav Ben Zion of Bobov, in the *Kedushas Tzion* (*Mo'adim*, p. 67), notes that the word "כביר" can be an expression of the community (see *Iyov* 36:5). Therefore, we can explain that "יחיד במלוכה" refers to Hashem, but "כביר כהלכה" means that we, the community, are the majority and the halachah goes according to us. We ask Hashem to shower us with only good and to send Mashiach so that the *malchus* of Hashem should be "נאה" and "יאה."

Echad Mi Yodei'a

Rav Avraham Gurwicz, in his *Haggadah V'Anafeha Arzei El*, explains that *Echad Mi Yodei'a* is not just a children's song. Rather it is a test at the end of the Seder to make sure our number associations and thoughts are always focused on Hashem and His Torah. Our minds should always connect these numbers with Torah ideas. Similarly, the Torah (*Shemos* 10:2) says, "...למען תספר באזני בנך ובן בנך את אשר התעללתי במצרים וידעתם כי אני ה'." This means, as the *Sefas Emes* (*Bo* and Pesach 5735) explains, the purpose of *sippur yetzias Mitzrayim* is to have *daas*, knowledge, of Hashem. After completing the story of the Exodus, we review and record all our knowledge. Why do we repeat and review each concept again? Because the way a person grows is by building off of the knowledge he already has. After learning and mastering each step you can then build up to the next one.[48]

THE HAGGADAH HALEKACH V'HALIBUV (5781) notes the seeming lack of humility in saying, "אחד אני יודע, שנים אני יודע‎—I know one, I know two, etc." How can a Jew speak in such a way? He suggests a beautiful insight based on the comments of Rav Yosef Engel in his *Beis Ha'otzar* (vol. 1, *maareches aleph-vav, klal* 33). We find throughout Shas that Rabbi Yehudah HaNasi often states his opinion by stating, "אני אומר‎—I say." This also seems to show a lack of humility.

Rav Engel suggests that in fact, this really is an expression of humility. We know that the Gemara (*Sotah* 49a) says that when Rabbi Yehudah HaNasi died, it was the end of true humility. If he was the paragon of humility, he couldn't have been boasting when he said, "I say." Rather, the intention of this phrase is the same as when we would nowadays write, "נראה לפי עניות דעתי‎—In my humble opinion." When Rabbi Yehudah HaNasi would state what he thought was the halachah, he would say this is what I think is the law is, but I am not stating it as a definitive fact.

Rav Engel brings another approach, that אני, according to the students of the Baal Shem Tov, is a reference to Hashem. In *Hoshanos* of Sukkos, we say, "אני והו הושיעה נא," and *Rashi* explains that אני is a reference to Hashem. The Gemara (*Sukkah* 53a) records that Hillel would say at the *Simchas Beis HaShoeivah*, "אם אני כאן הכל כאן‎—If I am here then everything is here." *Rashi* there says that "אני" is a reference to Hashem. Rabbi Yehudah HaNasi was therefore saying that "אני אומר"—whatever wisdom and opinion I have to offer—comes only from אני, i.e., Hashem.[49]

Therefore, on the night of the Seder we hope that we have come to a place where we can say "אחד אני יודע." Whatever I have to say about these things doesn't come

---

48 Regarding the custom to sing "Who Knows One?" in English, the *Likutei Yehudah* says that the Maggid of Kozhnitz would sing the song in Polish. The *Imrei Emes* explains that the Gemara (*Berachos* 13a) says the *Shema* can be recited in any language because it says, "שמע‎—Listen," meaning, in any language you can understand. Therefore, since *Echad Mi Yodei'a* is a declaration of the oneness of Hashem, it too can be said in any language one understands. The Ostrovtza Rav notes that if you add up the values of one to thirteen, it equals ninety-one, the numerical value of the שם הוי"ה and שם אדנות.

49 See *Kedushas Levi, Parashas Shemos*, s.v. "לכה ואשלחכה."

from the אני that is physical, rather "אני יודע"—whatever my knowledge is about these numbers comes from the "אני" that is Hashem.

RABBI MARCUS LEHMANN, in his Haggadah, gives a beautiful understanding of *Echad Mi Yodei'a*, based on the Haggadah printed in Frankfurt in 1898 with the commentary of Rav Tevele Bondi. He explains that the purpose of this poem is to answer the question of the angels at the splitting of the sea. At the end of the day, both the Jews and the Egyptians worshipped idols. So why should the Jewish People have been saved? The answer is this list of thirteen merits. The poem should therefore be understood as answering the question of "Who knows the first merit in which the Jewish People were worthy of leaving leave Egypt?" and so on until the thirteenth merit.

The following is a list of the thirteen merits, beginning with number thirteen.

13. The Thirteen Attributes of Mercy were revealed to Moshe not simply to be repeated, but to guide us in proper *middos* and ethics. The Gemara says that it is not sufficient to recite the Thirteen Attributes of Mercy; we are supposed to copy them. When Hashem decided to take us out of Egypt, it was because we distinguished ourselves with the proper *middos* of *rachmanim*, *bayshanim*, and *gomlei chassadim*—mercy, modesty, and generosity. Hashem saw that we had the potential to connect with His thirteen attributes because of our already inherent connection to other proper attributes.

12. The plan was that we would become a unified nation. Even though the twelve tribes initially had issues with one another, this was a superficial misunderstanding. In reality, the twelve tribes are unified.

11. This, in turn, allows us to be like the eleven stars to which we were compared in the dream of Yosef and in the promise to Avraham Avinu. A star bears witness to God's magnificent creations in the heavens, and we, as a unified people, bear witness to His ruling over humanity. By living our lives as Jews, always striving to grow spiritually, we shine brightly for the sake of Hashem.

10. The spiritual potential of the Jewish People was highlighted at Har Sinai and the revelation of the Ten Commandments. With the Ten Commandments we were shown that Hashem rules over the mind and spirit of every Jew.

9. At Har Sinai, even the souls of those unborn, represented by the nine months of pregnancy, were present. The months of pregnancy also represent the dedication of the women in Egypt who kept Jewish families together. We were saved in the merit of their having actively promoted the continuity

of the Jewish People. They understood the importance of spiritual striving—that there was something beyond the physical burden of our slavery.

8. This focus on the spiritual is also the message of the *bris milah*, which raises up the physicality of man to spiritual heights. *Bris milah* is a sign of the Godliness implanted in man.

7. Shabbos is also a sign that reminds us that physical work in this world is only blessed through resting on the seventh day. Shabbos infuses our physical work week with spirituality. Shabbos is a day of rest from physical and mundane activities so that we can realign ourselves, and recognize our spiritual purpose and task in this world.

6. We understand our purpose in this world through the Six Books of the Mishnah, the Oral Law, which enable us to understand the Written Torah.

5. Receiving the Five Books of the Written Torah was the purpose of leaving Mitzrayim. The Torah instructs us on how to bring spirituality into the world.

4. In doing so we look to the four matriarchs as guides to women of how to bring spirituality into the world.

3. And the men look to the three patriarchs who are the chariot of the Shechinah and spirituality in this world.

2. The message of placing the spiritual over physical is taught by the two *Luchos*, which would have been meaningless without the spirit of the Torah engraved on them. When Moshe threw the *Luchos* to the ground and they shattered, "לוחות משתברות ואותיות פורחות," the letters flew away. The *Luchos* actually broke because the letters flew from them; it was not the material element that held the spirit, but the spirit that held the material. The broken *Luchos* are there to remind us to not ascribe too much value to the physical world. Which leads to a recognition…

1. That there is "אחד אלקנו שבשמים ובארץ‎—one God, in heaven and in earth." The main merit through which the Jewish People earned their redemption was by coming to recognize Hashem and sanctify His Name throughout the world.

In summary, Hashem chose us for our *middos* so that we would act as a unified nation and publicly represent Him. We learned at Har Sinai to recognize the importance of the spiritual, manifested through the righteous women in Egypt, who continued the Jewish family, the performance of *bris milah*, and the observance of Shabbos. All of which are taught in the Oral Law and the Written Law, which we can also learn from the matriarchs and patriarchs, which is the lesson of the two *Luchos* and their breaking, which—when we understand their lesson of the importance of spirituality over physicality—lead us to a recognition of One God.

RAV YISSACHAR DOV OF BELZ asks why we only say *Echad Mi Yodei'a* at the Seder—why don't we say and review these important concepts every day? He explains that a wealthy person who is smart doesn't reveal to the whole world his entire wealth and value; it is a private matter. However, if you get him to drink a little, he begins to open up and he will be looser in telling you about all of his riches. The same is true of the Jewish People. After we drink four cups of wine, we openly and freely speak about the fabulous wealth and treasure that we possess. How proud we should be of our heritage, where we come from and what we can accomplish!

YET, WHAT IS SO SPECIAL and unique to the Jewish People about the nine months of pregnancy, when even non-Jews have this too?

A few answers:

- These nine months represent the ability to create continuity in Jewish people and to bring a child into the world (*Haggadah shel Pesach: Im biurim, halachos, v'hanhagos she'nishmeu mi'pi Rav Yosef Shalom Elyashiv*).
- Rav Yosef Shalom Elyashiv explains that this is a reference to the miracle that happened to Moshe Rabbeinu when he was born. The Gemara (*Sotah* 12a) says that the fact that Moshe was hidden as a newborn indicates that he was born three months earlier than expected. This enabled Moshe to be kept hidden from the Egyptians during those three months and eventually be saved.
- The *Minchas Elazar*, in *Shaarei Yissachar* (vol. 1, 133), says he heard an answer to this question from a chassid who was at the Seder with the *Divrei Chaim* of Sanz. At the same Seder the Rebbe of Tartzal offered the following explanation. Only the Jewish People are careful about the laws of *taharas ha'mishpachah*. It is very common that a Jewish child is conceived on the night the wife goes to the mikvah, when she is most likely to be ovulating. By observing the laws of *taharas ha'mishpachah*, we know the exact time of conception. Therefore, the *tishah yarchei leidah* are a hint to the Jewish People's laws of *taharas ha'mishpachah*.
- Rav Yitzchak Shmuel Schwartz, in *Sichas Avos* (p. 94), says that during these nine months, the child is in a place of holiness and the mother eats kosher

food, making the child more holy than the rest of the world. The *Devir Aharon* (*Pesach*, p. 305) notes that the Gemara (*Niddah* 30b) tells us that the child learns Torah with an angel and becomes *kadosh* during this time.

RAV GERSHON STERN, in *Yalkut Hagershuni* (*Osios, aleph, kuntres acharon, Haggadah Shel Pesach*) notes four fascinating comments about the first four steps of *Echad Mi Yodei'a*:

1. אחד מי יודע—Who knows that we need to have *achdus*? We talk about it all the time, but why is it so important? Because *Malachi* (2:10) says, "הלוא אב אחד לכלנו, הלוא א-ל אחד בראנו; מדוע, נבגד איש באחיו—Have we not all one Father? Has not one God created us? Why are people unfaithful to one another?" We know we need *echad*—as in *achdus*—because Hashem is one, and we need to act like Hashem and be one as well: as a united Jewish people.

2. שנים מי יודע—Who knows why we need to have both the laws that are *bein adam laMakom*, between us and Hashem, and *bein adam l'chaveiro*, between us and our fellow man? Why not simply excel in one or the other? Why isn't one more important than the other? Because both sets of laws were given by one God, "אחד אלקינו שבשמים ובארץ," who is not made up of any parts and rules over everything, all the different laws are of equal importance. The two *Luchos* are therefore of equal importance and are equally valued by Hashem.

3. שלשה מי יודע—Who knows why and when *zechus Avos*, the merit of our forefathers, is effective? We know that *zechus Avos* is effective when we follow the "שני לוחות הברית" and we believe with complete faith in One God who is in the heavens and the earth. *Malachi* (1:2) states, "אהבתי אתכם אמר ה'," Hashem says that He loves us. Why? He explains that Hashem loved Yaakov but He hated Eisav. *Bereishis Rabbah* (76:4) explains that Yaakov walked in the path of his forefathers and Eisav did not. This teaches us that the merit of the Avraham, Yitzchak, and Yaakov works when we have the two *Luchos* and *emunah* in One God.

4. ארבע מי יודע—Who knows why there are four mothers instead of three mothers to match the three fathers? Because Hashem wanted there to be two main wives of Yaakov. This would lead to the jealousy and fighting that would eventually bring the Jewish People down to Egypt. Our time in Egypt created the environment that fortified and sealed the knowledge of and belief in Hashem that would stay with the Jewish People forever. All of this occurred because Yaakov had two wives instead of one and there were four

mothers instead of three.[50] Therefore, the reason we need four mothers and three fathers was to make sure we would go down to Egypt, build up own relationship with Hashem, leave, and receive the two *Luchos* from our One God.

RABBI NAFTOLI HEINEMANN, of Monsey, New York, in *Dear Children* (*Bereishis*, p. 67), writes that the Haggadah demonstrates great significance in the number eleven and the eleven stars in Yosef's dream. What is so important about the eleven stars in the dream of Yosef? The brothers are in any case later mentioned as the tribes in relation to the number twelve, so what exactly do we gain by recognizing the eleven stars in the dream of Yosef? Furthermore, the eleven stars weren't even real—they were only part of a dream. The answer is that the dream tells us more than it appears on the surface. The Gemara (*Berachos* 55b) says that a person dreams at night about what he thinks of during the day. The brothers hated Yosef and they couldn't speak to him nicely. He was in a situation where his brothers hated him for all different kinds of reasons. They threw him in a pit, sold him to Arabs, etc. We would think that when Yosef thought about his brothers during the day, he'd think of them as evil people out to kill him. However, from the dream—a window into Yosef's subconscious—we learn that he thought of his brothers as stars and didn't see the bad in them. He viewed them as special people, symbolized by stars. The number eleven (representing the eleven stars) teaches us a very important lesson: a Jew should always see the greatness of another Jew. Even when another Jew is being difficult or challenging, we should try our best to view them as shining stars. Let us bring *ahavas chinam* into our lives.

Chad Gadya

The *Chida*, in the *Chaim Shaal* (28), writes the following about a person who made fun of *Chad Gadya*:

---

50 Rabbi Stern cites Rabbi Nosson Adler in his *Nesinah L'Ger* (*Devarim* 26:5) on the verse of "ארמי אובד אבי וירד מצרימה"—that Lavan tried to destroy our father and we went down to Egypt. Rabbi Adler cites his father, Rav Mordechai Adler—the rabbi of Hanover, Germany—who explains that Lavan was responsible for sending us down to Egypt because he switched Rachel and Leah, resulting in Yaakov having two wives. The jealousy between the two went down to their children and their fighting eventually brought the Jewish People down to Egypt.

This individual [who mocked Chad Gadya] has ridiculed what has been
the custom of tens of thousands of Jews in cities and suburbs of Poland
and Germany. Included in these thousands of Jews [who recite the Chad
Gadya poem] are world Torah luminaries of the highest level of holiness, as
well as the scholars of every generation. Even today, the Jewish People have
not been orphaned and there are many roshei yeshiva and great scholars,
may Hashem continue to sustain them, who all recite the poem of Chad
Gadya. This person who ridiculed Chad Gadya is a rasha for he mocks
a myriad of Jews... There is no doubt that Chad Gadya is not a meaningless
poem. We have already been informed that the secrets behind many of
these poems/prayers have been passed on [from one generation to another]
and from one rabbi to another.

The Question of the *Ben Ish Chai*

The *Ben Ish Chai*, in the *Haggadah Otzeros Chaim*, asks what *Chad Gadya* has to do
with the Seder. He notes that at first glance, it would seem that the dog was correct
for biting the cat, because the cat had committed a crime by devouring the goat.
If so, the stick was wrong for hitting the dog. Where is the justice? In addition, if
you follow the logical conclusion of *Chad Gadya* and understand that the cat is the
aggressor and the dog is the savior then the calculation ends up that Hashem is an
aggressor. This certainly raises a serious issue.

In truth, however, says the *Ben Ish Chai*, there is justice in the end. The cat was
wrong to eat the goat, but who appointed the dog to administer justice? Likewise,
Hashem had decreed that the children of Avraham be subjugated, but who appointed Pharaoh to carry out the decree of Hashem? Just as Egypt was punished
for appointing itself as the one to implement the decree of Hashem, so will our
other oppressors be punished for doing the same.[51] It is not our job to get involved
in a dispute and think that we are acting on behalf of Hashem. It was the mistake
of the dog to get involved with the cat and goat. And it is a mistake when we get

---

51 The same question and answer are given by the *Chazon Ish* in the *Maaseh Ish*
    (vol. 4, p. 184). Rabbi Nosson Adler gave the same explanation regarding those
    people who poured fuel on the fire of the dispute between Rav Yaakov Emden
    and Rav Yonasan Eybeschutz. It is also brought in the name of a young Rav
    Chaim Soloveitchik in *Reb Chaim Brisker* (vol. 1, p. 113).

involved in arguments as well. If you offset *Chad Gadya* on the assumption that the dog was mistaken, it comes out that Hashem is correct at the end of the day.

Perhaps we can suggest another approach to the question of the *Ben Ish Chai*. A stick is only a tool and cannot act on its own. A stick can be used for good or bad. The other items on this list are animals, people, or forces of nature that can act on their own. However, a stick stays still unless someone does something with it. If a person looks at a stick and thinks that the stick did something wrong on its own, they are forgetting that Hashem is behind the stick. So too, everything that occurs to us in this world comes through the providence of Hashem. It is not the leader of a country, a family member, or a weather pattern that is affecting us. Rather it is just a "stick" in the hand of Hashem. The person who looks at the stick and sees something bad, is the same person who looks at the end of *Chad Gadya* and views Hashem as the negative aggressor. But if you look at the stick and see that it is simply an extension of the Hand of God, then, after all the calculations are made, it is clear that Hashem is running the world.

WHAT FOLLOWS are some fascinating and varied explanations of *Chad Gadya* offered by five different commentators on the Haggadah. Some of these are presented here in English for the very first time.

The Vilna Gaon—Commentary on the Haggadah

- The first goats we encounter in the Torah are in the story of Yitzchak asking Eisav to prepare food for him in order to receive the blessings. This event took place on the first day of Pesach. Our father Yaakov needed to receive those blessings for the spiritual benefits to himself and his children, and he therefore needed to get hold of two goats for his father first. Yaakov wanted both goats—representing the blessings for spiritual and material success respectively—but he only got one. He ultimately received the blessings for spiritual success, but not the blessings of material success in this world.
- Yaakov gave these blessings and the firstborn rights to Yosef. Because of the firstborn's inheritance and his role as representative of the family, he has the privilege of wearing nicer clothing. This led to fighting among the brothers. The Gemara (*Shabbos* 10b) says one should not favor one child over the others since we see that this behavior led to the exile in Egypt. This is represented by a cat, because the nature of cats is to be jealous and fight.

- The children of Yaakov then went down to Egypt, which is represented by the dog. The idols of Egypt were dogs. They even had dog statues that attacked the slaves who tried to escape.
- *Shemos Rabbah* (9:2) says that Moshe then comes with his stick, which was used to hit Egypt, the dog. *Pirkei D'Rabi Eliezer* (39) says that this staff, the sign of leadership, kept us safe until the destruction of the First Beis Hamikdash. Both the miracles in the desert and the miracles of the Beis Hamikdash were in the merit of the staff of Moshe.
- However, the fire of *avodah zarah* burned very strongly and ultimately led to the burning of the Beis Hamikdash. The Gemara (*Sanhedrin* 102b) describes how King Menasheh appeared to Rav Ashi and described the "burning fire" for *avodah zarah* that existed in his time.
- After the destruction of the first Beis Hamikdash, the water—the Torah in the form of the *Anshei K'nesses Hagedolah*—was able to extinguish the fire of *avodah zarah* and establish the primacy of Torah and the Oral Law.
- The ox comes and drinks the water. The ox, according to the *Tikkunei Zohar*, is Eisav. This represents the destruction of the second Beis Hamikdash, which consumes the Jewish People.
- The butcher is Mashiach ben Yosef. We know that Yosef is the enemy of Eisav. The Gemara (*Bava Basra* 123b) says that the descendants of Eisav will be defeated by the descendants of Yosef. When Mashiach ben Yosef comes, he will *shecht* the ox and make it kosher. He will spiritually correct Eisav and remove the *yetzer hara*. We mistakenly think that when we say that the *yetzer hara* will be *shechted* in the future, it means it will be destroyed. Rather, a *shechitah* acts as a *tikkun*, a rectification. The *yetzer hara* will become good and our bad traits will become good. A true fulfillment of serving Hashem "בכל לבבך," with all of our heart.
- The Navi and the Gemara (*Sukkah* 52b) say that the angel of death will kill Mashiach ben Yosef in a final battle.
- Finally, Hashem will remove death in the days of Mashiach ben David and there will be no death, *yetzer hara*, or suffering. The Gemara (*Bechoros* 8b) says that the wise men of Athens asked Rabbi Yehoshua, "With what does one harvest a field of knives?" Rabbi Yehoshua answered, "With the horn of a donkey." They said to him, "But is there such a thing as a horn of a donkey?" He said to them, "Is there such a thing as a field of knives?" The *Vilna Gaon* explains that they were asking how the Jewish People could possibly defeat

Eisav when Eisav had received the blessing of violence and living by the sword. Rabbi Yehoshua answered that Mashiach will come on a donkey, and he is described as a *keren*, a horn. The wise men of Athens responded that there is no such thing as a donkey with a horn. Rabbi Yehoshua responded that just like a donkey with a horn is supernatural, so too, the coming of Mashiach will be supernatural and it will overcome whatever challenges Eisav presents.

In the eyes of the *Vilna Gaon*, *Chad Gadya* teaches us that all of history comes from the blessings of Yaakov and Eisav. We must never give up on Jewish history because we know with certainty that we will ultimately be saved by Mashiach ben David.

Rav Yosef Zechariah Stern—*Zecher Yehosef*

Rav Yosef Zechariah Stern was the rav of Shavel, Lithuania. He was an unparalleled genius with remarkable command of the entire of Torah literature. He offers a novel and fascinating approach to *Chad Gadya* in his Haggadah, *Zecher Yehosef*.

Melachim I tells of the passing of Shlomo HaMelech and the eventual split of the kingdom into Yehudah in the south and Yisrael in the north. The leader who first rebelled against the existing kingdom of Yehudah and created a new kingdom in the north was Yeravam. In *Melachim I* (chapter 12) we find that Yeravam, however, had an idea with tragic consequences. Realizing that Yehudah still had Yerushalayim and the Beis Hamikdash, he became concerned that his people would gradually long to return there. To prevent that, he decided to offer alternatives to the Beis Hamikdash. He built two golden calves and placed them at opposite ends of the country, for the people's convenience. Yeravam barricaded the roads to Yerushalayim, appointed non-Levitic Jews as priests, and made up his own holidays. This effectively prevented *aliyah la'regel* and the *Korban Pesach*. It was only in the days of Chizkiyahu that the kingdom of Yehudah and the remnants of the kingdom of Yisrael were reunited. It was in these days that the Jewish People were able to bring the *Korban Pesach* as a unified nation for the first time in a long time. The song of *Chad Gadya* was composed in honor of this occasion. It is in Aramaic because that was the language spoken by many at the time.

- The goat is the animal for the *Korban Pesach*. The sum of two *zuzim* reflects the cost of buying the animal for the *Korban Pesach*.
- The cat is Yeravam, who was a minister for Shlomo. The Gemara (*Horayos* 13a) says that cats are not loyal to their owners, and they lack *hakaras ha'tov*. Yeravam rebelled against the kingdom of Shlomo and stopped the Jews from bringing the *Korban Pesach*.

- The dog is Basha ben Achiyah. *Horayos* 13a teaches that the dog is loyal and helps his master. Basha was not a descendant of Nadav ben Yeravam. He was from the tribe of Yissachar, and he assassinated Nadav only two years into Nadav's reign. When Basha became king, he killed all members of the family of Yeravam, and did not leave any survivors, thus completely decimating the family of Yeravam as had been prophesied. Hashem did this in retribution for the sins of Yeravam that he personally committed and those that he caused the Jewish people to do. Basha was like a dog carrying out the plan of Hashem without fail.
- The stick is Zimri. When Basha died, he was succeeded by his son Eilah. Eilah reigned only two years, and then he was assassinated by Zimri, one of his head charioteers. Zimri struck Eilah when Eilah was drunk and easy prey. He then declared himself king by eliminating the descendants of Basha, just as the Navi Yehu had foretold. A stick is only a tool of the person who wields it. Hashem used Zimri just to punish Basha.
- The fire represents the short reign of Zimri, which came to an end through fire. When the army heard that Zimri had assassinated Eilah, they made Omri their king and went after Zimri. Zimri took refuge in the palace, but Omri burned it down and Zimri died. This began the line of Omri, which continued with his son Achav.
- The water is Yehu. In *Melachim II* (chapter 9) he is anointed king by Elisha HaNavi, thus ending the line of Achav. As he approaches Yehoram ben Achav, who was an evil king, the *Navi* describes his small army as a "שפעת," which shares a root with שפע, meaning a flow of water.
- The ox is Shalum ben Yavesh. He ended the line of Yehu (which was destined to last four generations) by killing Zechariah ben Yeravam and claiming the throne in his place. It says in *Yeshayahu* 1:3, "ידע שור קונהו—The ox knows his master." Shalum fulfilled the role of being a pawn of Hashem, Who had promised the reign of Yeihu would end.
- The *shochet* is Menachem ben Gadi. Shalum reigned for one month before he was assassinated by Menachem, who became king in his place. Menachem was another evil king. He tried to subjugate Tifsach, an adjacent city in Aram. Because they would not submit, he used unnecessary and unacceptable levels of force. *Rashi* notes that Menachem even cut open pregnant women. This is why he was called the *shochet*.
- The Angel of Death is Pekach ben Remalyahu. The line of Menachem ben

Gadi was stopped when Pekach assassinated Pekachyah ben Menachem. Pekach reigned for twenty years and was yet another evil king. In *Divrei Hayamim II* (28:6), it says that Pekach slew 120 thousand men from Yehudah in one day. These actions fit the title "Angel of Death." We find that Chazal referred to people who were exceedingly harsh as the Angel of Death.

- This entire sequence of events was part of Hashem's master plan, ultimately leading to Chizkiyahu reinstating the *Korban Pesach*. Hoshea ben Eilah assassinated Pekach and became the last king of the Northern Kingdom. The ten tribes of Yisrael were sent into exile by the kingdom of Ashur. This allowed Chizkiyahu from Yehudah to enter the scene. He defeated Ashur, reunited the kingdom, removed the golden calves, and finally reinstated the *Korban Pesach* for all the Jewish People. The point of *Chad Gadya* is that all of these events and the ending of each line of the monarchy were ordained by Hashem. It was all a long-term plan to bring the *Korban Pesach* back to the Jewish People.

Rav Yosef Zechariah Stern says that this is the *pashut p'shat* and that all other explanations are forced. I am inclined to agree with him.

Rav Yosef Messas — *Vayizkor Yosef*

Rav Yosef Messas, the great Moroccan sage and chief rabbi of Haifa, was a young married man and sitting at his father-in-law's house on Seder night. Someone asked what *Chad Gadya* was about and he was told it was "על פי סוד," based on secrets of the Torah. Another person responded that whenever people don't know an answer to a question, they simply say it is "על פי סוד," a secret. In response to this statement, Rav Messas sat and wrote his own explanation of *Chad Gadya*:

- The goat represents the Jewish People, who sit like a lamb among the wolves that are the nations of the world. The father is Hashem who "bought us" twice. The word *zuzei* is related to the word *zaz*, meaning to move. This alludes to two times Hashem "moved" for us.

  - The first was at *Makkas Bechoros*, where He passed through Egypt, "ועברתי בארץ מצרים." What does it mean that Hashem passed or moved through Egypt? Does Hashem need to pass through anywhere? The *Maharil Diskin* explains that Egypt is a large area and the exact point of midnight could be different based on where one is located in the country (similarly, there are different times for Shabbos in nearby cities). Nevertheless, Hashem killed each firstborn when it was exactly midnight in their location.

Therefore, it appeared as if Hashem was moving through Egypt. This was all done for the honor of the Jewish People.

- The second "move" was at the splitting of the sea, when Hashem revealed Himself to the Jewish People, in all of His glory.

- The Gemara (*Horayos* 15a) says that a cat always forgets. The cat is Pharaoh, who forgot about Yosef (as it says, "ויקם מלך חדש אשר לא ידע את יוסף") and attacked the Jewish People.

- In response, Hashem gave Pharaoh the punishment of *tzaraas*. The dog was the *tzaraas* that Hashem sent to Pharaoh. The *tzaraas* is like the bite of a dog in that it hurts the skin of the person.

- This led Pharaoh to slaughter Jewish children in the hope that their blood would cure his *tzaraas*. In response, Moshe came and took away the *tzaraas* so Pharaoh could be punished with the *makkos* instead. Moshe is the root and foundation of the Jewish People. Interestingly, we are told that the Jewish mothers were giving birth to six babies at a time, but Yocheved seemed to only have one at a time. This is because the children of Yocheved, specifically Moshe, were equal to all the Jewish People. The Navi Yeshayahu (11:1) refers to a root as "ויצא חטר מגזע ישי." Therefore, "ואתא חוטרא והכה לכלבא."

- Fifty days after leaving Egypt, Moshe went up to Har Sinai to receive the Torah. The Midrash says that when Moshe went up to Har Sinai, the angels wanted to burn him for taking the Torah. The fire is the fire of angels in Heaven, and the fire came to burn the stick, i.e., Moshe.

- Hashem told Moshe to grab on to the Heavenly Throne for protection and answer the angels as to why the Jewish People should take the Torah. Moshe answered the angels with a quote from the Torah. The Torah says, "I am Hashem your God, Who took you out of the Land of Egypt." Were the angels in Egypt? The Torah says, "Honor your father and mother." Do the angels have parents? Thus, the water, which is always a parable for Torah, extinguished the fire; meaning, the answers that Moshe brought from the Torah protected him from the fire of the angels.

- While Moshe was on the mountain, the Jewish People sinned with the Golden Calf. He came down from Har Sinai and broke the *Luchos*. The *tora*, the golden calf or ox, removed the protection of the Torah (the water) and led to the breaking of the *Luchos*.

- Moshe then ground down the Golden Calf, placed it in water, and made the Jewish People drink it. It was as if Moshe *shechted* the ox.

- Then the angel Micha'el came to kill Moshe and take his *neshamah*, but Moshe chased him away (*Devarim Rabbah* 11:9). So the angel Gavriel came to take Moshe, and Moshe sent him away. Finally, Hashem sent the Angel of Death to take Moshe (the same Moshe who "*shechted*" the Golden Calf) and Moshe took his *mateh Elokim*, the staff of God, which contained the names of God, and used it to send away the Angel of Death.

Rav Aharon ben Moshe Teumim—*Mateh Aharon*

Rav Aharon ben Moshe Teumim was appointed the rabbi of Cracow in 1690 after being the rabbi in Worms, Germany. He was arrested by soldiers on a Shabbos afternoon for no apparent reason, while in Chmielnik, Poland, for a meeting of the Vaad Arba Aratzos. He died from the cruel beatings of the soldiers. In his *Mateh Aharon* on *Chad Gadya* (usually published with the *Midrash Haggadah* attributed to the *Malbim*), he says that the famous poem is in fact the story of the selling of Yosef:

- The goat is Yosef, who is the tenth of the tribes (since Levi isn't counted among the tribes). He corresponds to the tenth month, which is Teves and whose astrological sign is the lamb or goat.[52] Yosef was sold because of his coat, which cost two *sela'im*.
- The cat represents the Yishmaelim who took Yosef and sold him into slavery. A main attribute of Yishmael is to have a lack of *hakaras ha'tov*, appreciation. *Rashi* explains in *Yeshayahu* (chapter 16) that Hashem gave Yishmael a well of water when he was dying of thirst, and in return, his descendants gave the Jewish People empty containers of hot air when they were going into exile. A cat is an animal that lacks *hakaras ha'tov*.
- The Yishmaelim sold Yosef to Egypt, which is represented by the dog. When the Egyptians took Yosef, it was as if they had bitten the Yishmaelim, who now lost out on the benefits of having Yosef.
- The stick is the staff of Moshe, which, according to the *Mateh Aharon*, was used to reveal the place where the Egyptians kept Yosef in the Nile, the main geographical point in Egypt (the dog).
- The fire is the fire used in making the Golden Calf. The Golden Calf undid all the good things Moshe had done to get the Jewish People out of Egypt.

---

52 For this and other reasons, Rav Shlomo Fisher, in his *Beis Yishai*, develops the novel idea that the sale of Yosef took place on the tenth of Teves.

In addition, a statue of a calf was made, which is a perversion of the symbol of the ox, the sign of Yosef.

- Moshe responded to the sin of the Golden Calf by grinding it up, putting it into water, and making the Jewish People drink it. Thus, water was used to correct the terrible events caused by the fire.

- This correction was later ruined by the idol of Michah, which was in the form of an ox. The *Midrash Tanchuma* (*Ki Sisa*) says that Michah created his idol with the tablet on which Moshe wrote, "עלה שור," in order to cause Yosef's bones to rise up from the Nile.

- Adam HaRishon's sin lowered the spiritual level of all beings. This was corrected by the infusion of holiness into the world during the revelation at Sinai and the giving of the Torah. But this in turn was ruined with the sin of the Golden Calf. What then, can help repair the spirituality of all living beings? The act of *shechitah* helps rectify the spiritual nature of birds and mammals, and rectifies the sins of *avodah zarah* that permeate the world.[53]

- This explains how the spirituality of animals is repaired, but what about people? The only true rectification comes at the end of a person's life when they can go to *Olam Haba*, which is the place of spiritual perfection. When the *neshamah* leaves this world and goes to *Olam Haba*, the *neshamah* reaches its place of spiritual rectification. This can only occur with the Angel of Death who ends a person's life in this world and directs the *neshamah* toward the next world. In the parable of *Chad Gadya*, the Angel of Death is simply the Angel of Death, and the *shochet* represents human beings, whose lives eventually end and move on to *Olam Haba*.

---

53 Rav Yaakov Lorberbaum, author of *Nesivos Hamishpat*, was told one winter that the *shochet* in his town had drunk a few glasses of whiskey before going to his job, to warm himself up. Rav Lorberbaum warned the *shochet* against this practice, but he didn't listen. Rav Lorberbaum then said to the *shochet*, "Now I understand the line in *Chad Gadya*. All the other parties in the story committed acts of violence against the others. The *shochet* was the only one who did a mitzvah, so why should he be punished? The answer must be that he was going to *shecht* after having consumed four cups of wine, and it's forbidden to drink and then *shecht*."

- Ultimately, all of this will be rectified by Hashem getting rid of the Satan/Angel of Death and bringing the final redemption. As Rav Aharon Teumim concludes, "ובא לציון גואל—The redeemer will come to Zion."

Why is the sale of Yosef the final message of the Seder? Because it is the bookend to the opening message of the Seder, as we mentioned above (see "Karpas").

Rav Reuven Margaliyos—*Haggadah Be'er Miriam*, with an explanation from Rav Yitzchak Zilberstein—*Haggadah Nifle'osecha Asichah*

Rav Reuven Margaliyos, the brilliant *talmid chacham*, cites *Bereishis Rabbah* (38:13), which discusses the story of Avraham and the idols. When Avraham broke the idols of his father, Terach, he was taken by his father to Nimrod to be punished for his actions. Nimrod told Avraham to bow down to the fire, and Avraham countered that he should bow to water, since water extinguishes fire. The following conversation ensued:

Nimrod: "So bow to water…"

Avraham: "Perhaps I should bow to the clouds because they send the water."

Nimrod: "So bow to the clouds…"

Avraham: "Perhaps then I should bow to the wind because the wind brings and scatters the clouds."

Nimrod: "So bow to the wind."

Avraham: "Then perhaps I should bow to man because man can stand up before wind."

In the end, Nimrod saw that he couldn't influence Avraham. He announced that Avraham was just trying to confuse him with words and speeches. Nimrod concluded that because his personal practice was to bow to the fire, he would throw Avraham into the fire. Nimrod said, "Let your God come and save you from the fire." Avraham entered the fire and was saved by Hashem.

The miracle of Avraham in the furnace reverberated throughout the world. However, the nations continued to worship trees and stones. The Egyptians worshipped their sheep, which gave them wool and milk. Therefore, the song of *Chad Gadya* was written to poke fun at the Egyptians, who turned a sheep into a god while worshipping and bowing down to it. This is their one goat, which was their *avodah zarah*. The song tracks a hypothetical conversation between a Jew and an Egyptian:

- The Jew asks the Egyptian, "This sheep can be bought for two *zuz*, and you bow down to it? Why don't you worship a cat, which is stronger than the sheep?" So, the Egyptian agrees to worship the cat.

- The Jew then asks the Egyptian, "Why not worship the dog, who can overpower the cat?" So, the Egyptian says he will begin worshipping the dog.
- The Jew then presses further and asks why the Egyptian doesn't worship the stick, which can be used to control and dominate the dog? So, the Egyptian agrees to worship the wooden stick.
- The Jew then suggests bowing down to the fire, which can consume the stick. So, the Egyptian agrees to worship the more powerful fire.
- The Jew then suggests worshipping the water, which can extinguish the fire. The Egyptian agrees to that as well, and decides he will serve the water.
- Asks the Jew, "Why not serve the ox, which can consume the water?" So, the Egyptian agrees to worship the much stronger ox.
- The Jew asks why the *shochet* is not a better option, as he can kill the ox with his knife. The Egyptian agrees to follow this logic and serves the *shochet*.
- With this, the Jew tells the Egyptian that he should serve the Angel of Death since the Angel of Death can kill the *shochet* and take the life of every human being.
- Finally, the Jew asks, "Who controls the Angel of Death and who can stop it? Is it not the King of Kings, Hakadosh Baruch Hu?!"

ABOUT THE AUTHOR

RABBI ISAAC RICE teaches Judaic studies and heads the halachah department at the SKA High School for Girls in Long Island, New York, and is a rabbi at Congregation Anshei Chesed in Hewlett, New York.